WRITING AND SOCIETY

Writing and Society is a clear and comprehensive account of the growth in popular literacy during the early modern period, linking the development of new readerships with the authors and works which addressed them. It is the first single volume to provide a year-by-year chronology of political events in relation to cultural production. This overview of relevant debates in literary critical theory and historiography includes facsimile pages with commentary from the most influential books of the period. Nigel Wheale describes and analyses:

- the development of literacy by status, gender and region in Britain
- structures of patronage and censorship
- the fundamental role of the publishing industry
- the relationship between elite literary and popular cultures
- the remarkable growth of female literacy and publication
- the impact of English policies of state formation on the traditions of the Celtic literary cultures

This ground-breaking book brings together the materials necessary to understand Elizabethan, Jacobean and Carolean culture in relation to early modern British literacy and cultural politics.

Nigel Wheale lectures in English Studies at Anglia Polytechnic University. He is co-editor of *Shakespeare in the Changing Curriculum* (1991) and *The Postmodern Arts* (1995).

WRITING AND SOCIETY

Literacy, print and politics in Britain 1590–1660

Nigel Wheale

London and New York

First published 1999
by Routledge
11 New Fetter Lane, London EC4P 4EE

Simultaneously published in the USA and Canada
by Routledge
29 West 35th Street, New York, NY 10001

Routledge is an imprint of the Taylor & Francis Group

© 1999 Nigel Wheale

Typeset in Galliard by Routledge
Printed and bound in Great Britain by
TJ International Ltd, Padstow, Cornwall

British Library Cataloguing in Publication Data
A catalogue record for this book is available from the British Library

Library of Congress Cataloguing in Publication Data
Wheale, Nigel
Writing and society: literacy, print and politics
in Britain, 1590–1660 / Nigel Wheale
p. cm.
Includes bibliographical references and index.
1. English literature–Early modern, 1500–1700–
History and criticism. 2. Politics and literature–Great Britain–
History–17th century. 3. Publishers and publishing–
Great Britain–History–17th century. 4. Literature and Society–
Great Britain–History–17th century. 5. Written communications–
Great Britain–History–17th century. 6. Great Britain–politics and
government–1603–1714. 7. Literacy–Great Britain–
History–17th century. 8. Printing–Great Britain–History–
17th century. I. Title.
PR438.P65W751999
820.9'358–dc 2198-54317
CIP

ISBN 0–415–08497–0 (hbk)
ISBN 0–415–08498–9 (pbk)

To any Reader He or She
It makes no matter what they be.
(John Taylor the Water Poet, 1624)

Piper sit thee down and write
In a book that all may read.
(William Blake, 1789)

CONTENTS

CONTENTS

CONTENTS

FIGURES

ACKNOWLEDGEMENTS

Writing and Society brings together diverse areas of work in early modern history and renaissance literary studies from the last two decades, and my greatest obligation is to the scholars whose research I have found so rewarding and which is incorporated in the argument. Anglia Polytechnic University generously enabled research and writing over several years through remission from teaching and grants for conference attendance, travel and other expenses. The librarians at Anglia, Cambridge University Library, and the English and History Faculty libraries were unfailingly helpful, as were staff at the Plume Library, Maldon; particular thanks to Miss Wilson for showing me the Spelman collection at Swaffham Church, just before its removal to Norwich Cathedral Library. 'Writing and Society' was taught as a module in the English degree at Anglia for several years, and student engagement was, as always, the critical test; thanks to all those who rose to the challenge, and to my colleagues David Booy and Edward J. Esche for their teaching contribution. In the department David Booy, Peter Cattermole, Mary Joannou, Rick Rylance and Rebecca Stott all read and commented helpfully, often extensively, on chapters, and Malcolm Gaskill and John Sutton were generous with their historical knowledge; Paul Shakeshaft contributed acutely to discussion of painting; and David Booy kindly shared his work on seventeenth-century 'self-writing'. Thanks to Keith Wrightson of Jesus College, Cambridge, for a seminar, bibliography and inspiration. Mrs Margaret Swain of Edinburgh kindly exchanged ideas about costume detail in Belcamp's 'Great Picture' and revealed the wealth of interest in Stuart embroidery; Paul McAvilley gave invaluable detail on the siege of Bristol, 1642, even though we've worn different sashes ever since childhood. Other friends have willingly acted as a 'focus group' and commented shrewdly on chapters: Cathy Davies, Andrew Duncan (pencerdd), Lisa Empson, Joan Grumman, Tom Lowenstein, Gilly Maude, Robert Milsom, Suzanne Reynolds, Denise Riley, Ewan Smith, Roz Symon, Martin Thom, Andy Thompson, Janet Todd, Jinny Webber and John Welch. Peter Riley as ever sent me off on new tangents, this time to early modern Celtic literary culture. I owe a particular obligation to Edward J. Esche for the stimulation of a fifteen-year conversation about Shakespeare, Marlowe, drama, truth and method; watching productions in the Swan, Other Place and Globe theatres on our departmental trips always provokes new insights and debate. Talia Rodgers and colleagues at Routledge have shown breath-taking tolerance. Thanks to Lisa Carden and Jason Arthur for liaison, and Katia Hamza for scrupulous editing. Thanks to RFL and JHP for an unmatchable education. At home I'm deeply grateful to Kate and Dan for their real and sustaining interest in my obscure preoccupations, shared in so many conversations and expeditions. This is a book full of detail, and all the readers in the world will not save me from Error; remaining omissions, mistakes and follies are entirely my own work.

Thanks to the following galleries, libraries, publishers, editors and authors for permission to reproduce paintings, pages and quotations: Abbot Hall Gallery, Kendal, Cumbria, for Lady Anne Clifford's 'Great Picture', attributed to Jan Van Belcamp; the Trustees of Dulwich Picture Gallery, London, for Joan Alleyn's portrait; The Frick Collection, New York, for Sir Anthony van Dyck's 'Sir John Suckling'; the Syndics of Cambridge University Library for reproduction of pages from sixteenth- and seventeenth-century texts; Dr Alan K. Bowman and the Society for the Promotion of Roman Studies for quotation from the text, translation and commentary on Claudia Severa's letter; Cambridge University Press for quotation from John Margeson's edition of *King Henry VIII* and Michael Hattaway's edition of *The Second Part of King Henry VI*; Edinburgh University Press for the extract from Derick Thomson's translation of *Seathan Mac Rìgh Eirann* from his *Introduction to Gaelic Poetry*; HarperCollins Publishers Ltd for quotation from *The Diary of Samuel Pepys*, volume III, '1667', transcribed and edited by Robert Latham and William Matthews; Little Brown for quotation from Hester Wyat's poem in Germaine Greer *et al.* (eds), *Kissing the Rod: An Anthology of Seventeenth-Century Women's Verse*; Oxford University Press for quotations from David Bevington and Eric Rasmussen's edition of *Doctor Faustus* and Stephen Orgel's edition of *The Tempest*; and Sutton Publishing for quotation from D. J. H. Clifford's edition of *The Diaries of Lady Anne Clifford*. Thanks to all the copyright managers, librarians, archivists and curators for their efficient responses, and to J. C. S. Barnes, Curator of Abbot Hall Art Gallery and Museum for discussion of Belcamp's 'Great Picture', also to R. Hall and Anne Rowe of Cumbria Record Office for information on their Clifford holdings.

Conventions

Spelling and punctuation from sixteenth- and seventeenth-century texts are modernized (with the exception of quotations in modern copyright) and material in square brackets explains or expands the sense where necessary; when old texts are quoted extensively they are also referenced to modern editions as available. It is a pity not to present early modern writing in its original form, for all of the reasons given by David Norbrook and H. R. Woudhuysen in the Preface to their *Penguin Book of Renaissance Verse* (Harmondsworth, 1993, pp. xxxiii–xxxv), but since we routinely read and hear modernized Shakespeare it is perhaps not unreasonable to revise other writing from the period to make it more readily understood. The main focus of this work is on selected aspects of literacy and publication between 1590 and 1660, but long-term developments are occasionally followed into the decades before and after this time-frame. Place of publication for books printed before 1800 is London unless indicated otherwise. Years are given from 1 January, rather than from Lady Day, 25 March, which was the custom in the period. Phrases quoted in chapter and section titles are referenced in the first endnote within the text. 'Stationer' refers to a member of the Stationers' Company, and 'stationers' to printers and booksellers in general; 'Bible' refers to the work as scripture, and 'bible' to a text as trade commodity.

1

'PAPER I MAKE MY FRIEND AND MIND'S TRUE GLASS'

Early modern literacy

Christopher Marlowe's new sin

Doctor John Faustus, born of lowly stock but raised up high through 'scholerism', has made a pact with Mephistopheles which he is beginning to regret. The Princes of Hell therefore stage a show of the Seven Deadly Sins to strengthen Faustus's resolve. Pride comes first, the origin of all the rest – Covetousness, Wrath, Envy, Gluttony, Sloth and Lechery. Marlowe's seven figures form a traditional parade, each characterized in ways that would have been familiar to audiences of the religious drama from previous centuries, now suppressed by authority and in 1590 on the point of extinction. But in the middle of the tableau the figure of Envy introduces a distinctive new note:

> I am Envy, begotten of a chimney-sweeper and an oyster-wife. I cannot read, and therefore wish all books were burnt. I am lean with seeing others eat. O, that there would come a famine through all the world, that all might die, and I live alone! Then thou shouldst see how fat I would be. But must thou sit and I stand? Come down, with a vengeance![1]

Marlowe's Envy is defined by social status very exactly, as dirty as a chimney-sweep, as common as an oyster-seller – oysters before the nineteenth century were cheap 'fast food', and 'oyster-wife' was a term of abuse by the 1640s. Envy is a child of the new urban street trades, only just making a living at the edge of city life, and this precision about social status is quite new in the long history of sin. Even more striking is the fact that Envy is provoked by an inability to read. For this starveling of 1590, to be illiterate is to be excluded from clerisy, from knowledge and the capacity to make a proper living; it is, in fact, to be condemned to exclusion in the under-class.

The convention of the Seven Deadly Sins is ancient but it seems that Envy provoked by literacy is a new variation on this vice which came to prominence during the fourteenth and fifteenth centuries as a predictable response to growing material prosperity in European society – 'For in oure dayes nis but covetyse' lamented Chaucer in the 1380s.[2] Edmund Spenser's ornate triumph of the Deadly Sins in *The Faerie Queene*, written at almost the same time as *Faustus*, is staged appropriately in the House of Pride. Spenser's Envy, in keeping with the old-fashioned register of his epic, displays more traditional attributes of the Vice figure than Marlowe's – he rides a wolf, is envious of his neighbour's wealth and rejoices in other people's misfortunes. But this Envy also has a new and specifically literary aspect:

> And eke the verse of famous Poets witt
> He does backebite, and spightfull poison spues
> From leprous mouth on all, that ever writt:[3]

These two new Sin-variants suggest that significant changes were occurring in English attitudes to literacy by the end of the sixteenth century, for both readers and writers, and they demonstrate the emergent status of literacy as both a 'life-skill' and a profession in the 1590s.

During the 100 years following Elizabeth's accession in 1558 the population of the British Isles began to move out of a condition of near-total illiteracy. Reading and writing may have been relatively common in some privileged strata of Romano-British society during the late Roman occupation. There is tantalizing evidence for this among the imperial army and its families stationed on the northern British frontier around AD 100, shortly before the construction of Hadrian's Wall, 'productions not of the world of Cicero or Pliny but of the vitally important sub-elite literate inhabitants of the empire'. One of the writing tablets that has survived at the Vindolanda site near Hexham is a birthday invitation from Claudia Severa to Sulpicia Lepidina, almost certainly 'the earliest known example of writing in Latin by a woman', but for the next 1,100 years literacy was not widespread in any western society. The skill survived as 'palatial', 'scribal' or 'professional literacy', a specialized competence employed in state and church administrations, and enjoyed as literature largely by the court and ecclesiastical elites. Before the nineteenth century reading was generally more common than the ability to write because the two activities were taught quite separately, and even when a person was able to sign their name it did not necessarily imply very developed writing competence. It is possible that literacy in all pre-modern societies was only ever the prerogative of social, religious and bureaucratic elites because bringing the separate skills of reading and writing to the general population called for a rare combination of political will, economic and educational resource, and – crucially – the development of stable urban societies. The literacy attainments of ancient Greece and Rome are often vaunted, but recent scholarship has estimated literacy in classical Attica at between 5 and 10 per cent, and not more than 15 per cent in Rome and Italy of the early Empire.[4] It may therefore be true that, for the western hemisphere, it was only in late sixteenth-century Europe that the numbers of people having one or both of the abilities to read and write began to move beyond the literacy rates of the ancient world. In 1500 at the beginning of the Tudor period probably 90 per cent of the male population in Britain were unable to read or write, and perhaps just 1 per cent of women could be counted as literate – even among the clergy in the fifteenth century nuns were likely to be illiterate. By the 1680s male illiteracy in Britain still stood at 70 per cent, female illiteracy at 90 per cent, though with the obvious and significant exception of London.[5] These figures are broadly comparable to rates throughout northern Europe, but this 20 per cent increase in male literacy, and the 9 per cent increase in female literacy, was all that was required to sustain the European cultural renaissance.

Marlowe's Vice figure is vehemently envious of Faustus because the scholar has gained his status through book-learning. Volumes are central to Faustus's power, and in staged

2

performance they are potent icons of his knowledge and magic. Lucifer hands Faustus a tome, advising him to 'Peruse it th[o]roughly, and thou shalt turn thyself into what shape thou wilt.' Book-knowledge conveys a metamorphic power to the adept, the ability to transgress the fixed grades of pre-modern society, to assume new rank and degree:

> The iterating of these lines brings gold;
> The framing of this circle on the ground
> Brings whirlwinds, tempests, thunder, and lightning.

Faustus's final cry before he is dragged away by demons is another desperate bargain, 'Come not, Lucifer! / I'll burn my books', uttered in the misplaced hope that this might be enough to save him: for Marlowe, Faustus's true sin against the spirit might have been this desire to renounce the knowledge which had created him.

Professional writers such as the dramatists, pamphleteers and poets seeking patronage were necessarily alert to these subtle but real developments in attitudes to learning among the urban population, and *Doctor Faustus* aired these new concerns about literacy and the status of knowledge at the beginning of the London theatre's spectacular development during the 1590s. Twenty-two years later, when the drama was diversifying and developing more sophisticated styles, another envious illiterate burned with resentment on the city stages. Caliban started from an even lower knowledge-base than Marlowe's Envy, without any language at all; he was taught the power of speech by Miranda and Prospero, but they failed to extend his skills' programme to reading and writing. Prospero must have possessed a book like Mephistopheles' text which could summon 'whirlwinds, tempests, thunder and lightning', and made good use of it during the opening action of the play to create the illusion of shipwreck. Caliban knew that these books were the source of Prospero's power, and during Stephano and Trinculo's attempted coup against Prospero he insisted that the library be seized first:

> Remember
> First to possess his books; for without them
> He's but a sot, as I am, nor hath not
> One spirit to command –[6]

These roles of Envy and Caliban when they were first performed must have functioned at least partly to flatter their London audiences and congratulate them on their relative sophistication as readers. A greater proportion of play-goers during these two decades would have been able to read than their predecessors, and they were certainly more literate than their contemporaries in the smaller English towns and villages. Joan, wife of the actor Edward Alleyn who first performed Faustus, may have experienced mixed emotions as she watched her husband taunted by the parade of the Seven Deadlies, because she was possibly one of the majority of city women who were only partially literate, able to read but not write (see Figure 1).

Figure 1 British School, 'Joan Alleyn', 1596

Oil on panel, 79.1 by 63.2 cm. By permission of the Trustees of Dulwich Picture Gallery, London

Joan Alleyn, 1596:
'My good sweetheart and loving mouse'

Philip Henslowe served during the later 1570s as apprentice or servant to Henry Woodward, a London dyer. On 14 February 1579 he married Agnes, his master's widow, two months after Henry's death: Philip was in his twenties, Agnes was perhaps twenty years his senior, and the mother of Joan, aged 8, and Elizabeth, aged 4. During the 1580s Henslowe carefully used the substantial capital he acquired through his marriage to buy properties in Southwark for renting, and in January 1587 he entered into a partnership with John Cholmley, a grocer, to construct a playhouse, the Rose Theatre. The outstanding actor of this period was Edward Alleyn, for whom Marlowe may have written the roles of Tamburlaine, Barabas and Faustus; Alleyn's company, the Admiral's, performed at Henslowe's Rose playhouse. The year 1592 was notable for both men: Alleyn starred in *Faustus*, Henslowe gained new status with an appointment at Elizabeth's court as a Groom of the Chamber, and on 22 October Alleyn married Joan Woodward, Henslowe's step-daughter. The couple were however separated during the first year of their marriage while Alleyn toured and Joan continued to live at home on Bankside; six letters survive which they exchanged between May and September 1593. Alleyn was anxious because the plague was at its height in London while he worked the provinces in relative safety – entire households were dying in Southwark, and he urged Joan to pray daily, wash the doorstep and spread 'rue and herb of grace' on the window sills. Joan seems to have replied via her stepfather, so it may be that she was a reader but not a writer. On 5 July Henslowe wrote to Alleyn on her behalf, 'your mouse desireth to be remembered unto you...and prayeth night and day for your good health and quick return'. Their marriage was childless, which may have been one of Alleyn's motivations for founding the College of God's Gift at Dulwich in 1616, for the care of orphans and elderly poor. Joan Alleyn died on 28 June 1623, and in the following December Alleyn married Constance, some forty years his junior, a daughter of John Donne.

The unattributed portrait of Joan Alleyn was painted when she was in her mid-twenties, and when Edward Alleyn was at the height of his fame, acting at the Rose Theatre. She wears a fashionably cut black gown, and holds the conventional small testament as sign of her piety, though it is bound in a red which nicely matches her figured gloves – decorated with roses.

Dulwich Gallery has a unique collection of paintings associated with late sixteenth- and early seventeenth-century theatre, some directly from Edward Alleyn, and others from the extensive collection of the Carolean and Restoration actor William Cartwright. Materials from S. P. Cerasano, 'Edward Alleyn: 1566–1626' in Aileen Reid and Robert Maniura (eds), *Edward Alleyn. Elizabethan Actor, Jacobean Gentleman*, Dulwich Picture Gallery, 1994, pp. 15–16; see also Neil Carson, *A Companion to Henslowe's Diary*, Cambridge, 1988, pp. 1–5, and *Mr. Cartwright's Pictures. A Seventeenth Century Collection*, Dulwich Picture Gallery, 1987.

The steady growth in the number of early modern readers and writers from the 1590s was inevitably related to an expansion in the numbers of books and pamphlets produced decade by decade. Until the 1640s the increasing publication rate was unspectacular but consistent; during the first half of Elizabeth's reign, from 1558 to 1579, approximately 3,850 titles were published by the London-based Company of Stationers, the tightly controlled guild whose members were the only tradesmen permitted to make and distribute printed materials, together with a small number of continental and provincial English printers. The pace quickened in the second half of the reign, to 1604, with about 7,430 titles published. By 1624 another 9,740 titles had appeared, and on the eve of the Civil Wars in 1640 there were a further 9,680. A significant development from the 1620s was a considerable increase in production of small cheap almanacs, tracts and broadsheets, catering for a new and growing 'popular' readership. In the contentious years 1642, 1643, 1647 and 1648 over 1,000 titles were published annually, not including newspapers, and during the second half of the century this yearly rate of production of books and pamphlets increased tenfold. Where 200,000 individual volumes were produced each year in the first decade, two million items were on sale annually by the end of the century, so that, despite their fragility, books are now the single commonest class of object to survive from past times.[7] Every representation of a volume and every reference to reading or writing in renaissance culture is therefore worth careful attention exactly because of this developing status of literacy and the related growth in production of books. Joan Alleyn's eloquent portrait suggests as much, as do the roles of Envy and Caliban, figuring the unattainable power of literacy for individuals at the base of early modern social hierarchy.

Just four decades later, vernacular writing for the new print culture was given remarkable recognition by the social and artistic elite in Anthony Van Dyck's portrait of the courtier and poet Sir John Suckling, painted around 1638 (see Figure 2). John Aubrey saw the picture in 1661 and described it as showing Suckling 'all at length, leaning against a rock, with a play-book, contemplating. It is a piece of great value.' Suckling's figure gazes out of a rocky wilderness, turning the pages of a thick folio volume printed in double columns. Suckling is hemmed in by boulders with only the suggestion of a distant prospect, and the colouring is a closely grouped spectrum of russets and tawny browns, intensified by the murky blue of his silk tunic. A few sere leaves on a single branch reinforce the suggestion of autumn, and both the palette and scene are characteristic of Van Dyck's use of 'stark natural elements' in his portraiture from about 1630. The subject's costume is eccentric even for Suckling, whose major contribution to the King's cause in the First Bishops' War of 1639 was to outfit a supremely dandified regiment which attracted intense ridicule. The courtier-poet (and inventor of cribbage) is shown in a costume which mixes classical and oriental influences, possibly related to those designed for his first play, *Aglaura*, which was staged in 1637 and printed the following year at enormous expense (Suckling paid). *Aglaura* is a confusing farrago of incestuous intrigues, but it begins in a rocky wilderness and Van Dyck's portrait may be alluding to the play's performance at Court. Suckling's likeness rests his bulky folio on a rock bearing an emblematic, teasing quotation, 'Ne te quaesiveris extra', taken from the first satire of Persius (AD 34–62), a poet whose tortuous style was admired by John Donne among others. Dryden translated the line 'Seek not thyself, without thyself, to find', and described the satire as a courageous, individual stand against false values: 'the chief aim of the author is against bad poets...Persius, who is of a free spirit, and has not forgotten that Rome was once a commonwealth...boldly arraigns the false judgement of the age in which

Figure 2 Sir Anthony Van Dyck, 'Sir John Suckling', 1638
Oil on canvas, 216.5 by 130.3 cm. Copyright The Frick Collection, New York

he lives'. The folio itself, however, is not written in Latin, but English; a label emerging from the fore-edge of the volume reads 'Shakespere', and the top margin of the right-hand page is lettered 'HAMLET'.[8]

Shakespeare's works appeared in the First Folio of 1623, seven years after his death, and he became only the second playwright to have his writing canonized in this way. (Jonson had been ridiculed for gathering together his own *Works* in 1616, since 'opera' – 'works' – was a category till then reserved for serious scholarly endeavours such as theology.) Shakespeare's Folio was the most expensive playbook published to that date, and when the second edition appeared in 1632 the Puritan polemicist William Prynne quickly complained that 'Shakespeare's Plays are printed in the best Crown paper, far better than most Bibles. Above forty thousand Playbooks have been printed and vended within these two years'. The Second Folio kept dangerous company: King Charles read and annotated his copy while imprisoned at Carisbrooke Castle, awaiting trial during 1648 – as Milton put it, Shakespeare was 'one whom we well know was the Closet Companion of these his solitudes'. For some of his accusers this alone was enough to condemn him, arguing that he had better spent his time by preparing his defence than reading a play-book. Charles and Henrietta Maria had a fondness for Shakespeare's dramas. The Queen stayed overnight at Stratford on 11 July 1642 as she made her way to join Charles at Keinton, underneath Edgehill, where three months later the first major engagement of the Civil Wars would be fought. In Stratford the Queen lodged with the fifty-nine year old Susannah Hall, now widowed, the Shakespeares' first child, 'Witty above her sex...Something of Shakespeare was in that.'[9]

Van Dyck's portrait may also have contributed to a debate current in the 1630s between English authors (typified by Ben Jonson) who modelled their writing on the classical example of the 'Ancients', and those who imagined they were following a new vein – inspiration from the self, and from 'Nature'. It would be an exaggeration to say that this portrait is 'proto-Romantic' in its endorsement of 'natural' sentiment against facile sophistication, but it has a place in the widening conversation about the tensions between tradition and individual talent, convention and innovation, which Swift's *Battle of the Books* summarized so aptly for the next century in 1704. Suckling's tastefully posed figure nursing its expensive folio may therefore also be placed in a rocky wilderness because by 1638 Shakespeare was associated with untutored brilliance, as Milton wrote in 'L'Allegro', describing the stage where 'sweetest Shakespeare fancy's child' warbles 'his native wood-notes wild'.

The representation of Shakespeare's works in this elite painting is therefore a telling indication of the growing cultural status of some English writers and their publications on the eve of the Civil Wars. Van Dyck rarely included books in his paintings, and Malcolm Rogers has argued that the Suckling portrait is probably 'the first pictorial reference to Shakespeare and his works', and more specifically, possibly 'the first portrait...painted in England to include an identifiable book in the vernacular (apart from the Bible and Prayer Book) not written by the sitter'. Suckling's portrait also seems to offer striking evidence for the development of a Hamlet 'cult' as early as the 1630s, where the obscure quotation from Persius becomes a rewriting of Polonius's advice, 'To thine own self be true.' Arguing from similar sentiments in the decade, Jonathan Bate proposes 'that Shakespeare was the first writer in Western high culture to be praised specifically for his supposed artlessness',[10] and if so, then Van Dyck's portrait is an elegant and complex contribution to this founding myth, the first painting to celebrate the 'native genius' – of an English book.

Debating early modern literary culture

The 'Middle Ages' were smoothly succeeded by the 'Renaissance' in European cultural histories until very recently. In this version of the narrative a long period of Christian hegemony was displaced by the 'rebirth' of more 'man-centred' values inspired by the discovery and popularization of classical, pagan learning through the efforts of 'humanist' scholarship. But during the last two decades 'Renaissance' as a description of the period 1400–1700 has been largely replaced in academic history and some cultural criticism by a more neutral phrase, the 'early modern'. This defines the period not retrospectively but prospectively, where the 'early modern' is the precursor of 'modernity', and not the reformation of secular antiquity. Two dominant trends in Anglo-American criticism have helped to bring about this sea-change: new historicism and cultural materialism, with feminist-inspired theory and research contributing to both. Each of these approaches, with varying emphases, questioned accepted descriptions of 'renaissance literature' by redefining the relationships between cultural production and socio-political context. This research has broadened the range of authors and works studied from the years 1500 to 1700, partly by juxtaposing 'literary' and 'non-literary' texts, and most significantly by establishing a place for women's writing in the curriculum. Early modern conceptions of the person have been at the centre of much of this debate, focusing on the nature of identity and the forms assumed by subjectivity in distant cultures and alien value systems.[11]

The work of the French philosopher-historian Michel Foucault exerted a major influence on this research, encouraging attention to the circulation of 'power' and its effects in early modern society. These critical positions viewed culture as a set of transactions within 'discursive formations', a crucial means by which social hierarchy was maintained through the reproduction of ideological values in specific texts, theatrical performances or paintings. The new historicism and cultural materialism therefore perpetuated a dominant form of European historiography from the 1960s and 1970s which was broadly materialist and structuralist. This approach sought to define the supra-individual forces which governed economic development, social relations and the discourses by which these processes were mediated through specific communities and lives. In this form, historical and cultural studies came closest to Durkheim's conception of the practice of the social sciences, mapping the 'deep structures' which were thought to promote social formation.[12] New historicist and cultural materialist criticism therefore represented a 'return to history' which intended to demystify the separate, idealist category of 'literature' through rigorous contextualization. Simultaneously, they would also reform 'old historicist' methodology by constructing accounts of former societies which bore more directly on late twentieth-century debates over gender, power and representation.

But it can be argued that both the new historicism and cultural materialism were still not fully historical because they made only selective use of the growing range of approaches which other historians of early modern society have developed.[13] The study of early modern Britain was transformed during the 1970s by the 'new social history' which extended research into the life of the middling and poorer levels of society. This work produced a more detailed knowledge of early modern social structure, mapping crucial areas such as the changing patterns of marriage, family organization, social mores, crime and punishment, and popular culture and belief, all in fascinating detail. The localized nature of social life was explored through studies of towns and villages, and the development of London was established even more clearly as a quite exceptional history. A genuinely novel area of all this research was the attention given to the stratified nature of early modern literacy and the ways in which the availability of the separate skills of reading and writing was broadly conditioned by status, gender and region. At the same time the older, grander narratives of constitutional and political history, against which both the 'new social history' and the 'new critical historicisms' were reacting, also continued to be vigorously debated. One perspective which developed from these arguments revised accounts of the causes and consequences of the British Civil Wars and the nature of the Restoration settlement, through focusing on the ways in which Ireland and Scotland ignited the conflicts of the 1640s.[14]

This British 'new social history' paralleled similar developments in European research. During the 1980s Italian and Spanish historians produced 'microhistories' which worked outwards from the minute particularities of specific lives through their filiations into the wider community, rather than downward from supposedly dominant discourses operating abstractly on passive individuals. These enquiries were influenced by developments in ethnomethodology and anthropology which moved the focus of historical enquiry from 'the structures and mechanisms lying beyond all subjective grasp that govern social relations' to 'the multiple rationalities and strategies put into operation by communities, kinship groups, families, and individuals'.[15] Increasingly, detailed European and British social histories such as these restored a notion of individuals as active agents within their life-worlds, able to negotiate with conventions of their time and place by finessing the inherent contradictions of social hierarchy and arbitrating between competing expectations. Social relations in the period suddenly became much more fluid seen from this perspective of individuals, families and communities making their way by strategic compromise with discourses which earlier work viewed as oppressively all-embracing. In Roger Chartier's description, these historians moved on from studying 'the imposed rules to the inventive use of those rules; from obligatory behaviours to the decisions that each individual's resources permitted'. This work demonstrated the legitimacy of the major objection to Foucault's construction of past society (and by implication, present politics), because, as J. G. Merquior argued, it was 'devoid of any vision of non-alienated social relations'. When adapted by new historicist cultural critics such as Stephen Greenblatt, this aspect of Foucault's influence had therefore encouraged analysis of culture and politics in which 'By means of a rhetorical personification, power has been essentialized so as to absorb all agency.'[16]

Research into the 'social history of the book' also began to grow during the 1980s in response to some related debates. This new attention to the nature of printed materials developed from long-established disciplines such as bibliography and textual criticism, the physical history of writing as studied by Italian palaeography, and more recent disciplines such as the history of education, literacy studies and the socio-cultural histories of the French Annales school. These approaches converged in an examination of the material conditions of book production and distribution, extending traditional bibliographical studies by considering the ways in which texts were disseminated and read by variant constituencies, and focusing on three broad concerns: first, literary activity understood in its widest sense, including the acquisition of reading and writing skills differentiated by status, gender, age and region; second, all aspects of the production of text, from patronage to publication and distribution, inevitably including questions of censorship; and finally, to close the circuit, the multitude of ways in which individuals interpreted text through specific acts of reading or listening, again influenced by the communal assumptions governing personal interpretation.

One consequence of these historical studies of literacy-in-society has been to reposition the meaning of 'power' as defined by new historicist and cultural materialist critics. Where Foucault-inspired approaches considered how power was imposed and internalized through discursive formations in early modern societies, the new histories of writing have explored the ways in which literacy contributed positively to the struggle for representation and expression. As the ability to read and write spread among many constituencies for the first time, individuals gained a new 'power' in the sense of a personal competence which they were able to deploy for their own purposes. *Writing and Society* contributes to the study of early modern literary culture by bringing together several areas of this scholarship. The first five chapters integrate recent work on education and literacy, gender and status, and the regulation and censorship of printing. Having established key issues in these areas, Chapters 6, 7 and 8 go on to develop sustained readings of specific individuals and works. These three chapters are intended to demonstrate how the combined perspectives of literacy, print and politics may reveal new ranges of material and develop new kinds of interpretation for early modern culture, and contribute to the understanding of 'Language in history: that full field...in which the conditions of production, in the fullest sense, can be understood in relation to both writer and reader, actual writing and actual reading.' This was the disciplinary convergence which Raymond Williams projected in his own *Writing in Society*, one of the places in which the present book, in certain ways, began.[17]

Early modern English society was differentiated by a complex hierarchy of wealth, status and codes of behaviour, forming the tacit assumptions by which individuals conducted their lives, but literary criticism influenced by new historicism and cultural materialism has perhaps been reluctant to reintroduce notions of social hierarchy which might be confused with an 'Elizabethan world picture' articulating an orderly 'great chain of being', one of the dominant critical perspectives which was most fiercely attacked as a nostalgic and intrinsically conservative construction of 'renaissance' literature by the new cultural criticism of the 1970s.[18] It may be for this reason that the new social history's researches on hierarchy, which have transformed the study of the sixteenth and seventeenth centuries in British history, have not been widely referred to in literary studies. Chapter 2, 'Status and literacy: the qualities of people', therefore coordinates an account of the commonly accepted descriptions of early modern social hierarchy debated during the period itself with findings on attainment in literacy. Seven ranks or degrees of society are described in terms of their wealth, social standing and political status, together with the extent to which men and women in each 'degree' are thought to have been able to read and write; specific authors are cited from each category. These ranks were endlessly discussed and disputed in their own period, and this debate was an intrinsic part of early modern self-image, the point at which individual identity merged with a larger sense of collectivity. It is therefore crucial to recognize that notions of hierarchy were current, and fiercely contested, in ways which were directly linked to the acquisition of literacy and associated prestige.

Chapter 3, ' "Towardness": aptitude, gender and rank in early modern education', indicates how social standing and gender might affect an individual's access to school in the sixteenth and seventeenth centuries. Despite early modern prejudice against women being admitted to learning, there was a slow but gradual increase in provision and, most interestingly, the contradictions inherent in patriarchal attitudes towards female education demonstrate how opportunities might be seized by individuals for their own purposes, against the commonplace prejudices of the time. These contradictory attitudes to gender and rank are examined in *Positions [concerning] The Training Up of Children*, an educational treatise by the leading Elizabethan pedagogue Richard Mulcaster.

Throughout the period just one guild or company of artisans was responsible for publication of all printed materials in Britain. The Worshipful Company of Stationers had sole charge of commissioning, printing and disseminating every pamphlet and book produced, and more than this, the Company was also entrusted by the state with responsibility for regulating and censoring all published materials. Chapter 4, ' "Mechanics in the suburbs of literature": printing and publishing 1590–1660' provides a brief history of the Stationers' Company, one of the medieval guild organizations at the heart of the City of London's politics. This institution struggled to maintain control of a printing industry which always threatened to outrun its authority, especially during periods of economic and political crisis such as the Civil Wars. The British publishing trade during its first two centuries was insular and parochial, and produced little in the way of book-work to compare with the achievements of continental renaissance printing, but this localism in one sense advantaged writers in English because a higher proportion of vernacular literature was therefore published. An author's relationship to his (or, very much more rarely, her) published work in the period was also radically different to anything we may imagine. Sixteenth- and seventeenth-century writers had no copyright claim on their text once it had been bought by a stationer, who could be both the printer and publisher (disseminator) of the item. Writing and publication were therefore in transition between pre-modern attitudes, where authors generally composed at the request of patrons and for circulation among a known community, and the modern anonymous market for multiple copies produced by the printing press. The address of some writing in the period is therefore curiously caught between appealing to an intimate, immediate coterie of familiar readers, and the anonymous consumption of meaning bought in the open market of the city street. In fact, improvements in the technology of paper manufacture during the fifteenth century had enabled expansion in the production of (handwritten) text before the introduction of printing, so the advent of the press was by no means a dramatic transformation of publishing practices.

New work on the social history of literacy has constructed a much more detailed account of press regulation and censorship than was previously available, and this research can be used to examine new historicist and cultural materialist assumptions about the ways in which the 'symbolic system' of early modern culture circulated and controlled meaning. Chapter 5, 'Censorship and state formation: heresy, sedition and the Celtic literary cultures', sets the day-to-day operation of literary surveillance and censorship within a framework of the state's management of the transition from universal Catholicism to national Protestantism. Fundamental to this fraught process was the need to regulate religious practice within every parish, and to confront the disparate cultures and belief systems of the outlying regions. Chapter 5 therefore indicates something of the nature of the literary cultures of Celtic Ireland, Scotland and Wales, where censorship took the form of language-suppression directed against indigenous speech and writing. Interest in the history of these non-English cultures is growing during the 1990s as the political landscape of the British regions begins to change and the debates over the 'Four Kingdoms' conducted during the constitutional and cultural crisis of the Civil Wars take on new resonance. Our developing awareness of early modern Celtic literatures therefore presents new opportunities to read them – even as translations – in relation to English writing of the period. Chapter 5 also examines the operation of censorship within English religious and literary culture in terms of the surveillance exercised by the Worshipful Company of Stationers over publication and, briefly, of the Master of Revels' supervision of play-texts. New research suggests that here Elizabethan and Jacobean censorship was very much more piecemeal and ineffective than has been thought, leaving writing, drama and opinion relatively free to evade the state's overview by various stratagems.[19]

The following three chapters present different kinds of detailed 'case study' as demonstrations of the ways in which awareness of issues surrounding literacy, publication, social rank and politics may reveal new kinds of material and contribute to new insights. One of the most productive areas of the 'new social history' has pieced together in considerable detail the nature of early modern popular culture, a fascinating world in transition between the beliefs and practices of rural, customary culture and the developing life of the towns and cities. Chapter 6, ' "Penny merriments, penny godlinesses": new writing for new readers', outlines some of the debates over the nature and extent of this emergent urban, increasingly print-based culture, and explores the career of a quite new kind of author, John Taylor the 'Water Poet' (1578–1653). Born into a modest family in Gloucester, Taylor failed to complete his grammar-school education and was forced to become apprenticed as a sculler in London, rowing people across the Thames for meagre payment. He fell in love with the muse at the height of the 1590s poetry boom, and from 1612 began to produce a stream of pamphlets in a variety of genres right up to the year of his death. Taylor may be accurately described as one of England's first self-taught professional authors writing for print publication, composing primarily for the new popular audience in London and the provinces, and his career demonstrates the changing nature of literary patronage, as writers desperately sought readers in the novel environment of a commercial market. Taylor's output also raises crucial questions about the 'literary value' of pamphlets which have till now been generally disparaged as possessing no more than contextual or ephemeral interest.

New historical and cultural materialist criticism by and large has not exploited the work of historians of early modern popular culture, but women's writing in the period has begun to receive much more attention owing to ground-breaking scholarship in gender studies and feminist-inspired research. Chapter 7, ' "Dressed up with the flowers of a Library": women reading and writing', discusses the reading lives of two women from sharply contrasting social backgrounds in order to dramatize central critical issues around the study of early modern female literacy. The importance of Christian belief and practice to life in the sixteenth and seventeenth centuries cannot be over-estimated, and Chapter 7 examines the place of reading and belief in the lives of two women from quite different strata of seventeenth-century Christian society. Mistress Dorothy Hazzard, a courageous dissenting citizen of Bristol, played a key role during the siege of her city by Prince Rupert's forces in 1643, and at a moment of personal crisis her reading of the Bible made a decisive change in her life. By contrast, Lady Anne Clifford (1590–1676) was born into one of the half-dozen families that constituted the Elizabethan social and political elite, and she held characteristic Anglican beliefs with a strong Calvinist vein. As part of her devotional life, Anne Clifford intermittently maintained a journal detailing her struggle to regain family estates which she lost in 1605 and only won back in 1643. To confirm her title and status in 1646, she commissioned and designed a massive dynastic portrait depicting her family's history in which a central part is the detailed representation of over fifty separate volumes identifiable by author and title. Lady Anne Clifford's *Great Picture* is a unique portrayal of a woman's reading life among the Jacobean and Carolean nobility, and a complex example of the interplay of visual and verbal meaning in seventeenth-century culture. A particular concern of this chapter is the need to consider the ways in which social status might qualify the effects of patriarchal prejudice and convention as they bore on the circumstances of individual women in their reading and writing.

Writing and Society concludes with a detailed chronological outline of the main political and constitutional developments from 1589 through to 1662. This supplies a framework to contextualize the descriptions of hierarchy, literacy and culture given in the preceding chapters, and lists significant publications and performances for each year.

'Vale, soror, anima mea': reading the moment of writing

One early September around AD 100, Claudia Severa, living somewhere near the Solway Firth, dictated her birthday invitation to Sulpicia Lepidina at Vindolanda, thirty miles to the east. The women belonged to the imperial military elite, Claudia as wife of Aelius Brocchus, an equestrian officer, and Sulpicia as wife to Flavius Cerialis, prefect of the Ninth Cohort of Batavians. A professional scribe took down the message in ink, writing on to a thin leaf of birch wood:

> Claudia Severa to her Lepidina greetings. On 11 September, sister, for the day of the celebration of my birthday, I give you a warm invitation to make sure that you come to us, to make the day more enjoyable for me by your arrival, if you are present [?]. Give my greetings to your Cerialis. My Aelius and my little son send him [?] their greetings.

The scribe wrote in his efficient secretary hand, but at the bottom right-hand corner of the leaf Claudia Severa added her own four lines in a less practised script:

> Sperabo te soror
> uale soror anima
> mea ita ualeam
> karissima et haue

Her ephemeral trace has survived nearly two millenia. So far, it is the earliest known Latin from a woman's hand: 'I shall expect you, sister. Farewell, sister, my dearest soul, as I hope to prosper, and hail.' The complete isolation of the fragment intensifies the call of its familiar emotions, perhaps expressing only conventional sentiments, but somehow offering more than these – the inversion 'anima mea' is a touching rhetorical moment, since the 'emotive and regular position of the possessive in the intimate form of address was before the noun or name'.[20] Simultaneously recognizable to a second-millenium reader, but also alien, the twelve words hint at an entire world of relationships and obligations which we may then begin to imagine, and research.

From the mid-seventeenth century onwards a growing number of ephemeral texts survive from newly literate classes of people, tentatively beginning to write as a form of self-expression and self-reflection in ways that are much more legible for us now. Hester

Wyat, otherwise unknown, wrote one poem which has survived in a copy made by a friend, 'In Answer to One Who Asked Why She Wrote':

> What makes me write my dearest Friend you ask
> For our Sex always thought too great a task
> I grant you this yet 'tis no ill spent time
> And my thoughts naturally fall into Rhyme
> Rude and unpolished from my pen they flow
> So artless I my native tongue scarce know
> Learning the Wit and judgement must improve
> Refine the verse and tender passion move
> Whilst me no muse assists nor God of Love

After the obligatory modest remarks that composition is too demanding for the female sex, and characterizing her own inspiration as an effect of 'nature' rather than education, Wyat describes a writing that is seemingly free of conventional motives and forms of inspiration. She is not moved by classical sources, nor by erotic investment; nor, most remarkably, is spirituality her inspiration, because during the 1640s and 1650s it was Christian belief which sustained the majority of women beginning to publish for the first time:

> So whilst in Solitude the days I pass
> Paper I make my Friend and mind's true Glass [Mirror]
> To that my self unbosom free from fear
> Of a false woman's tongue or Listening ear [...]
> With joy I from these noisy crowds retire
> And from my thoughts of my own Heart enquire
> Should we not to ourselves this great debt pay
> The little time that fleeting Life does stay
> Were worthless if unthinking thrown away
> Then I my secret thoughts collect and write
> Cause this improves me, most does most delight[21]

Written in rural solitude, undistracted by love, 'vice', or the inanities of socially constructed femininity, this poem is another exchange of intense affection between women friends, one page among the growing number of letters circulating as a new form of distant intimacy. But more than Claudia Severa's invitation, Hester Wyat's 'Answer' describes writing as an exercise in self-collection, the new competence which 'most improves' and 'most delights', and which may side-step and move beyond the otherwise crushing conventions of its time. The following chapters explore similar reading- and writing-moments experienced by children, men and women of all ranks in the late sixteenth and seventeenth centuries, together with contexts which illuminate literacy's extraordinary contribution to early modern British society.

2

STATUS AND LITERACY

The qualities of people

An Exhortation concerning Good Order and Obedience to Rulers and Magistrates

Almighty God hath created and appointed all things in heaven, earth and waters in a most excellent and perfect order. In heaven he hath appointed distinct or several orders and states of Archangels and Angels. In earth he hath assigned and appointed kings, princes, with other governors under them, in all good and necessary order. The water above is kept and raineth down in due time and season. The Sun, Moon, Stars, Rainbow, Thunder, Lightning, Clouds and all birds of the air, do keep their order. The earth, Trees, Seeds, Plants, Herbs, Corn, Grass and all manner of beasts, keep themselves in their order. All the parts of the whole year, as Winter, Summer, Months, nights and days, continue in their order. All kinds of fishes in the Sea, Rivers, and Waters, with all fountains, Springs, yea, the Seas themselves, keep their comely course and order. And man himself also hath all his parts, both within and without: as soul, heart, mind, memory, understanding, reason, speech, with all and singular corporal members of his body, in a profitable, necessary and pleasant order. Every degree of people in their vocation, calling and office, hath appointed to them their duty and order. Some are in high degree, some in low, some kings and princes, some inferiors and subjects, priests and laymen, Masters and Servants, Fathers and children, husbands and wives, rich and poor, and every one have need of other: so that in all things is to be lauded and praised the goodly order of God, without the which, no house, no city, no commonwealth can continue and endure or last. For where there is no right order, there reigneth all abuse, carnal liberty, enormity, sin and Babilonical confusion. Take away kings, princes, rulers, magistrates, judges and such estates of God's order, no man shall ride or go by the highway unrobbed, no man shall sleep in his own house or bed unkilled, no man shall keep his wife, children and possessions in quietness, all things shall be common, and there must needs follow all mischief and utter destruction, both of souls, bodies, goods, commonwealths.

Certain Sermons..., 1560, fol. R.iiii [r–v]

Certain Sermons Appointed by the Queen's Majesty to be declared and read...for the better understanding of the simple people

The first book of homilies was published during the minority reign of Edward VI in July 1547, supervised by Archbishop Thomas Cranmer. Together with the Book of Common Prayer it was a vital part of the attempt to establish the authority of the Anglican church at a dangerous period. The twelve sermons were essentially a defence of moderate Protestant beliefs and practices against Roman Catholicism on the one hand, and sectarian Anabaptists (or 'gospellers') on the other. They were to be read to congregations throughout the year 'because...the people continue in ignorance and blindness' (Bond: 4). Cranmer himself is credited with writing the crucial sermons on salvation, faith and good works. They transformed medieval homiletic conventions from a straightforward moral discourse on points of scripture into a rationale for the church as an integral part of a secular state. The reading of the homilies replaced the priest's own sermon and prepared the people to receive the sacrament. They were therefore a criterion for ensuring religious conformity in both priest and congregation by imposing 'a most quiet, godly and uniform order' (6) throughout the realm:

> the Tudor state, having eliminated all duality from government by placing authority over both church and state in the same royal hands, laid a greater and more practically enforceable stress on religious unity than had been associated with the medieval Catholic polity.
>
> (Collinson: 228–9)

The homilies were suppressed during the reign of the Catholic monarch Mary Tudor, 1553–8, but quickly reissued one year after Elizabeth's accession in 1558, with the new queen herself involved in revising the texts to make them more comprehensible for 'the simple people' (9). A second book appeared in 1563, less preoccupied with central tenets of Protestant faith and more concerned to encourage moderate behaviour and beliefs in daily life as well as in religion, but still requiring above all obedience to superiors, church and state. Throughout her reign Elizabeth firmly advocated readings from the homilies as a way of enforcing conformity. The elaborate 'Homily against Disobedience and Wilful Rebellion' was added to the existing two books in 1570 as a part of the response to the Catholic Northern Uprising (1569–70) and was divided into short sections so that it could be read with greater effect on succeeding Sundays. All editions of *Certain Sermons* issued before 1683 were set in black letter to foreground their status and authority, but from the 1590s they were subject to increasing attack from reform-minded clergy and believers who wished to promote the independent role of the sermon in worship. The final edition, 'required and authorized' by government, was the 1623 folio, carefully printed on good paper, as part of the Crown's response to the growing popularity of Puritan 'Prophecyings' or extempore preaching. But by 1687 an edition produced for the private edification of families within their households was one indication that the public authority of *Certain Sermons* was in serious decline. These homilies 'were probably, next to the Book of Common Prayer, as well known and as influential as any writings produced between 1547 and 1640' (Rickey and Stroup: viii).

Quotations from Ronald R. Bond *Certain Sermons or Homilies (1547)...*, A Critical Edition (Toronto, University of Toronto Press, 1987); the facsimile reproduction of the edition of 1623 with an introduction by Mary Ellen Rickey and Thomas B. Stroup (Gainesville, FL, Scholars' Facsimiles and Reprints, 1968); Patrick Collinson, 'William Shakespeare's religious inheritance and environment', pp. 218–52 in *Elizabethan Essays* (London and Rio Grande, The Hambledon Press, 1994). An electronic facsimile of the 1623 text, edited by Ian Lancashire with introduction and commentary, is available from University of Toronto, Center for Computing in the Humanities, Renaissance Electronic Texts 1.1, 1994 (www.utoronto.ca).

All which Homilies, her Majesty commandeth, and straitly chargeth all Parsons, Vicars, Curates, and all other having spiritual cure, every Sunday and Holyday in the year, at the ministering of the holy Communion, or if there be no Communion ministered that day, yet after the Gospel and Creed,...to read and declare to their Parishoners plainly and distinctly one of the said Homilies, in such order as they stand in the Book,...And when the foresaid Book of Homilies is read over, her Majesty's pleasure is, that the same be repeated and read again, in such like sort was before prescribed [the Injunctions, Lord's Prayer, Articles of Faith, and ten Commandments] be openly read unto the people...that all her people, of what degree or condition soever they be, may learn how to invocate and call upon the name of God, and know what duty they owe both to God and man.

'The Preface', 1559, in Bond 1987: 57–8

From 'degree' to 'political arithmetic': mapping social hierarchy

The Homily on 'Good Order and Obedience' of 1549 attempted to naturalize the conventions of late medieval society within God's providential framework for cosmos, nature, body, household and community. Each human category was also firmly patriarchal, a further regime of constraint. But many people hearing the sermon's liturgical cadences – 'good and necessary order', 'comely course and order', 'necessary and pleasant order' – repeated year after year in the later sixteenth century would have noted how it failed to account for the increasingly complicated culture in which they lived. The Homily is at odds with the more discriminating social categories which were being constructed to describe status and hierarchy in the 1590s, a set of working assumptions which survived in

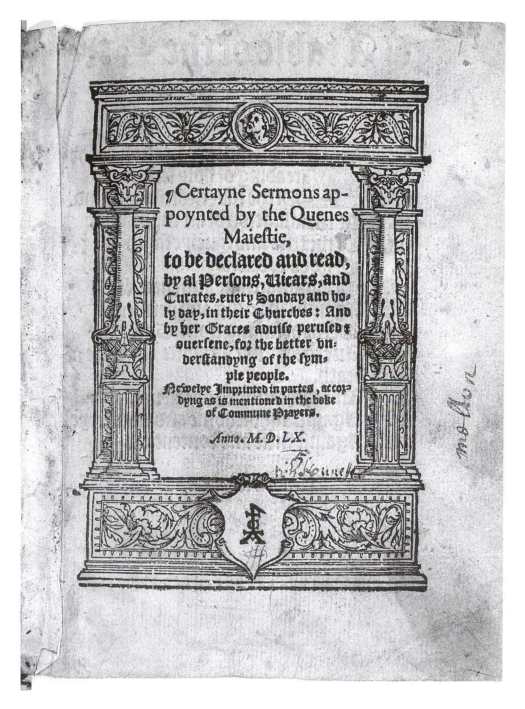

Figure 3 Certain Sermons appointed by the Queen's majesty to be declared and read ... for the better understanding of the simple people, 1560, R. Jugge and J. Cawood

Title page, Quarto, 19 cm. By permission of the Syndics of Cambridge University Library

various forms until the late eighteenth century, when it was finally displaced by the more strictly socio-economic model of 'class', and which was itself replacing the anachronistic medieval schema of the three 'estates'. Sixteenth- and seventeenth-century commentators wrote of 'orders', 'ranks' or 'degrees' within society, though they might also, more neutrally, describe the 'sorts' of people, a term which then had to be qualified as appropriate – 'better', 'meaner', 'learned', 'vulgar'.[1] From the 1640s the 'middling sort' evoked substantial new interests – the Levellers' *Declaration* of 1649 claimed to speak for 'all the middle sort and poor people' against rack-renters and unjust law. Seventeenth-century commentators also occasionally wrote of the 'class' of an individual, but it is anachronistic to think in terms of 'working-class' or 'middle-class' groups in this period, social formations which characterize the increasingly urban and industrializing societies of the later eighteenth century.

Social position in the early modern period, as now, was a complex mixture of wealth and status, and recent scholarship has for the first time begun to map the varying levels of literacy attainment in relation to social standing. In making descriptions of their contemporary society, early modern social commentators were also articulating their assumptions about the hierarchy of power and influence, and how the civility of ordered status was maintained. Their descriptions mingled political prescription with economic description. The place of gender in social hierarchy in the early modern period cannot be uncoupled from these complex, sometimes contradictory gradations because the social being of female and male was inextricably linked to position as well as to sex. Conventional attitudes of the time assumed that the female was at all points subservient to the male, as daughter and wife, and frankly as woman; this hierarchy 'was sustained informally through culture, custom and differences in education, and more formally through law'.[2] But the descriptions of women's reading and writing in Chapter 7 explore the ways in which individuals often flouted these commonplace assumptions as to what was appropriate gendered behaviour, complicating any straightforward notion that women were always necessarily and absolutely subordinated by patriarchal hierarchy.

'Order', 'rank' or 'degree' in early modern society indicated status deriving from a whole complex of qualities including family standing, gender, kinship ties, political connection and place in the community, property and how it was possessed, as well as conspicuous display and consumption as a function of wealth. The last might include construction of elaborate properties, lavish hospitality and expensive clothing, maintenance of a numerous household, and exercise of patronage, which could extend to writers and scholars. The nation's housing stock was rebuilt during this period, and the inhabitants reclothed in the lighter and cheaper 'new draperies', indicating the impact of freer capital and an increase in circulation of all kinds of goods. Sumptuary legislation attempted to enforce dress codes and correlate degrees of material display with social status, but always ineffectually. By the late 1570s William Harrison was lamenting the decay of honest plainness in English clothing: 'nothing is more constant in England than inconstancy of attire'. He deplored flashy eclecticism in dress, the aping of all kinds of foreign fashions, such that men 'bestow most cost upon our arses...as women doe likewise upon their heads and shoulders'. Flouting of the dress codes continued to grieve authority: thirty years later, on 22 February 1619, the Dean of Salisbury preached a fierce denunciation of luxurious raiments before King James and Prince Charles: 'They are not for every sole and private man to gather about him a gaping multitude, but for Magistrates and other remarkable persons, employed in governing estates, and serving of Kings.'[3]

For as much as people commented on the stratifications of their social world, they were also acutely conscious of the mobility of personal and family status. Sir Thomas Wilson grumpily observed in 1600,

> but my young masters...not contented with the states of their fathers to be counted yeomen and called John or Robert...must skip into...velvet breeches and silken doublet and, getting to be admitted into some Inn of Court or Chancery, must ever after think scorn to be called any other than gentleman.

Time and again, as here, education was regarded as the cultural capital which made a decisive contribution to social standing. It was an uncertain world where a family might rise or fall within a generation through the ravages of disease, fluctuations of trade and harvest, bad debts, fire, and in the mid-century, the devastation brought by the Civil Wars. Significant numbers of family fortunes also seem to have been drunk and gambled to nothing. But in broadest outline, the physical conditions of life probably improved for the majority of people between 1500 and 1700. The wealthy land-owning classes expanded and grew richer, the urban patriciate and the middling sort also prospered, and the more vulnerable majority of people were progressively less exposed to subsistence crises than their European counterparts. The population grew from 2.9 million in 1546 to 4.1 million by 1601, peaking at 5.28 million by 1656, and falling back to 4.9 million in 1686, then rising slowly to 5.05 million by 1700. The expansion of London was phenomenal: from 55,000 citizens in 1520 to 475,000 by 1640, despite high mortality rates from plague and other disease: 'let the Mortality be what it will, the City repairs its loss of Inhabitants within two years, which Observation lessens the Objection made against the value of houses in London', John Graunt, the first true demographer, cannily observed in 1662. This dramatic increase meant that young people formed a higher proportion of the population: 'As you walk in the streets or look into the register book of your churches,...you shall find more living under the age of thirty than above', noted Godfrey Goodman, chaplain to Queen Anne, in 1616. The 'nuclear' family structure of parents, unmarried children and servants, rather than an 'extended' family, was the English norm; the average size of household in Ealing at the end of the sixteenth century has been calculated as 4.75 individuals, and average life expectancy no more than to the late thirties.[4]

The groups listed below, in descending order of early modern status, are the categories most commonly offered at the time, though writers differed in details and about precedence. Examples of authors from each rank are cited to demonstrate the inter-relations of status, education, gender and authorship. Little indication can be given of the large regional variations in status and wealth, often very marked between the north, west and south-eastern areas of England. The social composition and structures in Ireland, Scotland and Wales were so different that they have to be omitted; nor is there space to include arguments about the relative changes in size and prosperity of different social groups within the English population. Rankings were constructed entirely in reference to male status and occupation; women were subsumed under each grouping as the help-meet or chattel of the male, and their labour was focused on household management and child-raising. Distinctions maintained between what was appropriate to each gender in the 'public' and 'private' spheres respectively are very revealing: much of the key evidence for literacy attainment is based on signatures attached to oaths and declarations which were issued by parliaments at moments of national crisis. The Protestation Oath of 1641 was designed to mobilize the country against any coup attempts by the King or his followers, and demanded the signature of all males aged 18 and above, 'both householders and others', requiring them to defend 'the true, reformed and Protestant religion, expressed in the doctrine of the Church of England'. The gravity of the national situation was therefore brought home to every community, and a far larger proportion of the male population signed the Oath than was ever involved in parliamentary elections. The exclusion of women from these nation-wide exercises of political and religious conformity is a stark indication of what was required of them: they were silently incorporated under their menfolks' affirmation of loyalty. The lack of female signatures also makes women's literacy attainments more difficult to assess. Recent research suggests that really significant increases in female literacy occurred from the 1650s onwards in London, coinciding with a distinct growth in numbers of publications by female authors; one in two women in the capital city could write their signature in the final decade. However these assessments of literacy rates, based only on the ability to make a signature, may significantly under-estimate the ability to read, particularly among rural populations, because the two skills were taught separately. Children from poorer homes may have been withdrawn from petty school at the age of 6 or 7 to begin work in the fields; they might gain elementary reading skills but remain unable to write. This pattern continued through to the nineteenth century when it is estimated that one-third more children were able to read than write. The percentages throughout this chapter should therefore be thought of as consistently under-estimating probable levels of writing ability. There is also scepticism about the apparent 'gender gap' in early modern literacy: more girls than boys may have been taught reading only, an unquantifiable skill. Margaret Spufford is forthright on this: 'There is absolutely no way of knowing how many women below the level of the gentry in England learnt to read.'[5]

The titled nobility: 'the Theatre of Hospitality'

The peers of the realm were a small group of families owning 15 per cent of the land: dukes, marquises, earls, viscounts and barons, either created by the monarch or inheriting title, and taking seats in the House of Lords. They increased from 60 in 1600 to over 160 by the end of the century (numbering only the males as holders of title). This inflation was created by the Stuarts as they doled out honours to secure their position or raise revenues. Baronets, an order established in 1611 by James VI and I, could inherit title but did not sit in the Lords. Knights 'be not born but made'; esquires were the lowest rank of titled nobility. This caste was highly endogamous, that is, it married from within its own members, and so was virtually impossible to enter from 'below'. The nobility held the major offices of state, tended to supply Members of Parliament for their counties, and also occupied key regional administrative posts. Conspicuous consumption and prodigious expenditure were essential expressions of their status, and this elite rebuilt, reclothed and educated itself vigorously from the mid-sixteenth century onwards. Sir Henry Wotton, in his *Elements of Architecture* (1624), wrote:

> Every Man's proper Mansion House and Home, [is] the Theatre of his Hospitality, the Seat of Self-fruition, the Comfortablest part of his own Life, the Noblest of his Sons' Inheritance, a kind of private Princedom; Nay...an Epitome of the whole World.

This exactly conveys the nature of elite (patriarchal) generosity which was theatrically staged for consumption and approval. King James spent £47,000 on jewels for gifting in 1604, when his income from estates was less than £125,000.

Literacy for the nobility (and gentry) was therefore both a functional skill and a competence used as a social marker: the leisured cultivation of (more or less) wide reading might be a reward in itself, but it also demonstrated the capacity to be able to indulge time and expense in non-functional pursuits, 'liberal' rather than 'mechanical' learning. Henry Peacham stressed 'the Dignity and Necessity of Learning' in his *Complete Gentleman* (1622): 'Since learning, then, is an essential part of nobility, as unto which we are beholden for whatsoever dependeth on the culture of the mind, it followeth that who is nobly born and a scholar withal deserveth double honour.'[6] At just what point the 'functional' literacy of the lower grades of society might develop into these less tangibly rewarding activities is an interesting question. Even the physical exercise of writing by hand was thought to be demeaning by some elevated persons. There is an echo of this in *Hamlet* as the Prince tells Horatio how on the voyage to England he changed Claudius's written commission:

> ...I sat me down,
> Devis'd a new commission, wrote it fair –
> I once did hold it, as our statists do,
> A baseness to write fair, and labour'd much
> How to forget that learning, but sir, now
> It did me yeoman's service.[7]

Men of consequence – 'statists' – deliberately chose not to write with a 'fair' hand because as a manual activity it was more suited to 'yeoman' (laborious) status. Hamlet demonstrated here another of his role's mercurial qualities when he switched so adroitly between the hierarchies of literacy.

Male literacy among the nobility was effectively complete, though there might be odd exceptions in the early seventeenth century. Philip, fourth Earl of Pembroke, a sophisticated courtier at the centre of power and one of the dedicatees for Shakespeare's First Folio, was said to be barely literate though he had sophisticated taste in painting: was he an early modern dyslectic? The Scottish Highlands and islands presented another exceptional case. Patrick Stewart, second Earl of Orkney, Lord of Shetland, ruled his remote territories with cruel despotism, and before his execution for treason in 1615 one account relates that he was unable to recite the Lord's Prayer, 'A creature unprepared, unmeet for death' as the Duke says of Barnadine in *Measure for Measure*. The Earl was given three days' respite 'to better inform himself'. In fact the story is probably folklore, revenge by way of rumour on an unpopular lord. The Statutes of Icolmkill, Iona (1609) actually required families of the western Isles 'being in goods worth [the value of] threescore cattle' to send their 'eldest son, or having no children male their eldest daughter to the schools on the Lowland...to speak, read, and write English', reinforcing an Act as old as 1496. This legislation was a defining moment in the process of undermining the position and status of clan leaders in the Highland areas. Patrick Stewart's foster-father had wanted him to travel to France 'or to some good college within England [to] learn virtue and good manners', a moral education which might not have come amiss. Gaelic was still current in the Highlands, and the Statutes were an early attempt to limit both the language and its culture, a campaign encouraged by King James (whose grandfather James was said to have been the last Scots monarch with any knowledge of Gaelic). The Protestant ethos of the Lowlands elite associated Gaelic with Catholicism, so church and state combined with increasing effectiveness against what was perceived as an ignorant and anachronistic way of life – very few books were printed in Scots Gaelic before the 1690s.[8] In Wales it was rare to find English speakers beyond the gentry, and overall literacy (in Welsh or English) has been estimated at 20 per cent: the Welsh-speaking population received no schooling, and the few grammar schools served the English-speaking gentry. Expansion in Wales occurred during the Commonwealth and Protectorate when some sixty schools were established by the Commissioners for the Propagation of the Gospel in Wales, though the majority of them had disappeared by 1660. Materials for statistical research into literacy rates for early modern Ireland are scarce; the arrival of Counter-Reformation teachings in the early seventeenth century had a significant impact among the Irish Gaelic population. High levels of book imports for the Anglo-Irish communities suggest a growing readership, though the fate of the 'Irish Stock' created by the Stationers' Company in 1618 suggests otherwise (see below); free schools were estab-lished in each county of the Ulster plantations.[9]

Sons of prominent English families such as Philip Sidney (1554–86) and Fulke Greville (1554–1628) followed the new trend of attending 'public' school rather than being privately taught within their families, going away to Shrewsbury, a fashionable institution in the 1560s, when exactly half of its 266 boys boarded as 'tablers'.[10] Sequestered tuition at home continued throughout the period for sons, and more particularly for daughters. Lady Anne Clifford was first taught by her governess, Mrs Anne Taylor, and then tutored by Samuel Daniel, who encouraged her love of poetry, particularly of Spenser. He also taught her future husband, the fourth Earl of Pembroke (but with poor results). Thomas Hobbes taught successive children of the Cavendish family for over thirty years; Andrew Marvell tutored Mary Fairfax, Sir Thomas Fairfax's daughter at Nunappleton in Wharfedale, and then went on to teach Cromwell's ward, William Dutton (the son of a deceased Royalist). Female literacy among the aristocracy presumably achieved the highest proportion for any of the social grades by gender because status granted leisure for the cultivation of wide reading and, very occasionally, for the indulgent transgression of writing.

Women of high status in sixteenth-century Irish society played a key role in the complex family and sept politics of the country, and were accorded legal privileges and a deference which could appear shocking to unsympathetic English visitors. They could also as a consequence be well educated, as suggested by the extraordinary career of Gráinne O'Malley, or Granuaile of later legend. Her family exercised their 'lordship of the sea' off the coast of Connacht from territory around Clew Bay, and by the late 1570s she was being condemned by Henry Sidney as a 'terror to all merchantmen that sailed the Atlantic'. In 1590 she took part in the western rebellion when she raided the Isle of Aran because it had been granted to an English administrator. Sir Richard Bingham, the English president of Connacht, was determined to finally subdue the area, and Gráinne O'Malley, along with other leaders, was reduced to poverty by 1593. From this low point she negotiated the right to present her claim for restitution of land at Elizabeth's court, having obtained safe passage to London. Among the British Gaelic cultures, the sophisti-cated households of the western Scottish lordships encouraged the earliest female writers; three Gaelic poems from the late fifteenth century are ascribed to Isabella, Countess of Argyle.

Britain produced no outstanding women of letters during the first half of the sixteenth century to compare with the likes of Italian and French writers such as Vittoria Colonna, Gaspara Stampa, Louise Labé or Marguerite de Navarre, again indicating a relative under-development of literacy and culture among the British urban elites and aristocracy. The first considerable Elizabethan Englishwoman of letters was Mary Herbert (née Sidney), Countess of Pembroke (1561–1621). A child of the political and cultural elite, she was sister to Sir Philip Sidney and daughter of Sir Henry Sidney, President of the Marches of Wales, who, as Lord Deputy of Ireland in 1565, had been charged with the forcible colonization of that country; her mother was Lady Mary Dudley, daughter of the Duke of Northumberland. Mary Sidney married Henry Herbert, Earl of Pembroke, in 1575: the bride was 15 and her groom 50 years old. She gave birth to four children between 1580 and 1584, and after the death of her brother and parents in 1586 the Countess became one of the foremost literary patrons of her time until the death of her husband in 1601. She contributed to the legitimacy of print as a medium for elite compositions by editing and publishing her brother's *Arcadia* and his sonnet sequence *Astrophil and Stella*, and offering patronage to writers including Fulke Greville, Edmund Spenser, Samuel Daniel and John Donne. She also made translations, including Philippe de Mornay's *Discourse of Life and Death* (1592, reprinted three times), Petrarch's *The Triumph of Death* (*c.* 1600) and Robert Garnier's *Marc Antoine* (1592), and wrote some original poems; her *Antonius* became a source for Shakespeare's *Antony and Cleopatra*. Her outstanding work was to complete a metaphrase (or 'creative translation') of the Psalms begun by her brother. Philip Sidney made ingenious versions of forty-three psalms, and his sister completed the remaining 107, demonstrating certainly an equal, if not greater, facility. The Sidney Psalter remained unpublished until 1823, but circulated widely in manuscript, read and admired by many, including Aemilia Lanyer, John Donne and George Herbert. Mary Sidney was aunt and godmother to Lady Mary Wroth (1586/7?–1651/3?) whose poetry (in manuscript) was widely valued: Ben Jonson dedicated *The Alchemist* to her. In 1621 she published *The Countess of Montgomery's Urania*, the first considerable prose fiction by an Englishwoman, including a poem sequence *Pamphilia to Amphilanthus*. Other authors from the female nobility include the diarists Lady Anne Clifford (1590–1676) (see Chapter 7, below), Mary Rich, Countess of Warwick (1624–78) and the biographer Lady Anne Fanshawe (1625–80). Margaret Cavendish, Duchess of Newcastle (1623–73), was not carefully educated but began writing compulsively even as a child. She became the most widely published authoress of her time, producing poems, plays, essays, letters and philosophical observations in profusion.[11]

The gentry: 'to be idle, and live upon the sweat of others'

The titled nobility were often called the 'nobilitas major' and non-titled families the 'nobilitas minor', or gentry, indicating that these were upper and lower tracts on a continuum of power and wealth, essentially one elite category. By strict definition the gentry was meant to be confined to 'the younger sons and brothers of esquires, and their male heirs', a rank immediately below the lowest rung of the aristocracy. But this was a permeable group, covering a great range of wealth; from 1580 to 1640 the landowning classes increased in number and prosperity relative to – and often at the expense of – the rest of society. This was the elite which had most to lose in periods of crisis, and during the Civil Wars 'few noblemen or greater gentry ranked amongst the militants on either side'.[12] The key factor was possession of sufficient capital in the form of land and rents, generating a surplus with which to subsidize cultivated, conspicuous consumption; gentle status also carried the obligation to take responsible public office. William Harrison's description demonstrates the competing values involved in the estimation of 'gentility':

> Gentlemen be those whom their race and blood, or at least their virtues, do make noble and known....Whosoever studieth the laws of the realm, whoso abideth in the university giving his mind to his book, or professeth physic and the liberal sciences, or, beside his service in the room [rank] of a captain in the wars or good counsel given at home, whereby his commonwealth is benefitted, can live without manual labour, and thereto is able and will bear the port, charge, and countenance of a gentleman, he shall for money have a coat and arms bestowed on him by heralds...and thereunto being made so good cheap, be called master...and reputed for a gentleman ever after.[13]

Harrison allows lineage, creation by the monarch, and also the attainment of law and liberal sciences as criteria which conferred this key status, but the deciding factor is income, relieving the individual of dependency on a master or on manual toil. In the northern counties a gentleman might have an annual income of less than £250 while the most substantial gentleman in Kent might take in £10,000. In any three decades of the seventeenth century one-third to half of the Lancashire families of gentle station lost their status, financially ruined, or failing to produce male heirs. Their positions were taken by families rising through urban trade, or – the larger group – by yeomen accumulating sufficient capital and kudos to assume their position.[14] The College of Heralds was supposed to oversee and regulate membership of the gentry by maintaining a bloodstock register of 'gentle' families, but this was ineffectual and status conferred by the estimation of the local community was more immediately important. Gentle families constituted about 2 per cent of the total population, owning 50 per cent of the land in England. If the aristocracy is included then just over 2 per cent of the total population owned 70 per cent of the kingdom by 1690, while in Scotland the nobility and lairds (a smaller, poorer rank than the English gentry) owned the entire landscape: there was no Scottish equivalent to the yeoman rank. Gentle wealth and status conferred tangible exercise of power in the localities; male gentry filled the lower and middling positions in county administration, acting as High Constables and, crucially, as Justices of the Peace, directly responsible for enforcement of law, and also taking leading roles in the county militias.

The often reprinted anonymous *Gentleman's Calling* (1660) cited five qualities essential for gentle status: wealth, authority, 'an ingenious and refined education', 'reputation and esteem' and 'time', that is freedom from obligation to work. A gentleman was therefore by definition literate; sons of the aristocracy and gentry attending the universities and Inns of Court were, however, less likely than their contemporaries from professional and trading families to complete their studies by taking degrees, since they tended to wear their learning more lightly as cultural capital and social grace rather than as a means to earn a living. Peacham's *Complete Gentleman* (1622) intended to remedy this amateur, content-less knowledge of the English gent:

there is nothing more deplorable than the breeding in general of our gentlemen, none any more miserable than one of them if he fall into misery in a strange country. Which I can impute to no other thing than the remissness of parents and negligence of masters in their youth. Wherefore…considering the great forwardness and proficience of children in other countries, the backwardness and rawness of ours; the industry of masters there, the ignorance and idleness of most of ours; the exceeding care of parents in their children's education, the negligence of ours…that leisure I had…I employed upon this discourse…[15]

'Gentility' was therefore an indefinable combination of breeding, quality and affluence, an attribute that mesmerized everyone who did not possess it: but the very emptiness of this virtue was also its weakness. Since it could not be defined, and was exercised through leisure and impractical qualities, it was also fiercely resented. Reviewing the Seven Deadly Sins as they were found in 'bawds', John Taylor the Water Poet defined Sloth as

a Gentleman-like quality, and a Lady-like disposition, to be idle, and live upon the sweat of others; Manual trades or handicrafts are counted base and mercenary, and good industry is contemptible; laudable endeavours Mechanical, and to take pains and labour, is drudgery and mere slavery.[16]

The wives, widows and daughters of the gentry were generally able to read and write because of their involvement in accounting for household expenditures and because literacy was a desirable accomplishment in making marriages. From a small sampling of female deponents among the gentry and professions in northern England from 1640 to 1699, one in four were unable to sign their names, and the figures for a comparable group in Scotland give one in three.[17] At least three of the authoresses who contributed to the successful genre of 'the mother's advice book' were gentlewomen – Elizabeth Grymeston, Dorothy Leigh and 'M. R.', and one, the Countess of Lincoln, was titled. Anne Bradstreet (1613?–72) was born into a Northamptonshire major gentry family with strong Puritan sympathies and by the age of six she was finding 'much comfort in reading the Scriptures'. After marrying in 1628, she joined the 'great migration' to Salem, New England in 1629. Her collection of poetry, *The Tenth Muse Lately Sprung Up in America* (1650), was published by her brother-in-law, and without her permission, in London. Other gentlewomen writers include Lucy Hutchinson (1620–78?), daughter of Sir Allen Apsley, Lieutenant of the Tower, and Lucy St John. As a child and young woman she was a voracious reader, outshining her three brothers who attended grammar school, and her mother became so worried about her 'excessive' studies that she confiscated her books. Dorothy Osborne (1627–95) was the last of eleven children to Lady Dorothy, daughter of the regicide Sir John Danvers, and Sir Peter Osborne, who held Guernsey for Charles – a clear example of a family fractured by civil war. Dorothy Osborne's correspondence with her husband-to-be, William Temple, during the 1650s is a remarkable and moving survival.

Some exceptional individuals could make the transition from status of gentry to that of substantial landed title. Richard Boyle, first Earl of Cork, and reputed to be the richest man in Britain by the 1630s, began life as a lawyer from a modest background. His children numbered eight daughters and seven sons, including the natural scientist Robert, Mary Rich, Countess of Warwick (who kept a diary) and Catherine, Lady Ranelagh, a member of the Great Tew Circle and in later life hostess of a cultivated salon. Boyle imposed a rigid regime on his children, sending his sons away to school by their eleventh year, and despatching daughters at the same age to live in the households of their future in-laws. Although Boyle gave a copy of *Arcadia* to his daughter Mary when she was only 10 years old, in general his daughters received minimal teaching from their chaplain.[18]

The professions and major trades: 'minds...more thoughtful and full of business'

As largely urban occupations, the professions and major trades were difficult to locate in the conventional hierarchy. They included the church (by far the largest group); the law, a significantly expanding vocation; medicine, and finally the army and royal civil service, only affording a small number of positions. The church provided aspiring men with the safest career structure in early modern Britain, though this was disrupted by the unfolding political and religious crisis. John Donne (1572–1631), related to Sir Thomas More through his mother, reluctantly took orders in 1615 at the age of 43, becoming Dean of St Paul's in 1621 via the patronage of Buckingham. Donne's father had been an important member of the Ironmonger's Company, but died when his son was four; his mother married a Catholic doctor, and Donne received a Catholic education at home, going on to Hart Hall (Hertford College), Oxford, sympathetic to recusants. George Herbert (1593–1633) was the younger son of an aristocratic family and, like Donne, lost his father at an early age. He gained scholarships at Westminster School and Trinity College, Cambridge and began a successful academic career but, again like Donne, turned relatively late to the church, becoming a deacon in 1624.

The church was also the only profession which males from non-gentry families such as the yeomanry might enter in any numbers, though these opportunities also decreased during the seventeenth century. There was a huge disparity of circumstances among the clergy, from the poorest curate earning as little as £5 a year, to the bishops who could enjoy income and status equal to that of the upper gentry. A major development was the professionalization of the clergy through education; the perception that priests were scandalously ignorant and unfitted for their duties had been one of the major arguments for the Reformation. When the Bishop of Gloucester examined his 311 clergy in 1551, over half could not list the Ten Commandments, thirty-nine could not locate the Lord's Prayer in the Bible, and thirty-four dunces could not hazard a guess as to its author. The reforming tendency in the church certainly altered this situation: in 1576, only 15 per cent of the Leicestershire clergy were graduates, but the proportion rose to 31 per cent in 1585, 58 per cent in 1603 and 90 per cent by 1640. The final reviser of the 1611 'Authorized' Bible was Miles Smith, chosen to write the Preface and who probably also composed the (rather unreadable) Dedication to King James. Smith's scholastic career is a good example of a talented youth from the provinces in the mid-sixteenth century progressing with the help of patronage and ability.[19] Born in Hereford around 1554, his father was a tradesman, a butcher or fletcher; a decade later, 30 miles to the east, Shakespeare was born in not dissimilar family circumstances. Smith distinguished himself by his precocious learning and went on to Oxford when he was 14 or 15:

> From his youth he constantly applied himself to the reading of ancient Classical Authors of the best note, in their own Languages...and lusted after no worldly

thing so much as Books;…And for his rich and accomplished furniture in that study, he had this Elegy given him by a learned Bishop of this Kingdom, that 'he was a very walking library.'[20]

Even though he was known to be 'very favourable to the Calvinian Party', Smith was chosen to work on the translating and revising of the 1611 Bible, 'wherein he was esteemed the chief, and a workman that needed not be ashamed'. When he died in 1624, he bequeathed his Hebrew Bible in five volumes, rabbinical texts and Talmudic lexicon to Hereford Cathedral, where they can still be seen in the 'chained' library.

Since members of the professions acted as the agents of the nobility and gentry they were often viewed as honorary members of the gentle order, and could style themselves as such – for example Michael Talbot, 'practitioner of physic, gent.' – but the new merchants were more difficult to categorize. The major trades were those based in wholesaling and retailing, rather than manufacturing or manual occupations, and to the extent that members of the professions and urban elites were breaking with settled assumptions about occupation and status, and were the way of the future, they did not easily conform to early modern assumptions about social rank. The 'political arithmetician' Gregory King esti-mated that in 1688 three out of four people lived in the small rural settlements of village, hamlet and farm, and contrasts between town lifestyles and the customary rural round were ever-present. Conventional attitudes associated the professions and major trades with the gentry, rather than with the yeomanry, the rural order which just failed to reach gentle status. Harrison wrote, 'Citizens and burgesses have next place to gentlemen, who be those that are free within the cities, and are of some likely substance to bear office in the same.' Peacham could not 'but account the honest merchant among the number of bene-factors to his country while he exposeth as well his life as goods to the hazard of infinite dangers'. These urban elites tended to form protective oligarchies, securing trade and perpetuating their family situation through tight control of the positions of authority in their towns and cities, such as councils or courts of aldermen; they have been character-ized as 'conservative, introspective magisterial cliques' rather than as an innovative entrepreneurial class. Their association with the middling gentry was strengthened because members of the trades and professions often came from gentry families, and could become richer than many of the middle-ranking gentry. Like their rural counterparts, they held positions of power and influence within urban institutions such as the guild companies, or took office as mayors and aldermen. The level of involvement of the urban populace in holding office was surprisingly high: in the London parish of Cornhill during the 1640s, some 1800 inhabitants required 118 elected officials, one in every sixteen parishioners holding some kind of position.[21]

Good education was a central concern for 'new merchant' families and their guilds and companies endowed grammar schools expressly to educate their own sons; there may have been more grammar and private schools in and around London by the 1640s than at any time before 1900. Half of the boys attending the Merchant Taylors' School in the 1580s were sons of men in the cloth trade; most of the remaining pupils were sons of minor tradesmen of all descriptions – shoemakers, innkeepers, fishmongers, plasterers, carpenters, as well as occupations of slightly higher status, such as goldsmiths, grocers and bakers. Edmund Spenser (*c.* 1552–99) was the son of a cloth merchant, and went on to Pembroke Hall, Cambridge. Christopher Marlowe (1564–93), son of a Canterbury shoe-maker, was educated at King's School in that city, and proceeded to Corpus Christi

College, Cambridge. Ben Jonson (1572/3–1637) was the posthumous son of a cler-gyman, educated at Westminster Grammar School by William Camden, owing him 'All that I am in arts, all that I know', but then began work as a bricklayer for his stepfather. Charged with manslaughter after killing an actor in a duel, Jonson's literacy saved his life as he was able to plead 'benefit of clergy'. Because he was able to read Psalm 51 verse one – 'Have mercy upon me O God, according to thy loving-kindess; according to the multi-tude of thy tender mercies blot out my transgressions' (1611) – the hanging was commuted to branding. Of men charged with capital crimes 32 per cent were able to escape execution through 'benefit of clergy' in Elizabeth's reign, and this rose to nearly 40 per cent under James. This exemption did not apply to female prisoners, since women could not enjoy the learned status of 'clergy'. The law was changed in 1624 when the benefit was allowed for women charged with stealing goods worth less than 10 shillings, and women were finally given the same standing as men as late as 1691. Nearly half of all convicted women, however, may have successfully 'pleaded the belly' by claiming to be pregnant, and so escaped hanging.

John Milton (1608–74), neither bricklayer nor duellist, enjoyed higher social standing than Jonson as the son of a London scrivener (a composite occupation, something between bank manager and solicitor), educated at St Paul's School and Christ's College, Cambridge. Samuel Pepys (1633–1703), son of a tailor, attended St Paul's during the 1640s, going on to Magdalene College, Cambridge. About 20 per cent of the boys from Merchant Taylors' went on to the universities or Inns of Court, and the remainder would have taken apprenticeships. The fact that only 3 per cent of the boys came from profes-sional families is a significant marker of the division between 'trade' and 'profession' at this early date. To board a boy at grammar school might cost between £4 and £18 per annum, plus another £12 for clothes, a further £90–150 to sustain a commoner for three years at Oxford or Cambridge, where incidental expenses could easily grow – a fine of two pence at Oxford for failing to attend a lecture, for example – then upwards of £50 each year to attend the Inns of Court. College fees were set according to the student's ability to pay, and sons of poorer families could to an extent work their way through university as servi-tors or sizars to wealthier students and the fellows, but generally the correlation between wealth, social status and educational attainment was grimly inescapable. Children of fami-lies below yeoman status whose total annual income might be £15 or less would find it difficult to progress beyond rudimentary learning in the petty school because their earn-ings only just provided the necessities of life. The only hope of advancement for these boys was to receive charity from an enlightened patron. And as the period progressed 'the poorer sort' were increasingly excluded from grammar school provision as the 'middling sort' claimed the places for their sons and, in growing numbers by the end of the century, their daughters. By 1656 more than half of the boys at the (admittedly fashionable) Bury St Edmunds Grammar School came from the aristocracy, and only 15 per cent from yeoman families; less noted schools such as Wolverhampton Grammar would have taken a higher proportion of town boys. William Harrison also commented on another difficulty for poorer students:

> In some grammar schools likewise, which send scholars to these universities, it is lamentable to see what bribery is used; for, ere the scholar can be preferred, such bribage is made that poor men's children are commonly shut out, and the richer sort received (who in time past thought it dishonour to live, as it were, upon

alms), and yet being placed, most of them study little other than histories [tales, romances], tables [backgammon!], dice and trifles, as men that make not the living by their study the end of their purposes...[and] standing upon their reputation and liberty, they ruffle and roist it out, exceeding in apparel and haunting riotous company....And for excuse, when they are charged with breach of all good order, think it sufficient to say, that they be gentlemen.[22]

The vagaries of trade and the significantly higher mortality rates in towns also meant that the fortunes of these merchant and professional families were even more unstable than those of the rural gentry. Accumulating capital as merchant venturers or lawyers in London or the larger ports and towns, professional men could buy the effective status of gentility through purchase of land. But for this, as for all qualities of people, status was a fragile eminence.

The nobility, gentry, professions and oligarchic merchants constituted nearly 5 per cent of the population, and were the political, social and economic elite, the dominant 'class' in modern terms, and in that they were overwhelmingly male, also the patriarchy. Only men from this elite could afford to progress to the Inns of Court; literacy was a near-universal attribute among them and, as the producers and consumers of print culture, most authors came from their ranks. David Cressy speculates that until the mid-seventeenth century these households could without difficulty have bought up the London stationers' entire annual output of 300,000 items. The tenfold increase in publications by the end of the century must have been responding to a growing number of readers of all kinds. The capital city necessarily dominated literary production: of sixty-two London playwrights working during the period, only eleven, or 29 per cent, were Londoners by birth, the remaining 71 per cent being born elsewhere and migrating to the city to seek their fortunes. But these percentages are comparable for other professions too: 90 per cent of Elizabethan and Jacobean 'great' merchants migrated to London, as did 75 per cent of the lord mayors. The 'established' hierarchy of early modern society was the product of an increasingly unsettled and unsettling culture: 'the minds of men in London are more thoughtful and full of business than in the country, where their work is corporal Labour and Exercises, all of which promote Breedings, whereas Anxieties of the mind hinder it'.[23]

Literacy rates among wives and daughters of the major trades and professions probably compared to those for the gentry, and helped produce notable writers. Elizabeth Cary, Lady Falkland (1585/6?–1639), the first Englishwoman to publish a complete drama, *Mariam the Fair Queen of Jewry* (1613), was the daughter of a prominent Oxford lawyer. She was such an apt child-scholar that she taught herself several languages; in 1602 she married into the titled elite, becoming Lady Falkland through her connection to Henry Cary 'whose mother removed all her books'. Rachel Speght (1597?–?) was the daughter of a London minister, and her *Muzzle for Melastomus* (1617) was one of the first refutations by a woman of commonplace misogynist polemics. Katherine Philips (1632–64) was the daughter of John Fowler, a successful London cloth merchant, and Katherine Oxenbridge, daughter of gentry. This was a devout Puritan family, and John Aubrey reported that Katherine Philips 'had read the Bible through before she was full 4 years old; she could have said I know not how many places of Scripture and chapters'. In 1640 she went to school in one of the Hackney academies run by Mrs Salmon, 'a famous schoolmistress, Presbyterian', where she developed a close circle of friends and began writing poetry; this was the origin of the coterie culture within which her writing subsequently developed. In 1648, aged 16, she married Colonel James Philips, a 54 year-old widower and significant figure in Welsh Puritan politics.[24] Many of the women coming to publication for the first time in the 1650s wrote devotional works and were of the middling sort: for example, Anna Trapnel (?–?), Fifth Monarchist visionary, the daughter of a London shipwright, and Margaret Fell (1614–1702), wife of barrister and MP Thomas Fell, who produced influential Quaker works from 1655 to the early 1670s. Lady Anne Halkett (1622–99), autobiographer and devotional author, was daughter of Thomas Murray, a tutor to Charles I, and her mother Jane had been governess to Princess Elizabeth. Bathsua Makin (1612?–74?), daughter of Sussex rector John Pell and his wife Elizabeth Holland, was celebrated as the most scholarly Englishwoman of her period, becoming tutor to Princess Elizabeth in the early 1640s. Makin's *Essay to Revive the Ancient Education of Gentlewomen* (1673) was influential for the developing arguments over female educational opportunities during the eighteenth century.

Yeomen: 'they that in times past made all France afraid'

A man holding what was thought of as a significant area of land, usually fifty acres or more, was regarded by his community as a yeoman, though use of the term was looser in the north-east. A yeoman's tenure might be freehold or by rent, or a mixture of these, but the freehold element had to be worth upwards of 40 shillings each year. This in theory 'freed' him from rented subservience and, crucially, conferred the right to vote in county parliamentary elections – the franchise derived from this landed (male) status alone. The yeomanry serviced juries, acted as constables and controlled provision of poor relief, working as agents of the gentry in administering order in their locality. Many of the substantial farmhouses surviving from this period were constructed by men of yeoman status. A vernacular building with no architectural pretension was one cultural indicator of the difference between families of gentle standing and those below them:

> Yeomen are those which by our law are called 'Legales homines', free men born English, and may dispend of their own free land in yearly revenue to the sum of 40s. sterling, or £6 as money goeth in our times....This sort of people have a certain pre-eminence, and more estimation than labourers and the common sort of artificers, and these commonly live wealthily, keep good houses, and travail to get riches. They are also for the most part farmers to gentlemen...and with grazing, frequenting of markets, and keeping of servants (not idle servants as the gentlemen do, but such as get both their own and part of their master's living) do come to great wealth, in so much that many of them are able and do buy the lands of unthrifty gentlemen, and often, setting their sons to the schools, to the universities, and to the Inns of the Court, or otherwise leaving them sufficient lands whereupon they may live without labour, do make them by those means to become gentlemen; these were they that in times past made all France afraid.[25]

Harrison again indicates the crucial combination of disposable wealth together with knowledge of the liberal arts without which the transition to gentle status could not be made. Fifty acres in the early seventeenth century should have ensured a tolerable living for a husband and wife with four children, providing enough security to carry them through lean years when those earning less would have become vulnerable to food shortages. From 1465 to 1634 it has been calculated that a quarter of the harvests were 'deficient' and more than 16 per cent were 'bad'. The least well-off yeomen enjoyed an annual income of £40–50, and the better-off might receive four times as much. Most yeomen are thought to have been able to read in the seventeenth century, but one in three could not write, again very much dependent on income and locality, and we might imagine that, compared with the gentry, a higher proportion of their wives and daughters would have been readers only. A significant number of spiritual autobiographies survive in print and manuscript from yeoman Puritans. The profusion of works dealing with husbandry would have found its readership here, and by the end of the seventeenth century there are indications that literate farmers were innovating more in the use of new root crops and grass substitutes than their non-literate contemporaries.[26]

Craftsmen, tradesmen, copyholders: 'Of the fourth sort of men which do not rule'

Early modern commentators became much less precise when they attempted to categorize people of status below the rank of yeoman, an undifferentiated mass sometimes called 'the rascability of the popular'. Even though these people formed the majority of the population, they were assumed to be of little consequence and so were less worthy of remark than the small minority of families holding significant wealth and power. William Harrison's description reveals these prejudices:

> The fourth and last sort of people in England are day labourers, poor husbandmen, and some retailers (which have no free land), copy holders, and all artificers, as tailors, shoemakers, carpenters, brickmakers, masons, etc....[They] have neither voice nor authority in the common wealth, but are to be ruled and not to rule other; yet they are not altogether neglected, for in cities and corporate towns, for default of yeomen, they are fain to make up their inquests in such manner of people. And in villages they are commonly made churchwardens, sidemen, aleconners [inspectors of bread, ale and beer], now and then constables, and many times enjoy the name of headboroughs [constables].[27]

Individuals involved in manual trades such as food production, clothing, furniture and farming tools also often worked on the land, since nearly all manufacture was carried on in cottages and houses. This mixing of activities which later become much more specialized and separate is referred to as the 'dual economy'. There was as yet no such thing as a (manu-)factory, the large-scale industrial organization of labour which first began in cotton manufacturing during the early nineteenth century. 'Whosoever labour for their livelihood and gain have no share at all in nobility or gentry', wrote Peacham. Literacy figures for these groups are almost meaningless unless they are located quite precisely in time and place, but David Cressy has provided some 'global' percentages which sketch the hierarchies of literacy to be found within the various trades. London, unsurprisingly, sustained a significantly higher proportion of literate tradesmen than the rest of the country. London grocers were almost certain to be literate; three out of four bakers were literate in both London and the country; from this point the figures show marked differences between the capital and elsewhere: 66 per cent of London weavers estimated as literate (51 per cent in the countryside); 57 per cent of London tailors (49 per cent in the small towns and villages); 60 per cent of London carpenters (38 per cent elsewhere); 22 per cent of London labourers (15 per cent elsewhere). Recent research has also begun to add detail to the literacy of female workers in late seventeenth-century London: court deponents from 1695 to 1725 included eighteen silk winders, none of whom were able to sign their name; char/washerwomen, of whom 11 per cent could sign; hawkers, 18 per cent; nurses, 35 per cent; servants, 40 per cent; needle trades, 70 per cent; shopkeepers, 81 per cent; midwives, 87 per cent, and schoolteachers, encouragingly, 100 per cent.[28]

By the late sixteenth century a handful of men from modest urban artisan families managed to become career-writers, sustained by the new print culture of London: Thomas Deloney (1560?–1600) was a silk weaver who in *Jack of Newbury* and *Thomas of Reading* wrote vivid prose fiction about the struggles and progress of tradesmen. Henry Chettle (1560?–1607), the son of a London dyer who was apprenticed to the stationers' trade, went on to become a prolific playwright. The career and works of John Taylor (1578–1653) poet and waterman, are discussed in Chapter 6 to illustrate this new class of author occupying a precarious position in the lower ranks of society.

By this point we have travelled a long way down the social scale, but it is here that we can locate a small group of craftsmen who occupied an entirely anomalous place in terms of status and education. Henry Peacham's final rank included 'mechanical arts and artists. Whosoever labour for their livelihood and gain have no share at all in nobility or gentry, as painters, stageplayers, tumblers, ordinary fiddlers, innkeepers, fencers, jugglers, dancers, mountebanks, bear-wards, and the like.' Playwrights, actors and musicians generally came from low-status backgrounds, but moved in elite company if they received court patronage. Contemporary suspicions about the protean nature of actors and acting could only have been reinforced by this exhilarating, unlocated existence, and all of the concerns about actors imitating their social superiors become comprehensible when they are seen against the period's anxieties about unstable social hierarchy. Edward Alleyn (1566–1626) was an adroit 'personator' who continuously changed roles throughout a successful life. His father owned an inn at Bishopsgate but Edward followed his older brother John into the theatre during the 1580s, and by 1594 he was the best-regarded actor in one of the leading London companies. Marlowe is said to have written the roles of Tamburlaine and Faustus to exploit Alleyn's genius, and he also played Barabas in the *Jew of Malta*, besides numerous other roles. It may be that Alleyn's grandiloquent, slightly old-fashioned manner was satirized by Shakespeare at the close of the 1590s in Hamlet's advice to the players. In 1592 Alleyn married Joan Woodward, stepdaughter of Philip Henslowe who owned the Rose Playhouse where Alleyn performed, and this brought him into partnership with his father-in-law (for Joan's portrait, see p. 4). From the late 1590s Alleyn and Henslowe actively sought the position of Mastership of the Bears, finally obtaining it in 1604. This involved the promotion of bear-baiting and other entertainments in the Bear Gardens at Southwark, and similar diversions for the Court at Greenwich and Whitehall. Although Peacham classed 'bear-wards' among low-grade riff-raff such as stageplayers, tumblers, innkeepers, jugglers and mountebanks, the Mastership of the Bears was a responsible and lucrative position on which Alleyn and Henslowe capitalized. In 1600 they began construction of the Fortune Theatre which soon developed a racy reputation, consistently drawing adverse criticism from the civic authorities. Consequently, the Fortune returned a good income, second only to what Alleyn and Henslowe earned from the entertainment provided by the dozen bears and 150 mastiffs of the Bear Garden next to the theatres. The creatures tormented in the Bear Garden attracted a keen following, and 'brave' animals were celebrated; John Taylor listed the livestock performing at the Bear Garden in 1638, including the bulls Goldilocks and Dash, the bears Judith and George of Cambridge, Beef of Ipswich, Rose of Bedlam and Moll Cut-Purse.

By 1605 Alleyn was sufficiently wealthy to be able to pay the enormous sum of £5,000 for the manor of Dulwich, and he eventually accumulated 1,100 acres in the area. Sir Francis Calton, the previous owner of Dulwich, regretted making the sale to Alleyn and he tried to repossess the land. Calton's grandfather had been granted the estate by Henry VIII in 1544 as part of the dissolution of the Abbey of Bermondsey. Alleyn fiercely defended his hard-won status:

> And where you tell me of my poor original and of my quality as a player. What is that? If I am richer than my ancestors I hope I may be able to do more good with my riches than ever your ancestors did with their riches….That I was a player I cannot deny; and I am sure I will not. My means of living were honest.

The unknown Cambridge scholar-dramatist who wrote *The Return from Parnassus* around 1600 disdainfully attacked journeymen playwrights and actors who, 'mouthing words that better wits have framed, They purchase lands, and now Esquiers are named', surely had in mind successful 'new men' like Alleyn and Shakespeare. But Ned Alleyn vigorously culti-vated his gentle status, accumulating a fascinating collection of over thirty paintings and an impressive library: he kept up with the works of his fellow tradesmen, recording for example the purchase of 'a book. Shakesper sonetts 5d', in 1609, the precise year of the *Sonnets*' publication. In 1619 Alleyn paid £8 for tapestries and commissioned decorative carving for his study; a chimney over-mantel was painted in gold, red, blue, green and yellow, and his cabinet would have rivalled that of many landed magnates in its cultivated opulence. At the age of 46, and having no children, Alleyn decided to establish a school and almshouses on his estate, and in September 1619 the opening of the College of God's Gift (now Dulwich College) was celebrated by a service and dinner attended by notables including Lord Chancellor Francis Bacon, Inigo Jones and Sir John Bodley. Alleyn continued to build on his status right to the end. His wife Joan died on 28 June 1623, and four months later Alleyn was negotiating to marry Constance, forty years his junior and a daughter of the Dean of St Paul's, John Donne. Alleyn died on 25 November 1626, remembered as the greatest actor of his generation, munificent founder of a school and hospital, and the 'Master Ruler and Overseer of Mastiff Bitches and the King's Games of Bears, Bulls and Mastiff Dogs'.[29]

A biography which is peculiarly tensioned by (lack of) status as well as by insecurities of gender is that of Aemilia Lanyer (1569–1645). As the daughter of Baptista Bassano, one of Elizabeth's court musicians, by his mistress Margaret Johnson, she became a servant to the Countess of Kent and then mistress to Lord Hunsdon, the Lord Chamberlain. When she became pregnant by Hunsdon in 1592 she was given in marriage to Alphonso Lanyer, another court musician. Hunsdon became patron of the Chamberlain's Men, the company to which Shakespeare belonged, in 1594. Aemilia Lanyer's poems in *Salve Deus Rex Judaeorum* (1611) are dedicated exclusively to female nobility in the court circles, including Lady Margaret Clifford and her daughter Anne, discussed in Chapter 7, and in this context demonstrate a vulnerable low-status author's desperate search for patronage and security. It also seems that 'England's first all-round professional woman writer',

Aphra Behn (1640?–89), may have been born into a family which made a living among the urban trades, as daughter of a wet-nurse and barber in Canterbury, and access to a privileged education may have given her the crucial advantage which allowed her to develop as an author.

The artificiality of these distinctions of rank and the ways in which actual lives could break through defensive categories are illustrated by the career and times of Shakespeare's father, John, successively urban craftsman, yeoman, burgess, and finally gentleman bearing arms. John Shakespeare, son of Richard, a copyholding farmer, is twice described as a 'glover' in records, and he made his mark with the emblem of a pair of glover's dividers, rather than by signing his name. Leather-working was a developed and substantial trade by the 1560s, but glove-making was particularly associated with poor workers, and was common in the west of England through to Herefordshire, Shropshire and Oxfordshire. The 'dual economy' is apparent in Shakespeare senior's activities because he also dealt in agricultural commodities such as barley, wool and timber. John Shakespeare certainly improved his status by marrying Mary Arden in 1557, the youngest daughter of his own father's landlord, a substantial farmer. She brought with her some valuable properties, and – crucially – connection to a minor branch of the Ardens of Park Hall, one of the great families of Warwickshire. We might expect a woman of her status to be able to read, if not write, but William Shakespeare's mother, like his wife, has left minimal traces in the contemporary record, though it may be she was 'familiar with a quill pen'. Marriage increased John Shakespeare's status, and he is consequently described in some documents as a yeoman, since his wife's property was of the appropriate extent.

In 1557 he took the first of his civic appointments, acting as borough constable (or headborough), and by the time of William's birth in 1564, John Shakespeare was a notable citizen in Stratford, being elected Alderman in 1565, Bailiff – that is, Mayor – in 1568, and Chief Alderman and Justice of the Peace in 1571. Is it possible that a burgess holding these important offices would have been unable to read or write? Was William Shakespeare taking obscure Oedipal revenge when he created Dogberry the illiterate parish headborough? Bailiff Shakespeare was perhaps one of those non-writing readers produced by the petty schools, but who did not have the time or opportunity to develop writing in his twenties, as some of his rank did. Even so, in 1568 he approached the College of Heralds for a grant of arms, and a 'pattern' was drawn up, but not granted. In 1596 he reapplied for a grant of arms, and was successful on the grounds that his great-grandfather had performed 'faithful and approved service to H7' (sic), being rewarded with lands, and that he himself had married into a family of status, the Ardens of Wilmcote. It may be that William helped his father financially by the mid-1590s, because the successful actor and playwright was able to buy New Place, the largest available property in Stratford, in May 1597. In 1602 John Shakespeare's right to arms was criticized, and the College of Heralds' reply demonstrates the concern with status, kinship and substance which gentle status required: 'the man was a magistrate...A Justice of Peace, he married a daughter and heir of Arden, and was of good substance and habilité' (appropriate qualities).[30]

We assume that John Shakespeare and Mary Arden were able to send their first son to the King's New (Grammar) School in Stratford, where he would have been soundly educated during the 1570s, the period of educational expansion and improvement. If he did attend Stratford School, then his schoolmaster was Simon Hunt from 1571 to 1575, the year in which William would have left school aged 11, and Hunt left for the Catholic

Seminary at Douai; Shakespeare had been taught by a 'crypto-Catholic' despite the ecclesiastical laws which tried to filter out non-Anglican teachers. John Shakespeare's son did not, however, proceed to university, but took his chance as a player in London, probably at some point in the later 1580s. William Shakespeare therefore did not become a 'university wit', though many youths of his own status did go on to Oxford and Cambridge. From 1570 to the 1630s over half of the undergraduates at Oxford were described in their college registers as being 'plebs', that is from relatively lowly backgrounds such as husbandmen, clothworkers, glovers and similar craft trades. Most of these students became priests, like Miles Smith of Hereford. Their contemporaries from gentle families were in the main acquiring cultural capital, rather than pursuing learning for the purposes of future employment and advancement. Students from the 'fourth estate' maintained themselves through grammar school and university by working as sizars or servitors, servants for dons or their richer contemporaries, or else with the support of scholarships. This window of opportunity for advancement through the universities diminished significantly after the 1630s, when the proportion of gentry in the student body increased. The cost of university attendance rose, and scholarships went increasingly to sons of middling families, often from the clergy. By 1637–9 the proportion of 'plebian' graduands from Oxford had fallen from over half at the beginning of the decade to 37 per cent – 27 per cent in 1711, 17 per cent in 1760, and just 1 per cent in 1810. It is probably the case that a larger proportion of males from 'the lower sorts' had access to Oxford and Cambridge during the Elizabethan and Jacobean period than at any subsequent time, including today.[31]

Was John Shakespeare a Catholic? Did his son adhere secretly to his father's religion? A Catholic profession of faith signed by 'John Shakespere' was discovered in the roof of the Shakespeare home in Henley Street in 1757, but it has often been dismissed as a forged product of eighteenth-century bardolatry and ignored by most scholars. The Spiritual Testament is now being taken more seriously, and Richard Wilson has revived the argument that William Shakeshafte, an actor known to have been in the service of the Catholic Hoghton family of Hoghton Tower, near Preston during the 1580s, was in fact Shakespeare. Edmund Campion was also based at Hoghton, with a very extensive library, and this may explain the anomaly of Shakespeare's provincial origin and apparent lack of 'further' education: 'of all Elizabethan and Stuart dramatists, he alone emerged outside the golden triangle of London and the universities'. A rigorous Jesuit education in service at Hoghton may have supplied the learning which we otherwise attribute (mystically) to Shakespeare's singular talents.[32]

Apprentices and servants: 'Seeking service and place'

Employment as an apprentice or servant was an inescapable rite of passage for many young people, a period in their lives which for the majority would be succeeded by marriage in their mid- or late twenties. One survey of six English localities found 62 per cent of 15–19-year-olds in service, 70 per cent of 20–4-year-olds, and 30 per cent of 25–9-year-olds. These occupations cut across several social groups, including the minor rural gentry, yeomanry, husbandmen and town tradespeople, and increasingly also some substantial urban gentry. Those economic migrants going to London 'for necessity, as poor young men and maids to seek services and places', stood a good chance of becoming literate or receiving further education as apprentices, particularly if they joined the distributive trades, with perhaps as many as three out of four being able to write as well as read. The fashionable retailing areas developing in London from the second decade of the century such as the New Exchange in the Strand – an early modern 'shopping mall' – created a demand for 'comely' shop girls who had to be numerate. Edward Barlow left home in the village of Prestwich, Lancashire in March 1657 to be apprenticed as a seaman in London. When he finally arrived in the capital he described crossing London Bridge and seeing 'many things…with long poles standing up in them and a great deal of ropes about them'. This apprentice-seaman had never seen a ship before, but he was able to make this 'defamiliarized' description in the journal which he began five or six years later.

Training by apprenticeship was described as 'mechanical' learning, and was differentiated by educational and social theorists as early as Sir Thomas Elyot from the 'liberal' and 'scientific' arts cultivated in the grammar schools, universities and Inns of Court. This was an irksome distinction to many, for example the members of the Stationers' Company who were struck by the elevated status granted to scholar-printers in France, Germany and Italy. Joseph Moxon made the most ambitious claim for English printers as scholar-typographers in his *Mechanick Exercises: Or the Doctrine of Handy-Works Applied to the Art of Printing* (1683). Apprenticeship in the major Companies could blur some of the snobberies attaching to the gentleman/tradesman distinction: nearly 14 per cent of the apprentices entering London Companies from 1570 to 1646 came from families of the minor aristocracy and gentry, and by the 1640s there were about 20,000 apprentices living in the city. Evidence for a high level of literacy among London apprentices can be found in the number of book and play dedications addressed to this group of young men.[33]

Husbandmen, cottagers, labourers, vagrants: literacy at the margins of survival

Husbandmen farmed smallholdings of between five and fifty acres, and they might experience hunger and deprivation in lean years. Particularly bad harvests occurred in 1594–97, 1646–50, 1657–61 and 1673–4. A husbandman farming thirty acres in the early seventeenth century might make £15 in an average year, spending £11 of this to feed his wife and four children, leaving a disposable income of £3 or £4, 'a tolerable, though by no means easy existence'. In a bad year with poor harvests there would be no surplus, and life could become very difficult. Some 40 to 50 per cent of the population were exposed to deprivation at these times – 2.5 million people by 1688. By the mid-seventeenth century England was becoming less vulnerable to subsistence crises than some other European countries, though in the 1690s parts of Scotland suffered famine which reduced many thousands to beggary. Literacy levels were low for people of this status, and probably did not significantly improve during the period – they would barely be able to meet one year's grammar-school charges from their disposable income, and there would be little enough money even for purchase of two- or three-penny pamphlets or a bible at three shillings and four pence.[34] Margaret Spufford comments:

> The importance of reading may have been still marginal at a social level below that of the yeoman in a world in which the regular functions were predominantly oral. Yet increasingly the attender at church, at manor and hundredal court, and even at market, would find the written and printed word was physically present, if not actually necessary.[35]

Cottagers might possess a few acres of land, but could not make a living from it alone, and so took paid labour from other masters. As the landowners grew and became more prosperous until the decade of the Civil Wars, people living by manual labour became relatively poorer, earning on average one shilling a day. The number of people relying on wages for their survival also increased, from perhaps one-quarter in the late sixteenth century to nearer a third by 1700. These families existed at subsistence level, so children were put to work as soon as they were able to make any contribution to family income. A 1570 census of the poor in Norwich recorded five- and six-year-olds at work, with teenage members of families providing the major income. The 'family economy' of the poor 'depended on the cooperation of all family members; no one was allowed leisure'.[36] Having no economic status, labourers, cottagers and the poorer rural tradesmen rarely held positions of any standing in their villages, and it is probably the case that there was little or no real increase in literacy rates among these people much before the eighteenth century. Despite these crushing odds against becoming literate, some among village tradespeople managed to write and probably many more were able to read, and it was this culture of cheap print and popular piety that sustained John Bunyan (1628–88). Bunyan was born at Elstow near Bedford and, after attending village petty school, took on his father's trade of brazier, selling and mending pots and pans. He was arrested in 1660 for unlicensed preaching, and during twelve years in Bedford jail he wrote nine works, including *The Holy City* (1665) and *Grace Abounding to the Chief of Sinners* (1666). The jail was built over the river and must have been a torment, but even so it was there that Bunyan began *The Pilgrim's Progress*, probably finishing his masterpiece during another spell of imprisonment in 1676.

From the vantage of the 1690s Sir William Temple reflected on the 'splenetic' nature of the English, and how this volatile humour had afflicted the country during the mid-century. He deplored the babel of

> Disputers upon Religion, Reasoners upon Government, so many Refiners in Politics, so many curious Inquisitives, so many Pretenders to Business and State-Employments, greater Porers upon Books, nor Plodders after Wealth. And yet nowhere more abandoned Libertines, more refined Luxurists, extravagant Debauches, conceited Gallants, more Dabblers in Poetry as well as Politics, in Philosophy and in Chemistry. I have had several Servants far gone in Divinity, others in Poetry; have known in the Families of some Friends, a [door]Keeper deep in the Rosycrucia Principles, and a Laundress firm in those of Epicurus. What Effect soever such a Composition or Medley of Humours among us may have upon our Lives or our Government, it must needs have a good one upon our Stage, and has given admirable Play to our comical Wits.[37]

Temple observed the culture of the poorer urban sort with condescending irony and he illustrates perfectly the social elite's uneasy fascination with the growth of a new, unseemly appetite for print among the lower orders. Disquiet over the effects of education on the social fabric were not uncommon from the Restoration onwards, as commentators and moralists sought to explain new aspirations among the urban poorer and middling sorts. We must therefore now review some of the central debates provoked by the faltering but real growth in educational provision between the late sixteenth century and the Restoration.

3

'TOWARDNESS'

Aptitude, gender and rank
in early modern education

Scripture for the boy who drives the plough

In the dawn hours of Sunday 14 July 1667 Samuel Pepys was feeling vexed with his wife Elisabeth as he waited impatiently for her downstairs in the company of Mrs Turner (who later in the day would solicitously massage Pepys's sprained ankle). The trio were to take a coach-ride into the country; the beer, wine and cold chicken were stowed in the coach-and-four hired the previous day, but Mrs Pepys was making a point by taking her time. Eventually the three set off after five o'clock, and began to enjoy the beautiful day, 'the country very fine'. Pepys drank a prodigious four pints of medicinal waters at Epsom 'and had some very good stools by it', tempers improved, and the company dined 'and were merry' at an inn. They returned over the Downs, and Pepys took a stroll

> where a flock of sheep was, and the most pleasant and innocent sight that ever I saw in my life; we find a shepherd and his little boy reading, far from any houses or sight of people, the Bible to him. So I made the boy read to me, which he did with the forced Tone that children do usually read, that was mighty pretty; and then I did give him something, and went to the father, and talked with him....He did content himself mightily in my liking his boy's reading, and did bless God for him, the most like one of the old Patriarchs that ever I saw in my life, and it brought those thoughts of the old age of the world in my mind for two or three days after.[1]

It is not clear from Pepys's diary whether his shepherd patriarch could read for himself, but figures on the growth of literacy by status during the seventeenth century suggest that his son might well have been the first scholar in this poor family. If so, he was a beneficiary of one strand in late medieval and reformation Christianity which was eager to bring scripture to the widest possible readership.

Throughout Europe from the fourteenth century onwards increasingly effective demands were made for a form of the Bible which would be easily available to all believers. In response to these pressures the Latin Vulgate text was translated into a growing number of languages during the late medieval period. In England alone over two hundred Wycliffite bibles survive from the late fourteenth century, part of the Lollard movement for more direct lay participation in the life of the church and a more personal experience of spirituality. But the state's nervousness about the spread of these potentially disruptive Lollard beliefs provoked a ban in 1408 on all further translation from scripture except under close supervision by authority. Laity wishing to read the Bible in English had to obtain an episcopal licence, and this further restricted the privilege to an affluent elite who could afford the charges.[2] Many devotional works did provide summaries and 'harmonies' of the gospels in English, but printed scripture in the vernacular only began to reach England by the 1520s, thanks to the efforts of William Tyndale, Miles Coverdale and a few other isolated scholars. Tyndale and his collaborators were determined to bring the whole Bible into English for as many as could read or listen, and one of Tyndale's most cherished declarations, reported by the Protestant martyrologist John Foxe, was worthy of Chaucer's poor Parson:

> And soon after, Master Tyndall happened to be in the company of a learned man, and in communing and disputing with him, drove him to that issue that the learned man said, we were better be without God's law than the Pope's. Master Tyndall, hearing that, answered him, I defy the Pope and all his laws, and said, if God spare my life, ere [before] many years I will cause a boy that driveth the plough shall know more of the scripture than thou dost.[3]

Next to the growing number of translations of the Bible, John Foxe's *Acts and Monuments* was one of the most widely read books among English Protestants in the later sixteenth and seventeenth centuries, popularly known as 'The Book of Martyrs' owing to its vivid narrative accounts and woodcuts of the persecution of early reformers. Foxe's report of Tyndale's remark may be a pious invention for the benefit of his readership, but it is certainly consistent with the translator's attempts to produce a version of the Bible which would be comprehensible to the widest readership, including, 150 years later, a shepherd boy on Epsom Downs.

Historians of literacy calculate that at the beginning of Elizabeth's reign only one in five English males could sign his own name, and only one woman in twenty. By the outbreak of the Civil Wars in 1642 one in three men could sign, and one in ten women. By 1700 almost one in two men were signing, and one in four women (if accurate, a rapid and telling increase among the female population). In the middle of the eighteenth century, 300 years after the invention of printing, half the English population still could not write – 40 per cent male, 60 per cent female – and it was only during the next 150 years that the conversion to mass literacy occurred at an increasing pace, until by 1914 over 99 per cent of brides and grooms were able to sign the marriage register.[4]

What these simple figures cannot show are the varying rates of growth in the ability to read and write during different decades – faster during the 1570s, much slower in the first decades of the seventeenth century, stagnating during the years of warfare; nor do they differentiate by status and region, or show how gender affected these variations. As David Cressy wrote, 'The local geography of literacy is still bewildering.' The term 'literacy' also covers a very wide spectrum of skills. Reading was taught as a distinct activity from writing, and it was only from the late eighteenth century that they began to be linked in children's education. As a general rule, in the early modern period only boys were encouraged to write, and the outwardly more passive experience of reading was conventionally considered to be all that was appropriate for the small number of girls who received formal academic education rather than learning domestic skills and social accomplishments. Many schoolmasters and mistresses routinely made an extra charge for teaching writing since the cost of materials was an added concern. Exceptionally, the burgh school in Ayr during the late sixteenth century admitted girls to learn both reading and writing, but the innovation did not last long, and by 1602 the girls had been sent off to the church 'song school', because the town magistrates felt that 'it is not seemly that sic [such] lasses should be among the lads'. Inventories however record a higher proportion of book ownership among women than the raw illiteracy statistics would suggest, and this hints at the existence of many more women who were readers but not writers. Books even made their way in some numbers to distant areas: by 1642 Euphame Halcro, dying in distant Orkney, had come into possession of her husband's books worth the very considerable sum of £46.[5]

Readers might also be differentiated through the demands made by the complexity of early modern pages: some books still abbreviated words using contraction symbols and some calligraphic forms were more like shorthand. For the new groups of partial readers, illustrated texts such as broadside ballads and elaborate iconographic posters (or 'tables') which could be pasted on to cottage walls provided complex text-with-image combinations. Reading was also closely related to listening carefully, and established schemes of rhetoric made the committing to memory of argument and instance a habitual practice. Note-taking from the elaborate rhetoric of sermons was commonplace, the notes then being read and repeated for private devotion in the family or among like-minded believers; print became stenography and circulated as quotation, instance and apothegm.[6]

Educated people today understandably view the slow but inexorable rise in percentages of readers and writers by class, gender and region since 1500 as a kind of triumphant progress, and sixteenth- and seventeenth-century educational reformers also argued passionately for the benefits of literacy. Some far-sighted proposals were made for expansion. William Dell preaching on *The Right Reformation of Learning, Schools and Universities* to the House of Commons in 1646 argued that a university or college should be established in every major English town and city, to be funded by the state with 'an honest and competent maintenance'. Students attending their local college might live at home, removing the need for scholarships, and would combine their studies with pursuit of a lawful calling or business, so that 'twenty would learn then, where one learns now'. Gerrard Winstanley, the True Leveller, addressed his definition of true 'Commonwealth's Government' to Cromwell in 1652, and was concerned to heal the division between tradesmen and scholars:

> But one sort of children shall not be trained up only to book learning and no other employment, called scholars, as they are in the government of monarchy; for then through idleness and exercised wit therein they spend their time to find out policies to advance themselves to be lords and masters above their labouring bretheren, as Simeon and Levi do, which occasions all the trouble in the world.

Other historians argue that among poorer people illiteracy was not generally regarded as a shameful stigma until the mid-nineteenth century, though as the figure of Envy from *Doctor Faustus* demonstrates, there is clear evidence in London print and theatre culture from the 1590s that literate townspeople might look down on their unlettered country cousins as clownish.

National debates about the desirability of mass literacy did not seriously begin until the early nineteenth century, and because early modern society was predominantly *un*-literate, it positively valued other forms of cultural competence and transmission such as effective speaking, customary songs, sayings and stories told from memory, and more purely visual representations. Therefore, as David Cressy argues, 'low literacy rates in the early modern period should not be taken as indicators of retardation or deprivation, awaiting rectification by progress'.[7] Non-literate individuals in past times could be justifiably suspicious of the ways in which writing might be used against them, for example in property and land ownership dealings, written testimonials, or in the exercise of oppressive laws which they were in no position to grasp. The demand to set down laws in plain English was a constant theme of Leveller agitation during the 1640s. The anonymous *Gold Tried in the Fire; or, the Burnt Petitions Revived* (1647) called for all legislation to be published in 'the English Tongue', 'and in the most usual Character of writing, without any abbreviations, that each one who can read, may the better understand their own affairs'[8]. The 'most usual Character' might mean roman font, rather than black-letter or 'bastard gothic', which by 1647 was used for works such as ballads and almanacs aimed at the popular readership, but which could also signify the Crown's pretensions, and might be read with suspicion. For all these reasons it is preferable to describe early modern non-readers and writers as 'unliterate', a more neutral term than 'illiterate', and first recorded from 1548, since 'illiterate' from Cicero onwards has generally carried pejorative meanings.[9]

From absey to grammar school

The population of Sweden was nearly completely literate by the late eighteenth century, a situation achieved before any other European state, not by virtue of schooling but by learning based in the household. Both Sweden and New England (also precocious) were small and culturally homogeneous societies where reformed religion encouraged literacy among believers. By contrast, in Britain as in most other European countries, there was no single system of learning, and social status, gender and locality all influenced the kind of education an individual might receive. At the local level it is very difficult to say why the inhabitants of some settlements became more literate than others, precisely because so many different factors were involved, and the presence of schools was not always decisive: informal learning was often the only option for many. Parents were urged to teach their children and read to their households; servants and apprentices were to be included in hearing scripture or sermons repeated, and many apprenticeships incorporated an element of education. For poorer individuals serving in households as indentured servants, there might be opportunity to build on rudimentary knowledge gained from their early schooling which had not been continued. In the mid-eighteenth century Lowlands a girl who had very little schooling learned 'by following the minister with my eye on the Bible as he read that portion of the Scripture he was going to lecture on'.[10]

The Reformation had tied church, state and education ever more closely together. Legislation passed during the 1530s and 1540s required the teaching of basic articles of religious belief in tandem with learning the alphabet, syllable guides and spelling lessons. Infants learned their letters from a hornbook, a square of wood shaped like a table-tennis bat on which were pasted the alphabet, syllables and the Lord's Prayer, the paper glazed over with transparent horn to preserve its text from grubby fingers. The alphabet was often preceded by a Greek cross, and the letters themselves were also commonly arranged in the shape of a cross, hence the name 'Christ-cross-row': the sign of Christ's sacrifice was internalized simultaneously with the alphabet. Pupils who did not progress to forming a proper signature would make their mark, often in the form of the cross which was all that they had mastered at petty school. Grammar-school masters were clerics or else

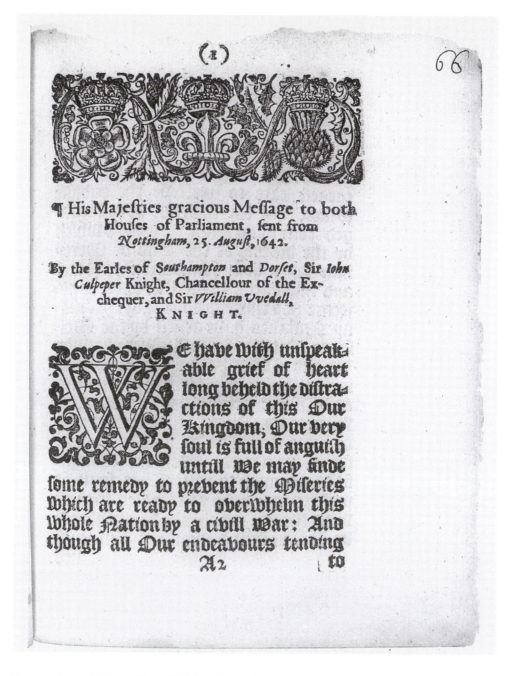

Figures 4.1 and 4.2 Font Wars: *His Majesty's Gracious Message to both Houses of Parliament, sent from Nottingham, August 25. With the answer of the Lords and Commons to the said Message: And His Majesty's Reply to the same, Sept. 2. Together with the Answer and humble Petition of both Houses to his Majesty's last Message: And also His Majesty's Message in Reply to the said Answer, Sept. 11. 1642.*
London. Printed by Robert Barker, Printer to the King's Most Excellent Majesty: And by the Assigns of John Bill. 1642

Pages 1 and 5. By permission of the Syndics of Cambridge University Library

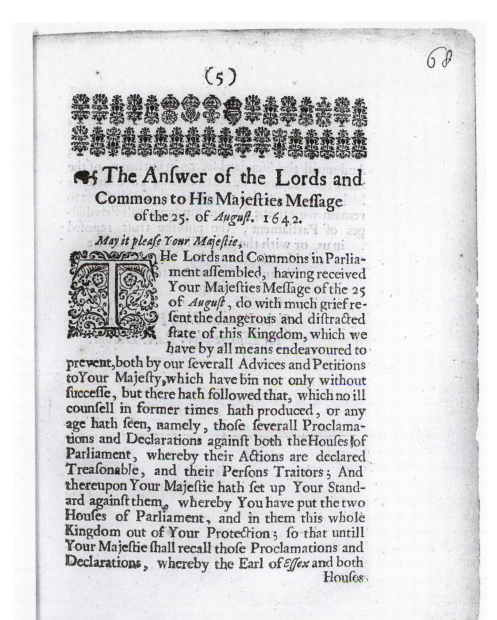

(5)

68

The Answer of the Lords and Commons to His Majesties Message of the 25. of *August*. 1642.

May it please Your Majestie,

THe Lords and Commons in Parliament assembled, having received Your Majesties Message of the 25 of *August*, do with much grief resent the dangerous and distracted state of this Kingdom, which we have by all means endeavoured to prevent, both by our severall Advices and Petitions to Your Majesty, which have bin not only without successe, but there hath followed that, which no ill counsell in former times hath produced, or any age hath seen, namely, those severall Proclamations and Declarations against both the Houses of Parliament, whereby their Actions are declared Treasonable, and their Persons Traitors; And thereupon Your Majestie hath set up Your Standard against them, whereby You have put the two Houses of Parliament, and in them this whole Kingdom out of Your Protection; so that untill Your Majestie shall recall those Proclamations and Declarations, whereby the Earl of *Essex* and both

Houses

The last hopes for reconciliation between Charles and Parliament were destroyed in March 1642 when the Commons assumed sovereignty and unilaterally confirmed the Militia Bill as an Ordinance, taking the defence of the country into their own power, regardless of the King's opposition. Charles travelled north throughout the summer as reports (often exaggerated) of the Catholic uprising in Ireland provoked outraged reaction in England. Charles finally raised his standard to summon troops to his cause at the top of the castle hill in Nottingham on 22 August:

> a general sadness covered the whole town, and the king himself appeared more melancholic than he used to be. The standard itself was blown down, the same night it had been set up, by a very strong and unruly wind, and could not be fixed in a day or two, till the tempest was allayed.
> (Clarendon, Book Five, *The History of the Rebellion*, Oxford, 1840, p. 312)

Three days later Charles was persuaded to propose negotiations with Parliament in the 'gracious Message' of 25 August, but it was received 'with unheard-of insolence and contempt'. Barker, as the King's Printer, formalized the King's authority and Parliament's subservience in his page-setting and strategic choice of fonts.

'ecclesiastical officers'; the local curate was required to catechize the children of his parish, and freelance teachers had to accept the Church of England's Thirty Nine Articles, the basic confession of belief and worship introduced in 1563, and to be licensed by the authority of a bishop. This was done to prevent the spread of Catholic or dissenting religious influences in schools, but curates might run classes in their villages without licence as a way of cutting costs. Licensed teachers serviced private, unendowed schools, or worked peripatetically through an area, teaching children their ABC. There were also probably more women teachers than have been recorded – individuals like Anna Hassall, who was teaching the sons of yeomen and husbandmen in Staffordshire in 1616. In his sermon on the *Reformation of Learning*, given in 1646, William Dell urged that 'godly men especially have the charge of greater schools; and also that no women be permitted to teach little children in villages, but such as are the most sober and grave'.[11]

Early modern education began through catechism, a question-and-response form which established learning as the internalizing of authoritative knowledge founded in memory, speaking and listening. This was a communal activity with little or no emphasis on individual initiative as we understand it. Thought and expression were schematized and rule-bound by elaborate rhetorical conventions which the author might draw on in composing and the reader or auditor could also use in comprehension. Grammar school and university education were organized around the gathering of maxims and quotations, and the ways in which these might then be framed using the copious strategies of rhetorical tradition. This radically conventional nature of early modern reading carried implications for all areas of expressive activity: thought, speech, written composition, graphic works, and even acting, were implicitly formulaic in ways that can seem constraining and unoriginal to our post-Romantic assumptions. Yet early modern authors and readers were perfectly capable of making challenging and even dangerous interpretations by extending the bounds of convention: 'The objects of a reader's enquiry were general: truths accessible (and for the most part already familiar) to all. But the means of extracting them were particular, indeed personal.'[12] The conventionality of learning and the continuous appeal to authority were beneficial for poets and dramatists because audiences and readers might bring elaborate frameworks of reference to what they saw and read. But for other kinds of intellectual labour this rule-bound learning could appear to be nothing short of disastrous. This was Francis Bacon's objection in his *Novum Organum* (1620):

> Again, in the customs and institutions of schools, academies, colleges, and similar bodies destined for the abode of learned men and the cultivation of learning, everything is found adverse to the progress of science. For the lectures and exercises there are so ordered, that to think or speculate on anything out of the common way can hardly occur to any man. And if one or two have the boldness to use any liberty of judgment, they must undertake the task all by themselves; they can have no advantage from the company of others.[13]

For the children of the gentry, learning began in the home, hearing scripture readings and repeating their catechism. Ralph Josselin's detailed diary records his 4-year-old daughter Mary showing scholarly aptitude in June 1646: 'A week of favours and goodness from God to us all…the towardliness of Mary to learn, give Lord to her the anointing of thy own spirit.' His son Tom began school at the age of 5 and was given his bible, quickly becoming a competent reader. Otherwise children learnt their letters at petty school, also called ABC ('absey') or dame school. Besides the petty, dame and grammar schools, there was a growth in 'return-to-study' options from the early seventeenth century offered by freelance teachers to all-comers. Small schools and academies developed to meet increasing demand, many of them sited in the north London suburbs. Local schools funded by citizens and well-resourced grammar schools endowed by individuals or guilds were established in market towns throughout England by the late sixteenth century, and most of the population was geographically close to a school of some sort, but fees prohibited entry for the majority. Girls at this point were generally removed from classroom instruction, and would only receive further tuition at home if they came from families of appropriate rank and wealth. It was not customary to teach girls Latin and Greek, but there were always exceptions. Elizabeth Jane Weston (*c.* 1582–1612) as a child removed with her family to live at the Imperial Court in Bohemia where she became fluent in German, Latin, Italian and Czech. She published two collections of Latin verse and conducted a learned correspondence with scholars throughout Europe. A boy's opportunities were conditioned by his family's wealth; if he came from a family of sufficient income, he could go on from his petty school to grammar school where he would begin to learn to write and 'cypher' (add, subtract and divide) and, if he was preparing for university, to study Latin. Some grammar schools also provided the 'elementary' reading induction of the petty schools, though it was not uncommon for writing and arithmetic to be taught outside the school by private scriveners, as at Manchester Grammar School as late as the 1660s.[14] Alternatively, the boy might attend a town school or fee-paying classes given by a private licensed teacher or local curate; if he was destined for employment in a 'mechanic' trade, he would not proceed with classics. Knowledge of Latin (and to a lesser extent of Greek) was a decisive marker in terms of status and gender. William Walwyn the Leveller agitator was clear about the divisive potential of classical knowledge. He wrote in 1649:

> I do not think any man much the wiser for having many languages, or for having more than one, and though I wish I had the Latin, yet I think it not worth that pains, and time, as is commonly spent in learning...which is all I have to say against Latin, or any kind of learning; except that part of it, which puffeth up, and makes men scornful pedants, despisers of unlearned and illiterate men.[15]

Children of the aristocracy or upper gentry would be taught by private tuition at home, though boys from this elite increasingly prepared for university at fashionable schools such as Shrewsbury and Westminster. Some schools separated their boys around the age of ten into those learning vocational skills and those acquiring the Latin that qualified them to proceed to university. If he was a candidate for higher education, a boy would begin classical studies with William Lily's Latin Grammar, the standard textbook used from the late 1530s until the 1750s in up to 10,000 copies each year (there were, alas, no royalties to authors or their descendants). Letter writing in English and Latin and direct translation aloud from Latin to English were recommended. Half an hour each week would be devoted to learning the catechism, and notes were to be taken at sermons, laying out the text quoted, doctrines explored, proofs of the arguments and application of proofs. The most proficient pupils would also be expected to translate the sermon into Latin either as a text, or viva voce. The well-organized early modern schoolroom was therefore an intensely competitive environment, with pupils continuously ranked against each other according to their competence in performing these exercises. John Brinsley published his *Ludus Literarius* in 1612, giving a vivid sense of how a committed grammar-school master conducted classes: his pupils were motivated to learn by striving to outdo each other from day to day, and with quarterly formal disputations organized in teams. Rhetorical display as a public performance was an unavoidable part of studies at the most sought-out London grammar schools, including the occasional performance of plays.[16]

Though boys were the focus of serious educational efforts, there are numerous examples of the pride which seventeenth-century parents took in their daughters' quickness: 'my eldest girl is...of a good memory and learns more than I can find means to have taught her', wrote Sir Thomas Meautys in 1636. Even so, early modern assumptions about female inferiority and dependency set girls on a distinct educational path. The sexes were educated separately, with fewer girls than boys being taught to write as well as read, and with no girls being allowed to progress to the full curriculum of grammar-school education after primary schooling. There are very occasional references to girls attending some grammar schools during the early seventeenth century – Alice Shaw at Rivington Free Grammar, Lancashire in 1615, for example – but co-educational schools only began to be established in the 1680s. The fact that some fashionable London schools from the 1580s began to stipulate that girls were not admitted might indicate that parents were trying to gain access for their daughters to this next level of public education, but without much success. Alternatively, the change in regulations at the London schools may have meant that a small number of girls who had previously attended the lower grades of school were now being excluded from institutions hoping to promote a more 'rigorous' image. In either case, a few establishments for the education of girls and young women of the middling sort were established during the early seventeenth century, clustering in the London suburbs around Hackney and responding to what must have been an increasing demand for 'secondary' education for daughters, another consequence of the expansion of schooling in the 1570s. This growing sense that daughters should be given the opportunity of schooling might also be reflected in the fact that well-to-do widows in Norfolk bequeathed similar amounts for charity in their wills as male testators, but left more for educational work than did their male contemporaries.[17]

The minority of young women receiving this new training were taught decorative arts and domestic skills rather than the grinding academic curriculum followed by their male contemporaries, as were the daughters of the nobility and wealthy gentry who continued to be tutored privately at home. The feminine 'decorative' skills could however be both demanding and learned in particular ways: Esther Kello (née Langlois) (1571–1624), daughter of a Huguenot family settled in Edinburgh, was taught calligraphy by her mother and became so accomplished that her work was presented to Elizabeth and James VI and I. Sophisticated needlework might draw on iconographical schemes as elaborate as those of many literary works, illustrating scenes from the Old Testament, or more rarely, from classical texts such as Ovid's *Metamorphoses*. Martha Edlin was 11 when she completed her miniature cabinet in 1671, marvellously worked with allegorical figures of Faith, Hope and Charity. Rosemary O'Day found that 'every town of any size had a girls' academy by the mid seventeenth century', teaching this mixed curriculum of studies and life-skills. But no women proceeded to the early modern equivalents of higher education in the English universities at Oxford and Cambridge or the 'post-graduate' Inns of Court in London, just as in Scotland no young woman went on to the universities at St Andrews (founded 1412), Glasgow (1451), Aberdeen (1495) or Edinburgh (1587). Gifted women from the social elite might however be invited to participate in coterie discussion groups and amateur societies. Lucius Cary, son of the Irish Lord Deputy Falkland and the highly educated Elizabeth Tarfield, drew together a seminar of writers and philosophers centred on his house at Great Tew, near Oxford. Catherine, brilliant daughter of Richard Boyle, contributed to discussions at Great Tew, and took care to have her sons educated by John Milton, who was appreciative of her learning.

Despite these barriers to female education, the image of a woman holding a book was one of the commonplaces of late medieval and early modern iconography. The Virgin Mary, awaiting the birth of Jesus, was often depicted poring over a Bible; this was an emblem of her saintly devotion but the image also suggested that the 'old law' of Judaism was about to be displaced by the word-made-flesh of Christ in the New Testament. A small but growing number of illustrations for Books of Hours made for the lay audience in fifteenth-century England portrayed Mary being taught to read by her mother, St Anne. Renaissance tomb sculpture throughout Europe also frequently presented the deceased wife or daughter holding a small mass book, signalling her devotion. Female studiousness in this way was a pervasive image suggesting the obedient learning of Christian precept and a chaste demeanour, and more and more women lovingly worked elaborate embroidered covers for their bibles and prayer books during the early seventeenth century (see discussion of Joan Alleyn's portrait above, p. 5). When Claudius and Polonius set Ophelia as a bait for Hamlet in Act 3 Scene 1, they ask her to read her book and become this image of obedient modesty. Ophelia is posed as an exemplary Christian daughter, true to the teaching of thousands of conduct books, sermons and elegies produced between 1500 and 1700, which defined the devout woman. But the example which this homiletic literature offered during two centuries changed very little, despite dramatic developments in belief and society, so again we should be wary of accepting these prescriptive books at face value. Hamlet, for example, easily saw through Ophelia's pose, and this might be a measure of the distance between the icons constructed in the conduct books and behaviour in everyday life. The preference of Stuart needlewomen for some of the racier themes from the Old Testament, such as the love of David for Bathsheba, Potiphar's wife's attempt to seduce Joseph, or Joseph being sold to the Midianites, may also indicate that some women elaborated a different kind of agenda in their craft-work. These paradoxical attitudes to female literacy are another example of the contradictory nature of early modern views on female status: encouraged to study devotional texts, yet discouraged from learning more widely, even though reading and writing are not skills to which limits can be set. Raphael's advice to Adam and Eve in *Paradise Lost* that they should remain 'lowly wise' exactly expresses this paradox which is also a plain contradiction: proper 'wisdom' cannot be constrained, and the innate desire for knowledge will lead humankind beyond an over-protective Eden and into the more testing world.[18]

'Education is the bringing up of one, not to live alone, but amongst others, because company is our natural cognisance'

Schooling and university teaching for boys and youths in the first two decades of Elizabeth's reign were expanding and becoming more effective. It may be no accident that the writers and readers who matured during the 1590s were 'bred as scholars' during this period of educational improvement. Richard Mulcaster was the first headmaster of the largest London grammar school, the Merchant Taylors, founded in 1561, where his pupils included Edmund Spenser, Thomas Kyd, Thomas Lodge, Lancelot Andrewes, and no less than seven of the forty-seven clerics who revised the 1611 'King James' Bible. In 1581 Mulcaster's *Positions [concerning] the Training Up of Children* was published, an original if rather windy set of proposals to reform Tudor education.[19] Mulcaster dedicated *Positions* to the Queen, declaring 'the very end of my whole labour…is to help to bring the general teaching in your Majesty's dominions to some one good and profitable uniformity' (3v–4r; 4–5). In this book Mulcaster continually emphasized the school's role as the nation-in-miniature – 'is not his master his monarch? And the school laws his country laws?' (152; 155). Uniquely among Tudor writers on education, he did not argue for learning as an induction to godly belief and true Christian practice. This had been the primary emphasis in Roger Ascham's *Schoolmaster*, first published in 1570 and a much more widely read treatise, with which Mulcaster's *Positions* was competing. The originality of *Positions* lies in this consistently secular conception of education as a public process, in contrast to earlier manuals such as Elyot's *Governor* (1531) or the anonymous *Institution of a Gentleman* (1555), both framed entirely in terms of the private education of the male social elite. Mulcaster argued eloquently for this group to be educated in schools – fee-paying, naturally – rather than sequestered in the family home with private tutors because

> *Education* is the bringing up of one, not to live alone, but amongst others, (because company is our natural cognisance) whereby he shall be best able to execute those doings in life, which the state of his calling shall employ him unto…according unto the direction of his country whereunto he is born, and oweth his whole service.

> (185; 186)

Mulcaster therefore denounced private education as a form of enclosure of the common good, which corrupted individuals by establishing 'a too private habit' (185; 186): 'For how can *education* be *private*? It abuseth the name as it abuseth the thing' (186; 187).

All rewarding education is tensioned between indoctrination of social norms and the desire to develop each individual's resources which may not square with dominant social arrangements, and Mulcaster's arguments are anxious and contradictory in these highly revealing ways. Early modern education was designed to reinforce the existing social hierarchy through training of a devout and efficient clerisy able to service the state apparatus, and by shaping obedient, god-fearing citizens and compliant wives. But Mulcaster's charged political agenda for education as a training in efficient subjection is troubled by his awareness of absolute paradoxes over gender and status. He had difficulty in reconciling a lively awareness of the scholarly aptitudes of girls and women with his society's conventional views, which generally denied females access to education beyond the elementary stage. Queen Elizabeth's learning and exercise of sovereignty were simultaneously the clearest example of woman's potential and a major embarrassment to Mulcaster's patriarchal reasoning. Similarly, Mulcaster struggled to accommodate the fact that some individuals did not always seem equal to the status which their birth and place in the social hierarchy conferred on them – why should some of the 'nobility' behave so ignobly? How is the essence of gentility to be defined in the 'true' gentle-man when the rank has become so permeable? These anxieties demonstrate how categorical assumptions about gender and status could be internally flawed even in the most apparently prescriptive texts:

> In the last title [chapter] I did declare at large, how young maidens in each degree were to be advanced in learning, which me thought was very incident to my purpose, because they be counterbranches [constituent subdivisions] to us in the kind of mortal and reasonable creatures, and also for that in each degree of life, they be still our mates, and sometime our mistresses [superiors], through the benefit of law, and honourableness of birth. Now considering they join [in every way] with us in number and nearness, and sometimes exceed us in dignity and calling: as they communicate with us in all qualities, and all honours even up to the sceptre [the monarch], so why ought they not in any wise but be made communicants with us in education and train[ing], to perform that part well, which they are to play, for either equality with us, or sovereignty over us?
>
> (183–4; 184–5)

Mulcaster discussed female education in Chapter 38, 'That young maidens are to be set to learning, which is proved, by the custom of our country, by our duty towards them, by their natural abilities, and by the worthy effects of such as have been well trained' (166; 169). They were, however, considered only within their circumscribed status: 'young maidens must give me leave to speak of boys first: because naturally the male is more worthy, and politically he is more employed' (132; 138). Mulcaster's 'Erastian' view that education was fundamentally a preparation for the subject's loyal and productive life within the state dictated that learning was 'first framed' for male pupils, who then through 'courtesy and kindness' 'lend' – significant verb – education to females. Therefore 'the bringing up of young maidens in any kind of learning is but an accessory by the way' (133; 138). But following on these conventional attitudes, Mulcaster's actual discussion of girls' education seems much more enabling; he is in favour of their being schooled because he is 'for them with tooth and nail' (167; 169). His first of four arguments is nationalistic; it is the custom of the country to allow girls education. Second, duty demands that we do not 'leave them lame'; third, 'is their own *towardness*', one of Mulcaster's key terms, in use from the beginning of the century to mean 'aptitude' or 'promise'; and finally there are 'the excellent effects in that sex, when they have had the help of good bringing up' (167; 170). Given their evident 'towardness', Mulcaster can only appeal to custom and practice in denying girls admission to grammar schools and universities, 'having no precedent thereof in my country' (168; 170).

Mulcaster's arguments about the innate superiority of the male sex by 'nature' are periodically undercut by the possibility that it is only 'nurture' which distinguishes male and female in learning – 'Or is their singularity less in nature, because women be less accustomed to show it, and not so commonly employed, as we men be?' (167; 175). *Positions* here fleetingly anticipates arguments that would only begin to be made systematically from the late seventeenth century, to the effect that women were subservient and incapable by reason of custom rather than by their 'nature'. This was Bathsua Makin's case in her *Essay to Revive the Ancient Education of Gentlewomen* of 1673. Mulcaster, however, could not begin to develop the logic of this insight, and went on to set limits to what women might know: males have no boundaries to their learning 'because our employment is so general in all things: theirs is within limit, and so must their [training] be' (174; 176). Yet his own experience was again at odds with his prescriptions: 'For though the girls seem commonly to have a quicker ripening in wit than boys have, for all that seeming, yet it is not so'; their maturity is in fact undermined by girls' 'natural weakness' and because 'their brains be not so much charged…as boys heads be, and therefore like empty cask they make the greater noise' (176; 177). Reading is useful for women to remind them of their religious beliefs and obligations, particularly if they are unable to hear these truths conveniently from a priest. Beyond this,

> I may not omit many and great contentments, many and sound comforts, many and manifold delights, which those women that have skill and time to read, without hindering their housewifery, do continually receive by reading of some comfortable and wise discourses, penned either in form of history, or for direction to live by.
>
> (177; 179)

Finally, again following convention, Mulcaster is uneasy about women being able to write: '*writing* [may] be discommended for some private carriages, wherein we men also, no less than women, bear oftentimes blame' (177; 179). By 'private carriages' Mulcaster probably means 'love affairs', using 'carriage' in the sense of 'personal conduct', and again he takes a balanced view, that men are as likely to 'misuse' writing in this way as are women. He concludes however that writing is to be encouraged as a wifely skill because it may contribute to 'the goodman's mercery', that is, to the husband's material advantage as head of the household.

Female literacy was tolerable when directed to works of piety and household management, and male literacy should also be harnessed to true belief and the work of the legitimate state, in the conventional early modern view. But many people were fearful about what might be unleashed by the power of reading and writing. Robert South

(1634–1716), Oxford public orator, was one of the most popular preachers of the Restoration period, speaking with a witty, modern directness that caught the mood of the new times. In 1683 he preached to Westminster School, his 'alma mater', on 'The Virtuous Education of Youth'. His topic was provoked by the Rye House Plot, a failed assassination attempt against Charles II and the Duke of York. South was appalled that 'there should be so numerous a party of men in these Kingdoms' who might be 'prepared and ready, nay, eager and impetuously bent to act over the same Tragical Scene', the killing of their monarch. South looked about to find why this should be, and he saw only a terrible decline in 'the Morality, nay, the very Natural Temper of the English Nation'. His catalogue is a predictable lament: children have no reverence for parents, servants are disobedient and untrustworthy; the 'Conjugal Relation' itself has coarsened, 'neither are Men so good Husbands, nor Women so good Wives, as they were'. South knew exactly where to lay the blame:

> But now, how comes all this to pass? Why, from the exorbitant Licence of men's Education. They were bred in lawless, ungoverned Times, and Conventicle-Fanatic Academies, in defiance of the Universities, and when all things were turned topsy-turvy, and the Bonds of Government quite loosed, or broken asunder. So that as soon as they were able to observe anything, the first thing which they actually did observe, were Inferiors trampling upon their Superiors; Servants called 'by Vote of Parliament' out of their Master's service to fight against their Prince, and so to complete one Rebellion with another; and Women running in whole shoals to Conventicles, to 'seek Christ' (forsooth) but [only] 'to find some body' else.[20]

South imagined the impressionable generation of babes born during the turbulent 1640s as hopelessly corrupted by what they saw in their ungoverned early years. Now men, they drink and duel, 'And Women [spend] both Time and Fortune, and perhaps their Honour too, at Balls, Plays and Treats.' Only true Education could restore morality to the youth of the nation, to be imparted through 'three sorts of Men', viz., parents, schoolmasters and the clergy. He urged his well-placed audience to

> employ the utmost of this your Power, and Interest, both with the King and Parliament, to suppress, utterly to suppress and extinguish, those Private, Blind, Conventicling Schools or Academies of Grammar and Philosophy, set up and taught secretly by Fanatics, here and there, all the Kingdom over. A Practice, which, I will undertake to prove, looks with a more Threatening Aspect upon the Government, than any one Fanatical or Republican Encroachment made upon it besides....So that what these Under-ground Workers have once planted a Briar, let no Governor think, that by all the Arts of Clemency, and Condescension, or any other Cultivation whatsoever, he shall be able to change into a Rose.
>
> (44–5)

South was alarmed by the spread of dissenting academies which had grown up immediately after the Restoration in 1660 as a response to the closure of Oxford and Cambridge to nonconformist entrants. These independent academies tended to provide a more demanding curriculum than the older grammar schools precisely because they had to substitute for a university education and train their pupils for success in trade and the professions.[21] South expressed the unease of a cultural and political elite threatened by the exercise of forms of literacy which it felt were running beyond its control, and he concluded by urging his select audience to support Free Grammar Schools as the only proper institutions for the breeding up of the nation's youth. These alone, like his beloved Westminster, would train up 'her Sons and Scholars to an Invincible Loyalty to their Prince, and a strict, impartial Conformity to the Church' (47).

Schooling was firmly identified as a deeply contentious matter by the second half of the seventeenth century, held widely responsible for contributing to the catastrophe of the Civil Wars. Education was viewed as either a powerful force for social cohesion and conservatism, or else as an encouragement to free thought which could militate against the interests of state and church. But beyond the schoolrooms and universities there was also a tide of books, pamphlets, ballads and newsbooks, which had been rising year on year since the early sixteenth century and which had from the Reformation given every European state cause for concern. We can now review the organization and regulation of London's renaissance publishing industry in its dealings with authors, readers and government.

4

'MECHANICS IN THE SUBURBS OF LITERATURE'

Printing and publishing 1590–1660

Printing in renaissance London

William Caxton published his *Dictes or Sayings of the Philosophers*, one of the first books to be produced from type in England, on 18 November 1477, at his premises in Westminster. Printing, or the use of 'artificial script' as it was first called, had taken about twenty-five years to reach London from Mainz, its place of origin. In the first years of the sixteenth century Wynkyn de Worde, Caxton's German-born foreman, set up his own shop at the sign of the Sun in Fleet Street, an appropriate venue for his ambition to reach out to a popular readership. Craftsmen producing manuscripts and hand-made books had traded in the vicinity of St Paul's from about 1200, and the area remained at the centre of the English book trade until the early eighteenth century. Piety was not the overriding motive for choosing this situation, but rather because 'Paul's, Fleet Street, Holborn, the Strand' were 'common-haunted places', as Robert Greene, one of the new breed of professional writers emerging in the 1590s, noted. Today the impressive chambers, library, and surprisingly quiet garden of Stationers' Hall, set back from Ave Maria Lane, remain as eloquent witness to the organization and locality which directed two centuries of book production in Britain.[1]

The printing trade in mainland Europe had established an effective and widespread network for distribution by the late fifteenth century, but the book as a commodity was much slower in making a progress through the British Isles. It was only by the late sixteenth century that books were being retailed in the larger provincial towns, and only during the later seventeenth century that printers began to set up in significant numbers beyond London: there were still only six towns throughout Scotland where books were printed or sold by 1668, though itinerant chapmen selling pamphlets from their packs were roaming the countryside from the mid-sixteenth century. English publishing concentrated on producing texts in the vernacular, a language of small commercial or intellectual value to most European readers, and there were few sales to be made by English publishers abroad. Some resourceful individuals made efforts to create trading links, but in general the great European fairs which attracted book-dealing – Lyons, Frankfurt and Leipzig – were not patronized by stationers from London: 'In continental terms, London only became a first-rank book-trades centre during the first half of the eighteenth century.' Book illustration was also slow to be developed by the London trade before the seventeenth century, since stationers either imported woodcut blocks from the Low Countries, or commissioned (generally inferior) copies. This relative immaturity of the publishing industry in Britain, and the unsophisticated design of English books compared with

55

European printing were weaknesses, but the concentration on publishing works in English inevitably encouraged writing and reading in the vernacular: 'Only in England and Spain did vernacular books outnumber Latin ones from the beginning....England entered the era of printing with a wealth of books in the English tongue.'[2]

Moreover no English stationer ever managed to achieve the status and affluence enjoyed by the elite scholar-printers of France, Germany and Italy. This was partly a result of the lack of any extensive market for scholarly texts in Britain, partly a result of the way in which the trade was structured. Pioneering publishers in Europe, such as Nicolas Jenson and Christophe Plantin, financed their ambitious editions through investments from merchant bankers or major institutions such as universities and civil authorities, but there were few astute collaborations like these available to English printers.[3] A more stringent professionalism also existed on the continent, as in the structure of formal examinations administered in France and Italy to refine skills and knowledge in the higher ranks of the trade. For these and related reasons, English stationers by the mid-seventeenth century could feel themselves to be at a distinct disadvantage:

> France especially is famous for the value she sets upon that Profession and Trade of Men (whom we in England incorporate by the name of Stationers) for there they are privileged above mere Mechanics, and honoured with a habitation, as it were, in the Suburbs of Literature itself.[4]

Despite this relative under-development of printing as an industry in early modern England, most London stationers produced readable work, and the trade was the means by which the Elizabethan and Jacobean literary renaissance was published and disseminated. In the first twenty years of Elizabeth's reign approximately 3,850 titles appeared, and from 1580 to 1603 this total increased to 7,430. Bibles or religious works of some kind constituted 40 per cent of this production: approximately one hundred editions of the Bible were printed in the period, and another thirty editions of the New Testament alone. Catechisms, or simple dialogues on the fundamental aspects of belief and orthodoxy, were also very much in demand, running to another hundred editions. The single most prolific category of religious publication was probably the sermon, with over 1,000 editions in English, not including both those given in Latin or translated works. An early register of borrowings from a 'public' collection survives for the library at Innerpefray, Perthshire, for the years 1747 to 1757: 60 per cent of all borrowings were religious items, even at this much later period. After holy writ and theological works, literature – understood in its broadest sense – formed the largest group of titles, and seems to have increased as a proportion of total output during Elizabeth's reign, rising from 13 to nearly 25 per cent by 1600 – but falling back to 13 per cent by 1640. Prose fiction of various kinds largely accounted for this increase, as new sorts of narrative displaced late medieval romances in the readers' favour, but cheap quarto playbooks were also a significant new vogue: fewer than thirty plays had been printed before 1558, while no less than 103 were published from 1590 to 1603.

Textbooks of various kinds formed the next largest group at 10 per cent of the total. One of the most profitable monopolies that a publisher could secure was the exclusive right to print legal texts, and Richard Tottel produced hundreds of editions of annual collections of Statutes and digests of common law precedent. The expansion in Tudor education was served by John and Richard Day, father and son, who produced the 'Absey book', or *The*

ABC with the Catechism, throughout Elizabeth's reign in tens of thousands of copies, out of which only four damaged leaves now survive. Illustrated ABCs had developed as early as the 1470s on the continent, but the first English pictorial primer only appeared in 1552. Boys going on to grammar school learnt their Latin through another monopoly text, the *Short Introduction of Grammar*, or 'Lily's Latin Grammar', which was a consistent earner for its publisher Reyner Wolfe, who turned out an astonishing 10,000 copies each year; this was the 'set text' until 1604, and stayed in use until the 1750s. Classical study texts were usually imported from Europe, but London printers produced over 170 translations from Greek and Latin between 1558 and 1603. The remaining 25 per cent of production consisted of a variety of conduct books, works of history, geography, science and pseudo-science, and the ephemeral but profitable output of newsbooks, pamphlets, scandal sheets and ballads; this cheapest end of the trade expanded significantly from the 1620s.[5]

To summarize, by 1600 approximately 200 different titles were being published in London each year by around twenty Master Printers, operating thirty-nine presses in all. Any attempt to understand this means of production which laboriously manufactured over 7,000 titles between 1558 and 1603, including the works of Sidney, Spenser, Marlowe, Shakespeare and the Geneva Bible, as well as countless ballads, almanacs and vivid pamphlets, must focus on the organization which jealously guarded its monopoly of the printing and distribution of books.

The Worshipful Company of Stationers

> Although publishing is, in its very nature, a highly individualistic and sometimes idiosyncratic occupation, one of the strongest themes running through the history of British publishing is the very tight organizational structure within the industry itself.[6]

The Worshipful Company of Stationers effectively controlled book production in the capital – and therefore the country – for nearly 200 years after its foundation in 1557. There were attempts to break its monopoly during the disturbed decade of the Civil Wars, but after the Restoration in 1660 the Stationers shaped the development of British publishing well into the eighteenth century, when commercial and political conditions created decisively new opportunities for authors and their works.

The term 'stationer' originated in the thirteenth century to describe any retailer trading from a fixed 'station' rather than selling as an itinerant trader. But the word applied particularly to sellers of books – which were still in this early period hand-written – and any associated activities such as copying texts, book-binding, or sale of paper, pens and inks. In the medieval period the 'stationarius' or 'bibliopola' was usually also a bookseller licensed by university authority and under their more or less strict supervision. The majority of stationers in sixteenth-century Oxford and Cambridge were Dutch, German or French by birth, again demonstrating the advantages gained by mainland Europeans in the trade. Until the mid-seventeenth century a stationer could be engaged in all aspects of book production and distribution, and it is only from the 1650s that the word took on its modern sense, first recorded as 'stationery' in 1727, applying to 'writing appurtenances' such as paper, inks and pens, rather than books proper: 'publisher' in the sense of a print-retailer also develops during the 1730s.[7]

Medieval stationers had organized themselves as a guild for the protection and regulation of their trade in the mid-fourteenth century, and as such they were no different from all the other artisan craft-workers of their time. Guilds developed during the later middle ages as organizations for the protection of their members, combining the modern functions of trade union, chamber of commerce and charitable society. The guilds sustained the practice of their particular 'mystery' – the work of their skill – through training by recruitment of apprentices and in regulating the size of membership, and they operated 'closed shops' by taking action against other groups or individuals encroaching on their trade. The London Stationers were therefore essentially a conservative cartel, with little incentive to innovate. Associated trades such as paper making and type founding were slow to develop in England, and English press technology lagged behind continental developments until the late seventeenth century. In this defensive spirit, the London Stationers were concerned to limit the share of publishing gained by 'aliens' – printers operating outside the guild, often Europeans possessing more sophisticated skills than their English counterparts. One anonymous author, denouncing the domination of the booksellers over the printers by the early 1660s, wrote:

> There is a clamour (and that not unjustly) against English printing, because we Print not so well here as they beyond the Seas....Some fault the Paper, and some the Ink; some say it is in the Water, others in the Letter; and a third sort, in the Workman: but it seems to be taken for granted by all, to be impossible to print so well here as there.[8]

In 1557 Mary Tudor and her consort Philip of Spain granted a Charter to ninety-seven of these 'free men of the mistery or art of Stationery' which constituted them as a corporate group with the exclusive privilege, applying throughout the kingdom, to print books. It is important to understand the reciprocal benefits – both to the Crown and to the Stationers – that this Charter formalized. Queen Mary was the monarch who had most to fear from seditious and libellous publications in sixteenth-century Britain, and firmly locating book production within a closely regulated group in theory gave the Crown absolute control over the printing and distribution of all texts: the first Master of the Company, Thomas Dockwray, was a prominent Catholic ecclesiastical lawyer, a strategic appointment. Regulative measures like these were being taken all over Europe: two years later, Pope Paul IV issued the first *Index* of works banned to Catholic readers. On the other hand, for Stationers included in the Charter, the arrangement granted all the benefits of monopoly in an industry where it was (and remains) notoriously difficult to maintain consistent income against expenditure. Just two years after its incorporation by Mary with a view to regulating Protestant literature, the Stationers' Company Charter was confirmed by Queen Elizabeth to oversee a precisely opposite regime. This is an early instance of the ideological opportunism of both Stationers and authority, equally prepared to evolve arrangements in an ad hoc fashion to preserve their power. The extent and effectiveness of the surveillance which the Stationers' Company maintained over all published material as a check against seditious and heretical works is discussed below in Chapter 5.

Individuals usually became members of the Company through an apprenticeship to a Master lasting for a minimum period of seven years. More rarely, they could buy membership if they belonged to a company which had equal or higher status than that of the Stationers: Abraham Veale, a member of the relatively wealthy Drapers' Company, bought his place with the Stationers in 1576. The Stationers were elevated to the elite group of Liveried Companies on 1 February 1560, though it is salutary to learn that these publishers who would soon be printing Marlowe, Shakespeare and the King James Bible were given status slightly below that of the Poulters' Company – the sellers of poultry and game. The Stationers were very late in achieving incorporation, and were taxed by the City at the same rates as the candle-makers and dyers since they were much less wealthy than more prominent Companies such as the Goldsmiths and Drapers, and they ranked twenty-seventh among the Companies. No one had made even a modest fortune by printing books in London before 1570, whereas in Venice one hundred years earlier, Nicholas Jenson had established many of the classic designs for renaissance volumes and accumulated a decent fortune in the process.[9] It also seems strange that a Company given control of all publication by government occupied such a modest place in the scale of London City wealth and status. But the onerous task of scrutinizing the content of all publications fell to the Stationers, and one historian of printing in the period is rightly sceptical about the potential of 'a couple of hundred squabbling small tradesmen' to operate as 'an effective arm of government'.[10]

Women occupied quite a significant place in the printing trade from the late sixteenth century, since the widow of a City Company member had by custom been able to become a freewoman – herself a member with rights – of her deceased husband's Company, and between 1580 and 1720 about 300 women have been identified as working as stationers, the majority after 1640. Throughout the period widows therefore played an active part in running print shops and taking significant shares in the financial stock of the trade (though as yet no significant links have been established between women printers and the growing number of female authors in the period). But no woman was recognized by the Stationers' Company as a Master (let alone Mistress) Printer. During a difficult period in 1636 when it was necessary to re-establish the claims of all those operating as Master Printers, neither Elizabeth Purslowe nor Ann Griffin were recognized with this status, even though their claims were as legitimate as those of their male counterparts. The first girl to be recorded as an apprentice was Joanna Nye, the daughter of an Essex parson, who was indentured to the engraver Thomas Minshall on 7 August 1666; her choice of apprenticeship is possibly an indication that the printing trade had grown in respectability during the period. In 1668 Elizabeth, daughter of the printer George Latham, became the first woman admitted to the Stationers' Company 'by right of patrimony'; sons had been admitted from the founding of the Company if their father was a Master at their date of birth. Printing may be exceptional in having offered even these limited opportunities to wives and widows, since London was described at the time as 'the great Stage and Shop of business, wherein the Masculine Sex bears the greatest part'.[11]

By the later sixteenth century the term 'guild' was falling out of use and these manufacturing cartels increasingly described themselves as 'Companies', a word which indicates how closely they were beginning to resemble modern trading organizations. The Stationers' Company at this point was therefore acting as a pressure group to further the business of its 'mystery' and to maximize income, but though by 1600 customers were complaining about the shoddy quality of some printers' work, there is no evidence of the Company ever seeking to improve or even maintain the quality of its members' output. In its role of a friendly society, a group such as the Stationers' Company became increasingly involved in the management of pensions for surviving dependants, and in relieving hardship among its members, as it matured as an organization. Finally, the Companies were absolutely identified with the status of the City of London, and much of their political activity and revenue-raising levies were devoted to defending the trading status of the area of London defined as the City; 'around the mid [seventeenth] century roughly three-quarters of the adult male householders in the City were freemen'.[12] It is therefore clear that anyone wishing to publish their work in late sixteenth-century London had to negotiate with a highly organized cartel whose members were jealous of their profits, privileges and powers, largely because of the precarious economics of their industry. The author sought to have his work circulated (female authors having hardly begun to enter the market by 1600) and the stationer-printer was eager to protect his investment and obtain a decent return. But having received payment for his text, the writer relinquished all further rights in his work which thereafter became the sole property of the stationer.

'Assignable productions of the brain': authorship and copyright

> We find proved and confessed that the nature of books and printing is such, as it is not meet, nor can be without their undoings of all sides, that sundry men should print one book.[13]

Who can say that they own a particular form of words or a specific idea? The concept of an intellectual property right vested in a text on behalf of its author is an intangible notion which was only developed gradually during the sixteenth and seventeenth centuries, and it was not until the eighteenth century that the singular concept of the author as legal owner with rights over their work was established. We therefore have to make an effort to reconstruct the early modern relation between a writer and their composition, an attitude informed by quite different assumptions as to ownership, copyright and self-expression. A Stationers' Petition of 1643 formulated an early version of intellectual copyright, but this was a significant departure from established book-trade practice:

> there is no reason apparent why the production of the Brain should not be as assignable, and their interest and possession (being of more rare, sublime, and public use, demeriting the highest encouragement) held as tender in the Law, as the right of any Goods or Chattels whatsoever.[14]

In fact authors had no contractual claim over their work in the early modern period: payment from the stationer or printer to the writer was very meagre, and with only rare exceptions there was no conception of authors being able to exercise copyright over their work. This apparent lack of authorial status in relation to the production and distribution of books can be partly attributed to surviving conventions of patronage. An author would rather be maintained by a patron with wealth, power and influence than be paid as a contributor, even the most important one, to the book trade. And although patronage still operated to the benefit of a few authors, it was never extended to stationers in England. Again this contrasted with continental practice: the leading financial dynasty in Europe, the Fuggers, gave enlightened patronage to a number of scholar-publishers, including Henry Estienne in Paris and Johannes Froben in Basel, while the French monarch François Premier sustained Robert Estienne.

There were broadly three ways in which ownership of a text could be exercised during the sixteenth and seventeenth centuries, and these categories applied throughout Europe: by grant of a royal contract; by establishing a privilege in a specific work; or by maintaining a monopolistic patent over a whole class of books. All of these forms of ownership and copyright were exercised by the publisher-printer-booksellers, and never by authors. In some exceptional cases, privileges to publish their own works were granted to individual authors, but Mark Rose argued that even here the bequest of ownership on the author was actually another form of patronage by the state: Venice granted a lifetime privilege to Ariosto for his *Orlando furioso* in 1515, and James VI and I honoured Samuel Daniel with a similar privilege for his prose *History of England* in 1612. But it was not until the early eighteenth century that writers began to have any significant claim on proceeds from their work, or any control over the form of its publication after it had been bought by the publisher. A legally sanctioned notion of authorial copyright, applying for a stated time and with agreed remuneration derived from future sales, was only established in the first decades of the eighteenth century in Britain. In this crucial aspect of publishing, at least, England had some claim to have 'led the way'.[15] But throughout the sixteenth and seventeenth centuries an author's return was often a very thin harvest.

The most potent early form of direct ownership of published work was the royal contract, or patent. In 1504 the Frenchman William Faques became the first King's Printer in England, responsible for publishing all statutes and proclamations for Henry VII. But princes had been slow to realize the possibilities of publication and so for fifty years before this date publishers had established their own forms of ownership in their production. The 'privilege' or exclusive right to print a particular work was first formulated by the early printer-publishers to protect their financial stake in that text; from the beginnings of printing the author had no privilege in his work. Within the first few decades after the invention of printing by moveable types in the 1440s, Venetian printers were successfully claiming privilege for the publication of particular works, and by 1518 similar protections were being exercised by leading London stationers. A substantial form of privilege was also developed which embraced complete categories of books: early examples of these which became very profitable in the period were law books, textbooks, official publications, books of music and liturgical volumes. The Crown also deployed privileges in respect of works which it wished to control, such as religious texts. Bibles, prayer books and catechisms all quickly became substantial earners for their publishers, and there were many disputes about the ownership of these titles, not least because it was often difficult to separate the categories of works for which specific privileges had been granted. This kind of exclusive privilege exercised over a whole class of publications was called a patent, and as a monopoly it could be resented by all the stationers who were excluded from enjoying its benefits. Monopolies in all kinds of commodities were a feature of early modern commerce, hated by consumers and adversely affected traders, and throughout Elizabeth's reign the smaller stationers, booksellers and printers complained fiercely against the monopolist patent-holders who were enjoying the profits from some of the most commercially successful titles, including popular materials such as ballads, prognostications, devotional chapbooks, sensational pamphlets and almanac books.

In order to claim exclusive rights of publication in a work, the London Stationers entered the title of a proposed publication in the Company's Register. An ordinance from the mid-century required every manuscript to be scrutinized by the Warden before it was entered in this way. Once more the requirement for surveillance of texts conveniently reinforced the operation of mechanisms which also regulated the trade. This legitimacy granted to a manuscript by the Stationers' Warden was quite separate from any approval granted by other authorities in the church or state bureaucracies, to which the Wardens would often appeal to protect their position. These rights in the work were established for the printer and bookseller, and the mere writer had no part in this ownership; possession of a manuscript, however it was obtained, enabled the Stationer to secure legal ownership through entry in the Register. Mark Rose contrasted this institutional form of ownership with the modern understanding of personal possession of a work by right of authorship: the Stationers 'participated, as guildsmen of various kinds had done for hundreds of years, in a community defined in terms of reciprocal rights and responsabilities', part of 'a regime of regulation rather than a regime of property'.[16]

The logic of this entry system in the Register seems clear, and we might imagine that Stationers would have felt the need to comply with it, either for their own benefit, or from fear of the expensive sanctions which the Company could exercise against infringements. But recent research indicates that as many as half of the titles published in the period were not recorded in this way at all: 'In 1596, less than forty per cent of printed books were entered…and only forty per cent of those were authorized.' There is even evidence to suggest that the men responsible for overseeing the authorization of books – the Master and Wardens – failed to register their own publications simply to avoid paying the registration fees of 6d for a book and 4d for a pamphlet or ballad: 'The benefits to be derived from printing – economic or ideological – outweighed the risks [of non-registration], even for some of the most established printers.'[17]

'Only for you, only to you': patronage, dedications, payment

The conventions of literary patronage were in crisis during the early modern period and developing in new directions. Among the non-English-speaking cultures of the 'four kingdoms' – the Welsh, Scottish and Irish Celtic regions – an older form of literary culture and patronage persisted, increasingly in tension with encroaching English ways. But the growth of commercial publication in London also had a profound impact on the nature of obligations which existed between authors and their patrons within English culture.

Nine out of ten books written in the sixteenth century began with a flattering dedication to a patron. Twentieth-century dedications are generally sincere addresses to an intimate friend or relation, or else are serious memorials, and early modern dedications could also have this kind of emotive status. Sir Philip Sidney's letter 'To My Dear Lady and Sister, the Countess of Pembroke', prefacing his prose romance *Arcadia*, has this kind of resonance:

> Now it is done only for you, only to you.…Your dear self can best witness the manner [of writing], being done in loose sheets of paper, most of it in your presence, the rest by sheets sent unto you as fast as they were done.[18]

Sidney's romance was also given to his sister in its title as *The Countess of Pembroke's Arcadia*, and so the dedication 'only for you, only to you' seems all the more sincere. But in a society that was supremely conscious of status and hierarchy, authors, who – unlike Sir Philip Sidney – were generally poverty-ridden and insecure, usually framed their dedications with a desperate degree of calculation. By addressing a person of status writers hoped to gain protection and reward for their work, either in money or kind, endorsement of their composition, and gain kudos for themselves. Inevitably the monarch was the most prestigious patron, and over 200 books and manuscripts were dedicated to Elizabeth, and nearly 100 to the chief architect of the Elizabethan state, William Cecil, Lord Burghley. Some individuals and families were celebrated for their active promotion of the arts and received numerous dedications, for example the Sidneys and the Herberts, the Countess of Pembroke acting as patron to a number of poets and musicians, including Samuel Daniel, Edmund Spenser and Thomas Morley; many scholars offered the fruits of their labours to patrons who had maintained them during their laborious studies. In some cases the stationer might act in the role of patron towards the author, maintaining the writer on his premises while the work was written, and calling on him to correct pages as they were produced. But for the majority of authors there were minimal financial returns. The Dutchman Abraham Ortelius, whose *Theatrum Orbis Terrarum* (1579) was the first comprehensive atlas, received very little payment despite the fact that his volume was an international best-seller. He wrote to his nephew in 1586:

> It seems to me that, as far as I have been able to find out in our own days, authors seldom receive money from their books, for they are usually *given* to the printers...[writers] also have some expectation from the work's dedication, through the generosity of a patron, in which they are often and indeed, I believe, mostly disappointed.[19]

John Stow's *Survey of London* (1598), a major work of scholarship compiled in the course of a lifetime, earned its author a meagre £3 and forty copies of the book. By the 1620s pamphlets and small collections of poems might earn their authors £2, but for many authors the only payment was in copies of their work:

> Many men's studies carry no other profit or recompense with them, but the benefit of their copies; and if this be taken away, many Pieces of great worth and excellence will be strangled in the womb, or never conceived at all for the future.[20]

Returns had hardly improved significantly by 1667 when John Milton received £10 for *Paradise Lost*, despite the fact that its 1,300 copies sold relatively quickly. It is difficult to find examples of authors who were lavishly rewarded during the English literary renaissance, with perhaps one exception. Shakespeare had left Stratford at some point in the late 1580s as the son of a very modest tradesman, but after ten years' astute work in the London theatres he was able to return to his home town in 1598 and buy the best house on the market. The theatre was the most likely way for a writer to earn serious money, though again this would not be recouped through sale of copies, but rather by a negotiated share of takings on the door. In its forty-five years' existence the Globe Theatre may have accommodated as many as fifteen million visits, so there were real profits to be made from successful drama. Edward Alleyn and Philip Henslowe, owners of the most popular venues, earned even more than the successful playwrights – and income from entertainments such as the Bear Garden next to the theatres was the biggest earner of all.[21]

By the 1590s the number of authors seeking patronage for their works had grown to the point where dedications were devalued currency, no longer the acknowledgement of a writer to a bountiful protector, and more often the desperate appeal for any recompense at all. The nurturing of connection between authors and potential patrons is best examined through individual careers, and Chapter 6 describes the difficulties encountered by John Taylor the Water Poet, one of the first artisan-writers, in maintaining literary patronage for his mass-market works after the 1620s. Chapter 7 reconstructs in some detail the dense webs of connection and patronage developed by one elite family, the Cliffords, over two generations, and Chapter 5 briefly describes the quite different traditions of patronage that prevailed in the Celtic lordship cultures of early modern Ireland, Scotland and Wales.

'Let not one Brother oppress another. Do as you would be done unto': printing from revolution to Restoration

During the 1580s there were numerous disputes between printers holding patents in specific works and pirate-printers who illegally produced copies of patented titles. Primers, catechisms and almanacs were the most commonly stolen works, but by the 1590s some play texts had also become desirable properties and were being surreptitiously printed – a cheap quarto titled *Hamlet*, for example, in 1603, probably done from memory by the actor playing Marcellus. Shortly after the death of Elizabeth in 1603, the Stationers sought to control this proliferation of unlicensed publication by reorganizing the rights in the printing of the most valuable titles. This was done by the creation of a property identified as 'the English Stock', effectively formed as a wholesaling organization within the Company which owned exclusive rights to the most profitable titles. This asset was valued at £9,000, divided into 105 shares. The English Stock represented a new, more efficient structure of ownership and revenue flow, at odds with the guild ethos of the Stationers' Company, since the oligarchy of the Master Printers remained firmly in control of the Stock. This arrangement bought off the majority of the Company's printers – at least for a while – through their shareholding status, even though this privilege was available only to a proportion of the membership. Shares in the Stock gave a fair dividend in return for investment and were eagerly sought after. This separation between a publishing elite earning its income through rights held in profitable titles, and the body of jobbing printers who physically produced the product, marked the beginning of a division within the industry that would become more pronounced in the course of the century, between men (and a few women) in possession of capital, and the greater mass of labouring wage-earners, and culminating in the eventual triumph of the booksellers over the printers in the last decades of the century.[22]

By the 1620s the Worshipful Company of Stationers was a middle-ranking fellowship of the City of London, working to protect the interests of its members. But the oligarchy of the old Companies was challenged on several fronts during the twenty years before the outbreak of the Civil Wars. All Companies found it increasingly difficult to control the growth of trade activities in the suburbs beyond the City, not to speak of the rest of the country, and in the course of the century the Stationers, together with many other Companies, were challenged by groups seeking to develop less restrictive working practices and exploit new markets. The mechanical reproduction of copies meant that the supply of books and pamphlets in early modern Britain easily outstripped demand, and the industry faced a constant problem of over-manning – there were too many apprentices being trained, hoping to become journeymen printers, who in turn wished to gain the coveted status of Master Printer. This elite within the Stationers' Company was the only group allowed to own and operate presses, and their numbers were very small, not exceeding twenty-five individuals, operating some fifty presses, before the 1640s. Only these Master Printers held the rights to print lucrative titles such as catechisms, books of psalms, almanacs and reading primers. Other members of the Stationers' Company increasingly resented this monopolistic arrangement, while the Master Printers themselves sought to limit and if possible reduce the number of presses in operation. The most valuable patent of all was that vested in the Royal Printer, which granted the monopoly on production of all bibles, service books and official materials. During the troubled decades of the 1620s and 1630s, resentment felt by the growing numbers of journeymen printers against the monopoly of the copy-holding Master Printers continued to grow, and the copyright of patented works was broken with regularity.

The Crown was also aggravated by the printing or importation of works critical of King Charles's 'personal rule' which had begun with the suspension of Parliament in August 1628, and a sustained enquiry into the affairs of the Stationers' Company was held from 1634 to 1636. The result was the Star Chamber Decree 'Concerning Printing' of July 1637, drawn up by Archbishop Laud and his office, which was another attempt to increase control over book production by legislation. We should be careful to understand the combination of motives at work in this Decree, as also in the founding Company charter of 1557, since, Sheila Lambert writes, 'the belief that the only relationship there could be between government and printers was one of repression is proving very hard to get rid of'.[23] In fact, a core group of Master Printers within the Company had actively sought the legislation because it legitimized their monopoly of patents in profitable titles. Laud was also being petitioned by unemployed journeymen printers to require the Master Printers to provide more employment for them, arguing that proper employment for printers would actually discourage the production of unlicensed and seditious works. The Decree perpetuated the arrangements of earlier, sixteenth-century legislation, but also set the agenda for the increasingly unsuccessful attempts to regulate printing and publication during the 1670s and 1680s, the failure of which created the preconditions for the Copyright Act of 1710.

Clause I of the 1637 Decree addressed the problem of publications 'seditious, schismatical, [and] offensive' to Church and State, in very comprehensive terms. Clauses II and III reaffirmed the licensing procedures which had been in place since 1557, but which had been widely ineffective. There was also a new requirement to provide two copies of each manuscript, which in an age before photocopying was a significant burden on authors. The categories of books signalled for particular attention in Clause III reflected the administration's disquiet over comment that had run too freely: 'all Books of History, belonging to this State, and present times, or any other Book of State affairs'; insecurity about legitimacy of rank and title was reflected in the attention given to 'all Books concerning Heraldry, Titles of Honour and Armes', and priority was naturally given to works of 'Divinity', closely followed by Physic [medicine], Philosophy, Poetry, and leaving nothing to chance, 'or whatsoever'. Clauses XXV and XXVI reiterated the right of the Master and Wardens of the Company to enter premises and search for unlicensed printing, a power granted to them in the original charter of 1557. This neatly served the interests of both the Crown in suppressing potentially troublesome works, and of the Master Printers who thereby were able to call in any pirated work that they discovered. Clauses V, VI, VII, XII and XXXII attempted to seal the kingdom against floods of unlicensed publication originating abroad by restricting licensed importation to the Port of London only. The clauses which increased punishments most severely were those directed against the printers, requiring a £300 indemnity for good behaviour from the twenty licensed Master Printers, and threatening the pillory and whipping to anyone working unauthorized presses. In its final clauses the Star Chamber Decree sought to limit the production of type itself (an innovation paralleled in French legislation of 1642).

By the autumn of 1640 King Charles's authority was catastrophically weakened with his defeat in the Second Bishops' War against Scotland, and the proceedings taken against him at the beginning of the Long Parliament. The Triennial Act of February 1641 proposed the abolition of the Star Chamber together with the Court of High Commission, and what was in effect a constitutional revolution continued throughout the summer, with the execution of Strafford and the Grand Remonstrance's denunciation of Charles in October. In this provoking atmosphere, the ordinary members of many city Companies expressed pent-up resentment against the oligarchies which presided over them, and the Worshipful Company of Stationers found itself in an extremely difficult situation. The two highest offices of Crown administration with which it was so closely associated had been swept away, its most successful members were suspected of royalist sympathies, and monopolists and patent-holders of all kinds were once more vulnerable to public attacks and parliamentary censure. Those members of the Company who felt that the Master Printers had too much control over the rights of profitable works seized their moment.[24]

Michael Sparke was a Puritan sympathizer who had already been punished for publishing William Prynne's *Histrio-Mastix* in 1632 (see Chapter 5), and he resented the Master Printers' monopoly in bibles, concordances, grammar books and law texts. *Scintilla, or A Light Broken Into Dark Warehouses* is a six-page anonymous pamphlet, printed in 1641, usually attributed to Sparke (though given by some to George Wither).[25] The pamphlet's epigraph, 'Let not one Brother oppress another. Do as you would be done unto', articulates egalitarian sympathies, a kind of early trades-union consciousness, and the lack of a printer's name shows that the pamphlet evaded formal registration. This 'Breviat' was intended to be given away freely as a piece of agitation: 'Printed, not for *profit*, but for the Common Weal's good: and no where to be *sold*, but some where to be given.' *Scintilla* is a detailed list of works subjected to price-fixing, 'for now six or 8 of the Eldest [the most senior Assistants in the Stationers' Company] combining, carry all to their own mark, and aim always at their own end.'[26] Sparke had been shipping bibles printed in Holland as a way of undercutting the prices fixed by English patentees, and *Scintilla* lists examples of how previous attempts to lower the prices of volumes and improve the quality of work had been foiled by the monopolists. He gives examples of price hiking and describes how book imports were confiscated. With a touch of 'puritan' hypocrisy, in view of his own involvement, Sparke piously comments, 'Great pity our Printing should be forced to be carried to Strangers, in my judgement: better to have our own Nation set at work.'[27]

Sparke's *Scintilla* was one of thousands of items published during the 1640s without reference to the elaborate safeguards established in the Decree of 1637. With the Court of Star Chamber and the 'Purgatory' of High Commission abolished, there were no mechanisms in place to regulate publication. Authors and printers produced an ever-increasing volume of work in response to the unfolding political crisis; the booksellers and Master Printers were by-passed as many of the ephemeral pamphlets and increasingly popular newsbooks were printed by the journeymen who had previously taken work from established Masters, and then sold direct to customers on the streets. As the constitutional conflict moved out of London and broke into open warfare in the regions, the propaganda war moved with it, again challenging the Stationers' cherished monopoly. Charles maintained a flow of increasingly ineffectual Proclamations, and Christopher Barker, as the King's Printer, produced these and other propaganda materials from various locations around the country after 1642.[28]

The scale and variety of materials published in the 1640s were without precedent (even if the majority of the items were just two- or four-sheet pamphlets) and it is fortunate that so much of it was collected and preserved – at increasing personal risk – by Milton's friend, the bookseller George Thomason, who amassed nearly 26,000 items, including 7,216 newsbooks and ninety-seven manuscripts, now in the British Library.[29] All parties involved in the Civil Wars produced propaganda, and from 1641 the newsbook was no longer a neutral record of largely foreign events, as it had been from its invention in the early 1620s, but became strongly parti-pris for one side or the other. Sir John Berkenhead's royalist *Mercurius Aulicus*, the first official newsbook published in England, was by far the most successful, produced at Oxford from January 1643 to September 1645. John Taylor the Water Poet fled from London in 1643 and turned his populist skills to writing for the royalist news-mongers. Parliament's attempts to legislate against the newsbooks were futile, as with the Ordinance of 1643, and the royalist propaganda was only ineffectually countered for Parliament by Thomas Audley and Marchamont Needham with *Mercurius Britannicus*.[30]

The freely operating printers who produced the flood of unlicensed materials during the mid-1640s gained strength and confidence, mounting several challenges to the oligarchy which controlled the Stationer's Company by asking for reforms in the composition of the Company's governing body. Similar demands were being made in other companies at the time. But the Stationers were also coming under increasing pressure from Parliament to reassert control over the disorderly tide of unlicensed writings; therefore it was the booksellers in the Company, suffering at the expense of the printers, who united to oppose any reforms and protect the value of their central asset, the English Stock. The stock-holders needed to 'regularize' printing production in order to regain their status and income: 'The Stationers, because of the unique commodity from which they made their living, could behave in no other way; copyright could not be protected without Government support.'[31]

An Ordinance for the Regulating of Printing was passed on 14 June 1643, attempting to restore the terms of the 1637 Act, but it was ineffectual, and it was against this legislation that Milton wrote *Areopagitica, or Speech for the Liberty of Unlicensed Printing* in 1644, one among a number of tracts debating the scope of toleration at the time. In his unlicensed pamphlet, which also forbore to name his printer, Milton denounced

> the fraud of some old *patentees* and *monopolizers* in the trade of book-selling; who under pretence of the poor in their Company not to be defrauded, and the just retaining of each man his several copy, which God forbid should be gainsaid.

He claimed that they deceived the House of Commons and supported repressive legislation. Milton himself was not against censorship as such: he argued that books should not be subject to the ill-informed selection process of state licensing, which kept arguments from the public domain. Once available to be read, a consensus might still decide that some books and their authors were malignant: 'Those which otherwise come forth, if they be found mischievous and libellous, the fire and the executioner will be the timeliest and the most effectual remedy that man's prevention can use.'[32] From 1649 to 1652 Milton held the post of Latin Secretary for the Commonwealth, and in significant respects became the kind of Licenser that he had denounced in *Areopagitica* five years previously.[33]

In January 1649, anticipating an outburst of publications critical of the execution of Charles, the Marshall-General of the army sought to enforce the 1643 Ordinance, again without success. The generals were not wrong; numerous works were quickly published which lamented the execution of the King, including *Eikon Basilike, The Portraiture of His Majesty in His Solitudes and Sufferings* (1649), supposedly Charles's final meditations, in fact ghosted by John Gauden, bishop of Worcester, rapidly going to nearly fifty editions; pro-royalist sentiment increased dramatically. The final piece of legislation for the regulation of printing to be framed before the Restoration was an Act of 7 January 1653, which was still too weak for the liking of the Stationers' Company, and they continued to lobby, unsuccessfully, for further controls. At the Restoration the senior members of the Company managed to reinstate the severe legislation of 1637 when 'An Act for preventing the frequent Abuses in printing seditious...Books...and for regulating of Printing and Printing Presses' was adopted in May 1662. In 1663 a discontented group of printers made a final attempt to break away from the Stationers' Company because it was now dominated by the booksellers who had continued to gather the rights in profitable works. But the future of the trade lay with the booksellers, not the printers, precisely because they controlled the copyright in texts. It was a Stationer who in 1666 made a clear case for authorial copyright, anticipating the first Copyright Act of 1710. The anonymous author of *The Case of the Booksellers and Printers Stated* wrote, 'the Author of every Manuscript or Copy hath (in all reason) as good right thereunto as any Man hath to the Estate wherein he has the most absolute property'.[34]

During the last three decades of the seventeenth century the publishing market outgrew the legislation which remained in all essentials the antique Tudor mechanism for the regulation of printing. The Stationers' Company could not prevent the setting up of presses in the provinces, and in London wholesaling combines of booksellers increasingly by-passed the old register-entry system of copyright control. The market grew to meet the demands of a diversifying, voracious new readership.

5

CENSORSHIP AND STATE FORMATION

Heresy, sedition and the Celtic literary cultures

'Peace, plenty, love, truth, terror': defining early modern censorship

In the final scene of Shakespeare and Fletcher's *King Henry VIII*, first performed as *All is True*, Archbishop Thomas Cranmer asks permission from Henry to give a blessing over 'the child' Elizabeth. Cranmer's speech is a paean to the future Queen, a blessing which is also a prophecy. From the troubled year of 1613 Cranmer's eulogy paints a nostalgic picture of a reign already firmly mythologized:

> Good grows with her;
> In her days, every man shall eat in safety
> Under his own vine what he plants, and sing
> The merry songs of peace to all his neighbours.
> God shall be truly known, and those about her
> From her shall read the perfect ways of honour
> And by those claim their greatness, not by blood.

Even more miraculous, from the ashes of this 'virgin phoenix' will spring an equally glorious (though as yet unknown) sovereign – King James VI and I himself. Cranmer then describes the virtues which will be the servants of 'this chosen infant' and inherited by her successor: they are 'peace, plenty, love, truth, terror', the last uneasily completing the verse line.

One argument for attributing this speech to Shakespeare rather than Fletcher is that the ambiguities of the word 'terror' are consistently explored in his drama from the earliest plays onwards. At the beginning of *Measure for Measure* the Duke describes how he has delegated all powers to Angelo, 'Lent him our terror, dressed him with our love', where 'terror' can be taken as 'the awe-inspiring ability to punish', but which is paired antithetically and provokingly – as in *Henry VIII* – with 'love'. Shakespeare's lines demonstrate how the state demands a subjection from its members which is inseparable from abject fear, even when, as here, its legitimacy is vested in a suckling child. Members of the audience may then draw their own inferences about how this 'terrific' power stands in relation to their lives and conduct.[1]

Elizabeth's administration began her reign in 1558 by confirming the role of the Stationers in overseeing publications. It simultaneously acted to control content of the drama with a Proclamation 'Prohibiting Unlicensed Interludes and Plays, Especially on

Religion or Policy' – 'permit none to be played wherein either matters of religion or of the governance of the estate of the commonweal shall be handled or treated'. This censorship was delegated to mayors and justices in the localities throughout the country, and was a shrewd way of ensuring that the religious plays of each region were overseen. The Proclamation also removed the possibility of using drama as a vehicle for political factions, which had been a new tendency from the 1530s. Over the next two decades the civic religious plays which had been performed for more than 150 years were given their final performances, in 1569 at York and in 1575 at Chester; the Coventry cycle was 'brought forth' for the last time in 1579. Here at least Elizabethan stage censorship was remarkably effective. The Mysteries had been largely amateur productions, playing in the provinces, but the opening of the Red Lion Theatre in Stepney in 1567 ushered in the professional, commercial stage and four more theatres followed within twenty years, creating a new source of anxiety for the censors, and fortuitously, a more coherent area on which to focus their concerns.

The London theatre industry which developed rapidly and successfully from the 1560s was mass commercial entertainment of a new kind, anathema to the City fathers who viewed the plays as godless, immoral and subversive interludes which drew rowdy crowds that were difficult to control and which might spread pestilence; more than this, they took honest citizens from gainful work and seduced them from true religion. The commercial theatres were therefore built south of the river and beyond the power of the City proper which operated from the Guildhall. But the drama thrived on a fundamental socio-political paradox because the plays were at the same time highly valued by the monarch as entertainment for the Court, and the Privy Council supported the establishment of the London theatres precisely because they could supply the dramatists and actors which they required. The Elizabethan and Jacobean drama was therefore bi-located, playing at the dubious margin of London in the suburbs south of the river, among the bearpits and brothels of Southwark to some 40,000 citizens each week, but simultaneously called into the centre of power and privilege to perform during the period of the Court Revels, and under the patronage and protection of nobility. The resonance of plays which dealt with the nature of political authority was fostered by this need to address at least two quite distinct audiences, together with a lively awareness that they also drew serious hostility from other vocal sections of society.[2]

The drama playing in these diverse London venues from 1560 onwards was therefore vulnerable to criticism, and the closure of all the public theatres in 1642 would seem to vindicate the argument that the forces of censorship and repression definitively triumphed over art. Yet there is little consensus about the nature and scope of early modern 'literary censorship' in current critical and historical accounts, perhaps because it is one of the subjects where scholarship most clearly reveals its own preoccupations. Social and political historians such as Christopher Hill and Margot Heinemann, writing from a libertarian Marxist position, argued that a pervasive regime of censorship had developed in seventeenth-century England, virtually totalitarian in its scope and effectiveness. Hill saw the Tudor and Stuart state as a repressive institution struggling to enforce censorship against radical, progressive views, a contention which reached its peak in the 1640s with the temporary collapse of all regulation, 'the most significant event in the history of seventeenth-century English literature'. Theatre historians such as Glynn Wickham and G. E. Bentley concluded that the Stuart and Carolean censorship of the theatre was so efficient that it succeeded in emasculating the drama by suppressing the political and dynastic debates which had flourished in history plays during the 1590s. Literary critics with new-historical, cultural-materialist or feminist perspectives also analysed literary production in terms of a dominant ideology which was contested by marginalized or oppositional voices, a struggle in which the instrument of censorship was seen to be central, either in specific acts of political intervention or through the diffuse but overpowering effects of patriarchal discourse. Annabel Patterson argued that authors and dramatists 'negotiated' their meanings within the prevailing political climate and accommodated to the censorship by expressing themselves indirectly through 'functional ambiguity' and use of 'aesopian' fables.[3]

However, recent archive-based studies which have examined the records of the offices responsible for censoring publication and performance argue against this 'repressive' model of cultural production. Cyndia Clegg studied the paper-trails left by Star Chamber and other state institutions and found that there were multiple, conflicting interests at work which militated against the efficient operation of a continuous and uniform surveillance, let alone censorship:

> the fabric of Elizabethan press censorship and control is a crazy quilt of proclamations, patents, trade regulations, judicial decrees, and privy council and parliamentary actions patched together by the sometimes common and sometimes competing threads of religious, economic, political, and private interests.

Clegg discovered only four occasions during Elizabeth's reign when the Bishop of London or the Archbishop of Canterbury, the official Licensers, acted against published works which were not involved with theological argument. That is to say, the ecclesiastical authorities ultimately responsible for oversight of all publishing seem to have been surprisingly unconcerned with the content of non-religious texts. She concluded that the Elizabethan state was only able to respond in an ad hoc manner to works which provoked a response after publication and which were perceived as explicit criticisms of prominent individuals or state conduct. Elizabethan press censorship was therefore located pragmatically and 'quite precisely in the politics of personality, patronage and national interest'.[4]

Similarly, Janet Clare argued against critical constructions which simplify the operation of censorship in the period as a 'dominant ideology' which was 'challenged' or 'transgressed' by specific plays and texts. By their very nature, censored material and the motivations of writers, actors and bureaucrats remain elusive, and arguments which try to particularize them are necessarily speculative. As with Clegg's study of the Elizabethan press censors, Clare found that the drama censors from 1560 to the mid-1620s acted with 'no consistent political, moral or cultural criteria', but intervened in a spirit of crisis management as government responded to changing circumstances. The serious apprentice disorders and food riots in London during 1592 and 1596–7 may have provoked the Office of the Revels to suppress references to the deposition of the monarch in Shakespeare's *Henry VI Part Two* and moderate the representation of Jack Cade's revolt (for which see Chapter 8, below). Similarly, Edmund Tilney, the Master of the Revels, personally edited the playbook of *Sir Thomas More* in the early 1590s, and again focused on scenes portraying riot in the city. His comment was, 'Leave out the insurrection wholly and the Cause thereof…and not otherwise at your own perils.' Yet even here, in one of the most well-documented cases of the censor's intervention in a play text, there is no scholarly agreement about the way in which the dramatists responded to the censor's threat: the insurrection was revised (by Shakespeare, some argue) but not cut. The deposition scene (4.1) in Shakespeare's *Richard II* was certainly censored in all Elizabethan editions of the play, but when it was restored in 1608 the title page actually made a selling-point of the new material – 'With new additions of the Parliament Scene, and the deposing of King Richard. As it hath been lately acted...'.[5] It may be that dramatists and acting companies were as opportunistic as the censors, and when the immediate cause for concern had faded – in *Richard II* the unsettled times and growing insecurity among the political elite as Elizabeth's reign drew to a close – materials which had previously given offence were restored to performance and text.

Libel was a serious offence in Elizabethan and Stuart England, defined as malicious speech or writing about individuals or the state, and it figured as a crime in nearly 580 Star Chamber cases between 1603 and 1625, and at a fairly constant rate. But no professional authors or dramatists were punished for libel under Elizabeth or James. Among the 2,000 plays composed between 1590 and 1642, there is only evidence of censorship being exercised on about thirty occasions, and few of these were directly political interventions. This may suggest that dramatists wrote with the surveillance of the Master of Revels very much in mind, self-censoring their work. Other scholars maintain that it was precisely because the theatre was perceived to be powerless that it could stimulate discussion on serious political and social issues. Paul Yachnin has argued that Elizabethan and Jacobean dramatists capitalized on renaissance conceptions of the autonomy of poetic discourse so as to insulate their plays from charges of political critique. The possibility of making meanings and drawing conclusions was offered to the audience through the plays' inherent ambiguities, and different constructions might be made by different constituencies (Shakespeare was peculiarly adroit in this way, writing plays which continue to resonate with ever-larger audiences). For this argument, the survival of the dramatists and companies from the 1590s depended on increasing professionalization and making alliance with powerful patronage which would protect them from the criticism of the City and dissenting pulpits. This development was crowned in 1603 when the most successful companies were taken under royal patronage as the King's, Queen's and Prince's Men. Shakespeare's company was, predictably, the first of these. By encouraging the view that drama was in fact a category of pseudo-statement, neither true nor false, but fictive, the theatre profession may have been able to divert some censorious attention away from the plays, while also maintaining considerable freedom of expression. This argument therefore helps to explain A. B. Worden's conclusion that:

> when we observe the breadth of political exploration which did secure untroubled presentation on the stage, we must suspect that the government lacked not merely the power, but the inclination, to impose conditions of writing that can helpfully be called "repressive".[6]

This chapter frames the question of early modern censorship in two ways: one, narrowly, as the intervention of government in day-to-day publication and performance where control was necessarily opportunistic, and in some cases actually counter-productive to the state's interests. The second approach contextualizes censorship more broadly, as the long-term impact of government on cultures and forms of expression which were considered to be inimical and where the consequences could be far-reaching. This dual focus may provide a way of reconciling the apparently contradictory arguments between social and literary historians and critics, since in the course of 150 years the English state did undeniably have a major influence on central areas of cultural life. The most thorough act of censorship was accomplished by the nation-wide iconoclasm of the Protestant Reformation in which every aspect of religious life and belief of Christians whom the state defined as heretical, whether Catholic or dissenting Protestant, was overseen and regulated, not infrequently through the exercise of 'terror' and violence. The civic religious drama surviving from before the Reformation was discouraged and suppressed during the first three decades of Elizabeth's reign as part of this lengthy, iconoclastic conversion of Britain from a Catholic to a Protestant culture. Another unarguable act of cultural suppression was the closure of the public theatres from 1642 until after the Restoration in 1660. And in Ireland, Scotland and Wales, traditional, non-English literary cultures were severely affected by successive administrations.

Widening the definition of 'censorship' to include the fate of the Celtic literatures may be an over-extension of the strict meaning of the word, but in so far as political elites – both Scottish and English – had during several centuries attempted to develop 'language planning' legislation against Gaelic speakers and writers, then 'censorship' is an appropriate description. Suspicion of the Gaelic cultures had been intensified by the anti-Catholic sentiments of the Reformation, and the creativity and patronage of the indigenous literary cultures of Ireland, Scotland and Wales went into decline and faced eventual extinction during the seventeenth century, a direct consequence of political and economic strategies implemented from the reign of Henry VIII to Oliver Cromwell's Interregnum, and beyond. English state policy was overwhelmingly concerned to shape national religious life and the cultural fabric of the non-English regions; to that extent censorship played a crucial role in the process of British state formation and modernization that accelerated inexorably throughout the early modern period.[7]

The Stationers' Company, overseer of the intellectual economy

Claudius becomes uneasy as he watches Hamlet's production of 'The Mousetrap', and he voices the early modern censor's concern when he asks his son-in-law, 'Have you heard the argument? Is there no offence in't?', to which the Prince disingenuously replies, 'No, no, they do but jest, poison in jest. No offence i'th'world.' Hamlet adapts 'The Murder of Gonzago' by adding 'some dozen or sixteen lines' which will confront Claudius with his crime so as to provoke reaction in him. This was one of the hoariest – and least convincing – defences of theatre which was periodically argued during the 1590s, 'That guilty creatures sitting at a play...have proclaim'd their malefactions.' But what is significant for the argument of this chapter is that Hamlet's subversion of the play does manage to escape censorship by posing its serious allegation against the King indirectly, and in this way revealing the most dangerous truth in the state – for those who are alert to the message.[8]

Attempts by authority to proscribe the circulation of specific texts were already well established before the arrival of the printed page. Throughout the fifteenth century the English church had been anxious to restrict the laity's access to bible translations in manuscript, as described in Chapter 3. But government efforts to regulate the new mass-productive technology of printing became increasingly common throughout Europe during the first three decades of the sixteenth century. This censorship was provoked by the early success and efficiency of the continental book trade, and by the prolonged crisis of the Reformation in which publication inevitably played a decisive role. In 1521, responding to the impact of works by Luther and Melanchthon, François Premier required all religious publications to be submitted for scrutiny by theologians at the Sorbonne. A Proclamation issued by Henry VIII in 1528 sought to limit the number of foreign printers active in London, and Henry further attempted to restrict printing in his kingdom to native stationers in 1534, at the same time increasing surveillance of all imported books. A royal Licenser for English publications was finally created in 1538, and the scope and responsibilities of this position formed the basis for subsequent practice in England, and was incorporated into the system of regulation established for the Stationers' Company itself in 1557.

By the middle decades of the sixteenth century an increasing number of complaints against London stationers for named 'seditious' works were being made by the Privy Council or the Star Chamber, and the 1557 incorporation of the Stationers' Company was conceived as a way of requiring publishers and printers to police themselves more effectively. The Privy Council was the single most powerful group in government, advising the monarch and supervising the work of the Treasury, foreign policy and home affairs. The quaintly named (though widely feared) Star Chamber was the same Council convened as a legal body in the Star Chamber of the Palace of Westminster, established in the fifteenth century as a special meeting which dealt swiftly with serious political misdemeanours. These highest levels of state administration sought effective ways of controlling the circulation of printed materials, and recent research by Peter Blayney suggests that Elizabeth's most trusted councillor, Secretary Cecil, may have involved himself with the formation and administration of the Stationers' Company at crucial phases of its development.[9]

Lacking extensive means of surveillance and control, the early modern state sought ways of encouraging its citizens to regulate their beliefs and actions through self-scrutiny, and the Charter of the Stationers' Company effected this kind of supervision, establishing control over the making of books with the intention of preventing publication of 'seditious and heretical' works. The Register entry system, described in Chapter 4, was intended to ensure that all books were 'seen and allowed' by appropriate authority, though as we have seen, a high proportion of published works were not scrutinized at all. The Master and two Wardens of the Company held the most powerful offices, with the absolute right to enter the workshops of printers and binders and the shops of Stationers retailing books to search for texts which were being printed or sold unlawfully. Offenders could be fined £5 and imprisoned for three months; 'powers of this kind were common to all the City livery companies and were fully recognised at law'. The 1557 Charter also confined the production of books to London, which suited the printer-publishers, who were therefore more easily able to regulate their monopoly – earlier in the century London stationers had intervened to prevent the development of book production elsewhere in the country. Centralization also helped the Crown in its surveillance of publications. The church as an arm of the state was closely involved in this process of scrutiny, seeking heretical and schismatic books which might undermine the orderly regulation of religious observance.

A mutually beneficial relationship therefore existed between the Stationers and the authorities which was fundamental to the operation of the Company throughout the seventeenth century. Commercial efficiency in regulation of the trade aided the religious and political policing of what was written and read. This was exactly the argument made by Christopher Barker, the Queen's Printer, as early as 1582:

if no man were allowed to be a Master Printer, but such whose behaviour were well known, and authorised by warrant from her Majesty, the art would be most excellently executed in England, and many frivolous and unfruitful Copies kept back, which are daily thrust out in print, greatly corrupting the youth, and prejudicial to the Commonwealth in many ways.

Surveillance by the Stationers' Company could be vigorous at difficult times. In 1586 the number of searchers of premises was increased from twenty-four to twenty-seven, going about their business in groups of three. The Company however only exercised this jurisdiction over its own members; other agencies searched the general population, and no one was exempt from their attentions. Even John Stow, the eminent chronicler of London, was visited by search teams and his library inventoried. So while it is possible to argue that 'the British book trade has over the centuries suffered remarkably little control from the state or from other institutions', the first 150 years of the Stationers' Company probably saw the most significant degree of direct governmental regulation over printing, owing to the shared interests of both the trade and Crown in the orderly development of the new industry.[10]

The Stationers and the licensing process could be over-ridden by Privy Council or the monarch as required: in February 1587 the Council ordered the calling in and revision of the second edition of Holinshed's *Chronicles* because they considered that it had revealed materials of concern to the state by discussing Irish and Scottish affairs. Other instances of vigorous press surveillance included the campaign in 1589 to discover and punish the author of the Martin Marprelate tracts, popular Puritan-inspired satires directed against the bishops. Simultaneously the theatre was recruited to the government campaign against extreme Puritanism, when Lyly, Nashe and Greene were commissioned to write a satire against Marprelate which proved very successful. A decade later in June 1599 all satires were called in and burned and the Privy Council required all histories to be submitted to it for licence. Cyndia Clegg argues that this robust move against satire is an example of the way in which Elizabethan censorship responded to particular infractions which affected current policy, and relates the campaign to the defence of the Earl of Essex against popular criticism just at the moment when his expedition against Ireland was about to be launched:

> few of the books printed in England that were unlicensed by the Stationers or unscrutinized by official reviewers were actually treated as transgressive by the state....That is, reception, far more than regulation, determined whether or not a particular text was transgressive.[11]

Tudor and Stuart administrations simply did not have the time or resources ruthlessly to pursue and suppress every sign of printed dissent. Pity some of the humble functionaries overwhelmed by their task. One parish clerk who was required to read and censor all ballads before they were printed simply broke down, no doubt with stress-related illness, and refused to carry on until sternly commanded by Archbishop Laud to return to his tottering pile of manuscript. There were all kinds of other materials which might need attention; in a society of very partial literacy, books and pamphlets were only one of many forms of expression which could give cause for concern. The explosive success of commercial theatre from the 1570s necessitated the reshaping of the Master of the Revels' office, from an organizer of entertainments to an editor of dramatic content. Speeches delivered to gatherings, such as sermons, the deliberations of the courts, and the coterie circulation of manuscripts and correspondence wove an intangible web of discussion and rumour which was impossible to police effectively. Therefore, although the ordinances for the regulation of printing in the period seem to be comprehensive, and to our eyes even fearsomely strict, there are many indications that publishers, readers and writers ignored the arrangements, or found ways of circumventing them.

Avoidance of the censorship laws can be found in surprising places: the Roman Catholic edition of the New Testament, published at Rheims in 1582, was one of the translations which the teams working on the 'Authorized' version of the Bible for James VI and I during the first decade of the seventeenth century were allowed to consult, on highest authority. Other instances include the list of books belonging to Andrew Perne, a Cambridge don, made in 1589, and including as many as 420 Catholic texts, which in strict terms should have been proscribed works. More surprising still, Archbishop John Whitgift had granted a licence to the Stationer Ascanius de Renialme in 1586, allowing him to import Catholic books, and from late sixteenth-century inventories of Cambridge libraries it seems that 'Catholic books were accessible to those who wanted them, and that the tidy-minded Whitgift was regularizing a trade that had always been tacitly allowed'. Books banned on the highest authority could also gain sales precisely because of their notoriety. Walter Ralegh was committed to the Tower in 1603 under sentence of death; in 1607 he began his *History of the World*, a modest project to occupy his enforced idleness. The folio was published in 1614 and began to sell quickly, but James ordered its suppression 'for being too saucy in censuring princes'; because Ralegh was 'civilly dead' he was therefore an 'unperson' with no right to expression in the public sphere. Yet when Ralegh was conditionally released in 1616, a page-for-page reprint of his *History* appeared within a year, and the book went on to become one of the century's best-sellers.[12]

Next to outright sedition against the state, the expression of religious dissent gave the most cause for concern to early modern government because well-ordered religious practice was so essential to national stability and unity. Individuals and groups whose beliefs were thought to be subversive of the one true, state-authorized religion were subject to the most sustained surveillance and drastic persecutions; 123 Jesuit missionary priests were executed in the cruellest way during Elizabeth's reign as they continued to serve the English Catholic community. Clandestine publishers and readers of suspect works had to fear a visit from the sadistic Richard Topcliffe and his 'pursuivants'. Topcliffe was the Queen's executioner and interrogator-in-chief, responsible for the judicial torture and execution of many unfortunate souls. Recusants – practising Catholics – were most frequently the object of Topcliffe and the searchers' attentions and their methods sound depressingly familiar today:

> They come either in the night or early in the morning, or much about dinner time....They willingliest come when few are at home to resist them, that they may rifle coffers [chests] and do what they list. They lock the servants and mistress of the house and the whole family up in to a room by them selves while they, like young princes, go rifling the house at their will. The manner of searching is to come with a troop of men to the house as though they came to fight a field. They beset the house on every side, and then they rush in and ransack every corner – even women's beds and bosoms – with such insolent

behaviour that their villanies in this kind are half a martyrdom. The men they command to stand and to keep their places; and whatsoever of price cometh in their way, many times they pocket it up, as jewels, plate, money....When they find any books, church stuff, chalices or other like things, they take them away.[13]

The authorities were most consistently zealous in their search for Catholic texts, 'though prosecutions rarely proceeded for these books alone', but dissenting Protestant believers posed a more immediate threat to the unity of the national church and the body politic. 'The Bible, the Bible only I say, is the religion of Protestants', William Chillingworth wrote, resoundingly, in his *Religion of Protestants a Safe Way to Salvation*, a humane and tolerant argument made in defence of the established church in 1637. But in the January cold of 1644 a copy of *The Religion of Protestants* was intolerantly thrown after its author into his open grave by Francis Cheynell, a Puritan divine who could not accept Chillingworth's wide sympathies. The dissenters' emphasis on study of scripture encouraged Puritans to demand greater access to the Bible, for literate and unliterate believers alike. 'Puritan' was from the 1560s a term of abuse directed at anyone who seemed overzealous in their belief, and by 1600 hypocrisy was often identified in the popular mind as the defining character of a Puritan. It was the Puritans' reverence for the working of individual conscience, and their rejection of conforming ritual which made them resentful of attempts to impose uniformity of worship at the expense of individual belief. Dissenting Christians from the 1570s therefore objected to the institutional hierarchy of lordly bishops, and by the 1620s they were characterized by their appetite for rigorous sermons, a preference for singing metrical psalms in the Geneva settings, and by a strict observation of Sunday as the Lord's Day, for which they were also called 'Sabbatarians'. These 'godly' believers disapproved of infant baptism and formalities such as the wearing of surplices by priests, displaying and bowing to the crucifix, and kneeling during Communion. These practices were described as 'Arminian' after James Arminius, a Dutch Protestant theologian who had opposed Calvin's theology of predestination. For making these kinds of objection the dissenters were also characterized as 'precisians'.

Individual congregations had begun to separate themselves from the national Church during the 1570s, usually following charismatic priests such as Robert Browne, and 'puritans composed within the Church and nation a religious sub-culture of committed rather than merely formal and conventional protestantism which, if not separated, was distinct and, in the language of the age, "singular".' Chapter 7 explores the personal and religious crisis of Dorothy Hazzard, a distinctly 'singular' person, caught in a terrible dilemma of belief in 1641. But these godly individuals only constituted a small percentage of the population and 'Most people assumed that they could win heaven by practising the social virtues and presuming upon God's mercy at the last.'[14]

The publications which gave most concern to authority before the 1640s were books and pamphlets written and read by these precisian believers which were critical of forms of worship and discipline in the established church. By the mid-1620s London printers would only publish veiled and mildly critical dissenting works, and more outspoken publications had to be produced in The Netherlands for clandestine shipment back to England. This was a substantial trade, for the most part made up of unexceptionable textbooks, tracts and bibles undercutting those produced by the London Stationers. But Holland was also the source of 'libels', usually brief verse satires (hence 'libelli', or 'short books'), and of the more extreme dissenting works. These became so numerous that in 1624 King

James issued a Proclamation against both 'popish' and 'puritanical Books and Pamphlets, scandalous to our person or state'.

William Laud's appointment as Archbishop of Canterbury in 1633 installed the Arminian tendency as the dominant view in the church and by proceeding to vilify dissident clergy and laity Laud alienated a significant proportion of the middle-ground believers who subscribed to what he denounced as 'puritan' belief. Sir Benjamin Rudyerd, no radical dissenter, friend of Ben Jonson and William Herbert, and who had tried to mediate between Charles and Parliament in the late 1620s, was forthright about the effects of Laud's policies when he spoke in one of the first debates of the Long Parliament in 1641: 'They have brought it to pass that under the name of puritans all our religion is branded....Their great work, their masterpiece now, is to make all those of the religion the suspected party of the kingdom.'

The dissenting Conventicles, or separated congregations, which had been a notable feature of the Elizabethan church, now became an obvious target for Laud's undiscriminating suspicion of all 'puritan' activity. Clandestine publications, which were distributed and discussed at dissenting meetings, played a central part in fuelling Laud's misapprehensions during the 1630s, beginning with Alexander Leighton's *Sion's Plea against the Prelacy* (1629). Leighton urged, with apocalyptic fervour, the abolition of episcopacy. In his view, bishops were the incarnation of Antichrist, and had always promoted treason: even the Gunpowder Plot had been organized by Archbishop Bancroft so that he might become pope! Leighton also described the assassination of the Duke of Buckingham as a providential sign directing Parliament to begin a holy war against episcopacy and all its works. Leighton was tried for sedition by the Star Chamber in the Spring of 1630 and in the suspicious climate of the moment, the court saw him not as a strident, misguided individual, but as an agent of a wide and dangerous conspiracy, in Laud's words 'desperate against the hierarchy'.[15]

Leighton's mutilation, fining and imprisonment had the inevitable consequence of creating a hero and martyr for thousands of individuals who would never lay hands on a copy of *Sion's Plea*. The Star Chamber next prosecuted the Puritan polemicist William Prynne, whose *Histrio-Mastix* had appeared in 1633, a lengthy, vitriolic attack on the stage and everything which Prynne associated with corrupt 'Arminian' behaviour. Prynne had been outraged by Henrietta Maria's appearance in Walter Montagu's *The Shepherd's Paradise*, staged at Court, and he was fined, mutilated and imprisoned for uttering libellous and seditious opinion. He responded from prison by publishing a series of pamphlets attacking Laud and episcopacy, and he was again tried, fined and further mutilated in 1637 with John Bastwick and Henry Burton. These three, together with Leighton, in the popular view became martyrs to Laud's intolerance, and his use of the Star Chamber against dissenters guaranteed its abolition in the constitutional revolution of 1641, by which time the court had become synonymous with royal absolutism. It is therefore possible to argue that state efforts to regulate and censor the publication of opinion through printing or drama were often piecemeal and ineffectual, and when they were perceived as being effective, they could be seriously counter-productive. The political and religious censorships exercised during Charles's eleven years of personal rule did have the material effect of uniting many subjects of otherwise moderate opinions against the statesmen and institutions which exercised them.

'Ireland is but swordland': literary patronage, censorship and persecution in the Celtic cultures

> For we understand them no more than they us. By the same reason may
> they as well esteem us beasts, as we them. It is no great marvel if we
> understand them not; no more do we the Cornish, the Welsh, or Irish.
>
> (John Florio's translation of Montaigne,
> 'Communication with animals', 1603)[16]

English was not the only literary culture of the early modern British Isles. There were also the sung poems and writing produced in Ireland, Scotland, Wales and Cornwall in their related forms of Insular Celtic, a language and culture which pre-dated English. Systems of patronage and literary conventions in the surviving Celtic cultures were radically different from those for writing and reading in English, and tragically, they faced eclipse during the seventeenth century. There was a final flowering of poetry in both Irish and Scottish Gaelic and also in Welsh 'free-metre' verse from about 1620 to 1720 as the older bardic conventions were overtaken by new popular forms of composition, but the social and linguistic matrix of these ancient cultures was fatally eroded by the mid-eighteenth century, encroached on by the economic and cultural domination of English.

Ireland and Scotland were fundamentally involved in the constitutional crises of the 1630s and the British Civil Wars which followed, and historians have begun to re-examine the part played by conflict between the three kingdoms during these decades. As Derek Hirst argued, 'Events and aspirations in Scotland and Ireland, two polities much less committed to polite assumptions of consensus, imposed their own momentum [in 1640]....The outlying kingdoms at last took their revenge for decades of subordination.'[17] The major regions of England such as the south-east, south-west and north-east were relatively distinct in economic and social terms, but Ireland, Wales, and the Highlands and western islands of Scotland were sharply differentiated by language and culture. The Irish (Gaeilge), Scottish Gaelic and Welsh languages (together with Breton, Manx and Cornish) had all evolved from ancient Insular Celtic, and poetry composed using the conventions of oral tradition was highly valued in these cultures. The lack of attention given to these literatures in general surveys of the period is understandable but unfortunate, not only because of their intrinsic interest, but also because of the fateful conflicts between these areas and the dominant English polity at the time. It is impossible to have precise estimates of the casualties inflicted on the different regions during the 1640s, but it seems likely that Scotland and Ireland suffered disproportionately in the fighting and consequent devastations; the consistent use of 'scorched earth' tactics in Ireland from the late sixteenth century onwards caused widespread deprivation and famine, and not least among the casualties was an extraordinary literary culture.[18]

Ireland in the later sixteenth century was an increasingly disrupted society as the two cultures which had uneasily co-existed from the time of the twelfth-century Anglo-Norman invasions came into growing conflict. Dublin, Kildare, Louth and Meath, the four counties of the English settlement known as the Pale, included some of the best agricultural land, their inhabitants spoke English, though some had adopted Irish, and their English was the dialect of Bristol and south-west England, already 'strange' to incoming Elizabethan bureaucrats. The generally poorer northern and western districts were occupied by indigenous Gaelic speakers, but were politically fragmented between the rule of independent lordships; both the Old English and the Gaels shared Catholicism as their religion (though a small minority of Old English Protestants also existed). Comparable but more attenuated traditions of the Celtic lordship society were also to be found in parts of Wales and throughout the Scottish Highlands. At the end of the sixteenth century the elite and peoples of the Irish Gaelic territories therefore had more in common with the Scottish Gaelic culture of the western isles and Highlands than with the 'Old Englishry' of Dublin and the counties of the Pale. From 1603 a third demographic group intervened forcibly in Ireland: the 'New' English who appropriated and settled large areas of Ulster, turning what had been a settled Gaelic territory into a Protestant stronghold. Both the Irish and Scottish indigenous cultures which were organized as septs and clans holding local territories became catastrophically weakened in the course of the seventeenth century, as they were progressively displaced by English language and culture, and all too often persecuted through punitive laws. Early Tudor Irish policy had included the deliberate suppression of Gaelic which was to be achieved by seizure of lands and the replacement of Catholicism with state Anglicanism. An Act for the English Order, Habit and Language was authorized by the Dublin Parliament in 1537, requiring as far as possible use of 'the English Tongue and Language' in Ireland. But by the 1560s the desire to promote the reformed religion modified attitudes to Gaelic, and Queen Elizabeth herself was impatient to have the Bible translated into Irish, going so far as to provide a press and type for its production. A Gaelic New Testament was finally published in the year of her death.[19]

Bardic poetry enjoyed a favoured place within Gaelic lordship culture since the court poets celebrated the glories and promoted the continuity of particular dynasties in highly stylized language and forms, generally sung and accompanied on the harp. W. P. Griffith wrote that, 'The function of poetic literature in Wales was to eulogize the patron.' In Wales these traditional forms of panegyric or praise poem could not easily accommodate the novel skills of the English-speaking elite as they returned from grammar school, university and the Inns of Court, and their new culture was viewed with suspicion as a threat to indigenous language and customs. Philip Sidney had reason to be acquainted with Irish and Welsh culture through his family. He noted that in Ireland, 'where truly learning goeth very bare, yet are their poets held in devout reverence', and in Wales, 'yet do their poets even to this day last: so as it [bardic tradition] is not more notable in soon beginning than in long continuing'. Katherine Philips, living in West Wales in the 1650s, was 'possibly unique in a seventeenth-century author with an English background' when she equated the achievements of ancient 'Brittish' poetry with the classics of Greece and Rome in her poem 'On the Welch Language' – though the likelihood is that Philips herself could not speak or read Welsh. Only Irish Gaelic was given any representation in the university curricula of the period, consistent with Elizabeth's desire to establish Anglican Protestant Christianity and gain a firmer administrative grip on the province.[20]

The bards and annalists of the Irish Gaelic communities helped to promote the dynastic ambitions of their households, and their contribution was by definition parochial. It has been argued that this poetry was therefore unfitted to cope with the radical cultural and political changes working through post-Reformation Europe, and that it largely failed to address the revolution brought by Tudor rule in Ireland. Recent historians have also argued that the surviving literature in Irish Gaelic before 1600 never articulated what could be described as a 'nationalist' opposition to English rule; this interpretation has been made against the view of earlier twentieth-century scholarship which was motivated by its own nationalist agendas. Gaelic Irish culture had never evolved a unified monarchy or state apparatus and so the basic preconditions for development of an idea of nation were not present: 'Bardic poetry of the classical period, 1200–1600, supports the view that Gaelic political consciousness was tribal rather than "national". ' Though their traditionalist, bardic education and outlook prevented them from arguing effectively against the New English incursions from the 1580s, the professional poets certainly responded to the impact of expanding colonization. Tadhg Dall Ó hUiginn (1550–91) was one of the outstanding bards of his generation, living in Connacht and Donegal, and patronized alike by Gaelic chieftans and Old English nobility. In praising the McWilliam Burke family, one of the powerful Old English dynasties of north Connacht, Ó hUiginn began by asserting that all inheritance in Ireland derived only from conquest, including the Gaelic Irish presence: 'Ireland is but swordland. Let all be defied to show that there is any inheritance in the land of Fál save that of conquest by force of battle.' And when the bardic poets did begin to acknowledge the decisive changes occurring in their society, their response could be the familiar complaint of poets down the ages: Mathghamhain Ó hIfearnáin lamented, 'who will now buy a poem?…it were nobler to become a maker of combs – what use is it for anyone to make poetry?'[21]

During the crisis years after the defeat of the Earl of Tyrone in 1603 and the escape into exile of many of the Irish political and scholarly elite, the energies of surviving Gaelic bards were mostly taken up with a bitter, trivial feud between the poetic schools of Ulster and Munster. This was a continuation of the older traditions of contention or 'flyting', but in the new times it was seen to be an irrelevance, 'hounds of great knowledge wrangling over an empty dish'. After the 'flight of the earls' in September 1607, the theme of lament for a dying culture grew increasingly common in bardic and other poetry, and the need for repressive measures against Gaelic language and culture lessened. The patronage of the lordship culture faded as English and Scottish landlords occupied the lands. In 1618 the London-based Stationers' Company attempted to create an Irish Stock venture by setting up 'a factory of booksellers and bookbinders' in Dublin, no doubt hoping for sales among the New English settlers. But there appears to have been little demand for their publications, and the Dublin factory was used to manufacture books for the English market, including the 1621 edition of Sidney's *Arcadia*.[22]

It was the reception of Counter-Reformation learning and the realization that indigenous Irish Catholicism required new tactics to defend itself against English Protestantism that decisively turned Irish Gaelic writing against the English presence from the 1620s onwards. Séathrún Céitinn (Geoffrey Keating, 1570?–1644?) belonged to a long-established Old English family and was one of the most significant Irish Gaelic authors of the mid-seventeenth century. He trained as a priest in Europe and his prose *Foras feasa ar Éirinn* (*Foundation of Knowledge about Ireland*), a history up to the time of the 'New' English incursions of the late sixteenth century, circulated widely in manuscript. The most recent scholarship has allied Céitinn's history with the writings of contemporary 'humanist antiquarians throughout Europe' who were constructing myths of origin that would bring political bearing on to their present. Céitinn begins to use a new collective term 'Éireannaigh' – Irish – to define the Gaels and Old Englishry united against the Protestant New English incomers, adding coherence to an emergent identity.[23]

As well as the formal literary culture of bardic poets in Ireland there were numbers of story-tellers, travelling harpers and ballad singers (often women) who made a living by visiting prosperous houses and performing or composing praise-songs to the households both within and beyond the Pale. The demography of early modern Ireland was already complex; legislation from as early as 1360 had attempted to create an 'apartheid' between colonists and natives, forbidding inter-marriage and the speaking of Irish by English settlers, but intermingling was inevitable and an 'Anglo-Irish' music and culture developed. Members of Old English Catholic families who had been a presence in the four counties of the Pale for several centuries could choose – like Céitinn – to write in Gaelic so as to be read by the scholarly elite of the indigenous Irish communities in the north and west. Irish Gaelic poetry and music were appreciated in the Old English culture of the Pale, encouraged for example by the Protestant, anglicized O'Briens, Earls of Thomond, who continued to patronize Gaelic poets into the early seventeenth century. Irish music was also enjoyed by English and Scottish colonists and in England; Irish airs such as 'Calino Castureme' found in the Fitzwilliam Virginal Book were played on the lute and virginals or sung at London theatres from the 1590s, and a vogue for Irish harp music developed in the capital from the 1620s. Queen Elizabeth kept an Irish harper, Donal 'buidhe', at court, and English settlers in the four counties of the Pale often entertained the itinerant poet-singers.

But as the Tudor campaigns of colonization in Ireland provoked increasing resistance, the laws directed against Gaelic language and culture grew more punitive. As early as 1534 poets, harpers and 'chroniclers' were identified to Thomas Cromwell as fomenters of abuses, extortions and robberies in their praise-songs. During uprisings the poet-bands fell under suspicion of acting as couriers between groups and entertaining rebel households at 'cuddies' or 'night-suppers', where they stirred up loyal passions and the spirit of resistance. Edmund Spenser is best known to English students of their literature as the author of *The Faerie Qveene*, but Irish readers are more likely to remember that he also worked in Ireland as secretary to Lord Grey, the Lord Deputy, and was a key administrator involved in the 'plantation' (settlement) of Munster. Spenser regarded his years in Ireland as a form of exile, and in the mid-1590s he wrote his *View of the Present State of Ireland*, a chilling analysis offering proposals for the more effective colonization of the province. Spenser confessed to admiring Gaelic bardic poetry for its 'sweet wit and good invention', and he had 'caused diverse of them to be translated unto me', but he also censured the bards:

> They seldom use to choose unto themselves the doings of good [loyal] men for the ornaments of their poems, but whomsoever they find to be the most licentious of life, most bold and lawless in his doings, most dangerous and desperate in all parts of disobedience and rebellious disposition, him they set up and glorify in their rhymes, him they praise to the people, and to young men make an example to follow.[24]

The English administration therefore targeted the itinerant singers when resistance became troublesome to them and attempted to ban poets and story-tellers from the settled areas and households. Under martial law in occupied districts the harpers, rhymers and bards were singled out for punishment and even execution because of their role in fomenting anti-English feeling. William Lyon, the first Protestant bishop of Cork, Cloyne and Ross, and militant anti-Catholic, wrote to Lord Hunsdon the Lord Chamberlain (patron of Shakespeare's acting company) on 6 July 1596:

> Some strict order must be taken for idle persons...rhymers, bards, and harpers, which run about the country, eating the labours of the poor, carrying news and intelligence to the rebels, and bruiting [spreading] false tales. Also, the rhymers make songs in commendation and praise of the treasons, spoilings, preyings, and thievings made.

The final months of Elizabeth's reign coincided with the defeat of Hugh O'Neill's nine-year rebellion even as, at the English court, the Earl of Shrewsbury recorded, 'Irish tunes at this time are most pleasing.' As part of the action against O'Neill's followers, the Lord President of Munster ordered his forces 'to exterminate by martial law all manner of Bards [and] Harpers' because of their incitement of rebellion. Elizabeth herself, it is said, in her last weeks gave the order 'to hang the harpers wherever found, and destroy their instruments'. Her godson, the poet Sir John Harington, was ordered by James VI and I to 'banish bards and rhymers...and whip them if they did not quit after proclamation duly made'.[25]

Poetry occupied if anything an even more revered position in Scottish Gaelic culture, and the 'filid' – highest caste of poets – and bards had sung praise poems, verse annals and battle incitements for their clan patrons across the centuries, many of which were still practised in the early modern period. Besides bardic poetry a wealth of work songs, love songs, keenings (laments) and devotional poetry has survived in Scottish Gaelic from the sixteenth to the eighteenth centuries; a similar flowering of more popular, non-professional forms occurred in Irish Gaelic at the same time, as 'the weakening hold of a bardic orthodoxy on the Irish language would in fact ultimately lead to the birth of modern Irish'. Many of these anonymous Scottish poems have female narrators, and as women's work songs it is safe to assume they were composed by their singers (who were almost certainly not writers). *Seathan Son of the King of Ireland* (*Seathan Mac Rìgh Eirann*) is the most celebrated. Dating perhaps from the late sixteenth century it exists in a number of versions, one nearly 200 lines long, a passionate and lyrical keening for a husband killed in battle:

> I was in Islay and in Uist with thee...
> I was in the land of birds and eggs with thee...
> I was three years on the hills with thee...
> dearer Seathan behind a dyke
> than a king's son in silks on deal flooring,
> though he should have a restful bed
> well-planed by wrights
> and protected by the power of druids;

In the medieval culture of Gaelic Ireland there had been a tradition of hereditary bardic families which included poets, historians, doctors and judges, who formed a unique class between ordained priesthood and the laity. They did not however admit women to their studies, and this elite bardic caste remained a male estate, despite hints at the existence of female 'filid' in earlier, perhaps legendary periods. In the *Táin Bó Cuailgne*, for example, Fedelm a poetess and seer of Connacht meets Queen Medb as she returns 'From learning verse and vision [filidecht] in Scotland'.[26] But by the fourteenth century Irish Gaelic women poets are generally only mentioned among the lowest ranks of entertainers such as fortune tellers and balladeers. More poems, however, survive in Scottish Gaelic composed by women, either in the anonymous work-songs, or in the last stages of the clan bardic poetry which was vigorously practised from about 1640 to 1720. The compositions of around fifty poets have come down to us from this time, and among the most accomplished are several women. The best known Scottish poetess of the later seventeenth century is Màiri Nighean Alasdair Ruaidh (Mary Macleod), who composed from the 1640s until the end of the century. She was born around 1615 at Rodel in Harris, and entered service as a nurse in Dunvegan Castle, the stronghold of the MacLeods. She was an unliterate singer, and only sixteen of her compositions have been passed down, but her Gaelic is celebrated for its musicality. With her contemporary Iain Lom she is said to have introduced a less laboured, more personal note to the traditional panegyrics and laments of clan bardic poetry, making song-poems where 'the tunes themselves are great, very great, or simply ineffable'. Some echoes of her musical culture at Dunvegan might still be played in the pipe pibroch passed down from Donald Mór [MacCrimmon], piper at Dunvegan during the 1620s and 1630s.[27]

English efforts to establish colonies in Ireland began as long ago as the late twelfth century with the Treaty of Windsor. Wales had been conquered in the same period, and the Acts of Union passed between 1536 and 1543 imposed English county administration and justice throughout the Principality; Welsh was banned from use in all courts and government. The conception of a 'Great Britain' which would incorporate Scotland was first argued vigorously in the late 1540s, fuelled by nationalist Protestant sentiments. Henry VIII described himself as 'King of Ireland' in 1541, and when James VI of Scotland took the English throne in 1603 he assumed that his rule extended to all of Ireland. A central element in this growth of English political and economic hegemony over the disparate Celtic cultures of the British isles was what would now be called 'language planning' or 'linguistic engineering', that is promotion of the dominant speech at the expense of the subaltern. On 23 August 1609 the political elite of the western isles met on Iona to agree the Statutes of Icohnkill before their Bishop, 'it being understood that the ignorance and incivility of the said Isles has daily increased by the negligence of good education and instruction of the youth in the knowledge of God and good letters'. The eldest son of any family owning more than sixty cattle would go south to a Lowlands school in order to learn to 'speak, read, and write English', and in the absence of 'children male', it would be the eldest daughter. The Statutes also noted that 'the whole Isles have been the entertainment [of] idle bellies, especially vagabonds, bards, idle and sturdy beggars, expressly contrary [to] the laws and loveable Acts of Parliament'. Therefore, 'no vagabond, bard, nor professed pleasant [individual] pretending liberty to bard and flatter be [tolerated] within the bounds of the said Isles' except those maintained by named lords and gentlemen. All other vagabonds, bards and jugglers are 'to be taken and put in secure restraint in the stocks', thereafter to be expelled 'forth of the country with all goodly expedition'. What songs, poems and ballads were expelled, along with the untidy beggars, rhymers and 'Egyptians' against whom local authorities were acting throughout the British Isles with increasing severity from the mid-sixteenth century?[28] The poetry and cultures of the early modern Celts were richly diverse and attract growing interest today, an appreciation which can be turned against the propagandist representations by which they are more generally known to the English-speaking world through *Henry V*'s Fluellen and Macmorris.

6

'PENNY MERRIMENTS, PENNY GODLINESSES'

New writing for new readers

Literacy and social change: 'More solid Things do not shew the complexion of the Times so well as Ballads and Libels'

The urban literate and the rural unliterate lived in the same society, but in what sense did they share the same culture? There were crucial abilities which differentiated people by status in early modern England. Grammar-school boys with a working knowledge of Latin possessed one of the most valued skills which could enhance their life-chances, enabling them to progress in education and employment. Part of their cultural credentials included the ability to quote impressively or recognize classical allusions in supremely learned vernacular works such as Jonson's *Sejanus* or Milton's *Paradise Lost*. Bizarre as it now seems, possession of a classical language was in effect a defining skill in this pre-industrial society, without which a male would find it more difficult to rise in status and esteem. Peter Cook's pub-bore E. L. Wisty, lamenting to Dud that he was condemned to be a coal miner because he did not have 'the Latin for the Judgin' ' contains a painful truth about English society, then and now. Ralph Verney in 1647 was worrying about his 8-year-old daughter Peg's education: 'she grows a great girl and will be spoiled for want of breeding…being a girl, she shall not learn Latin, so she will have the more time to learn breeding hereafter; and needlework too'. Readers and writers without Latin in some ways occupied a different cultural ambit. As authors they tended not to compose in the high-status literary forms modelled on classical conventions – elegy, ode, epithalamium, epic – and some knowledge of French or Italian was probably also necessary to compose conventionally sophisticated sonnets. Milton wished that he had published his divorce tracts in Latin rather than English because this would have restricted their readership to more 'sober' judgements – perhaps what he meant was that they would then have been beyond the reading powers of most women. All of the dramatists in the period were grammar-school products, and their plays were informed, however indirectly, by classical conventions of tragedy and comedy.[1]

There were, however, many readers without the benefit of grammar-school Latin who were consumers of these high-status works, and who read the classics in translation. Reading aloud to friends and neighbours who might be unliterate was also common entertainment. *The Civil and Uncivil Life* (1579) cosily describes rural gentry reading from their expensive folios just brought down from London to an audience of 'our honest neighbours, Yeomen of the Country, and good honest fellows, dwellers thereabout: as Graziers, Butchers, Farmers, Drovers, Carpenters, Carriers, Tailors and such like men, very honest and good companions'. Citizens without benefit of the classics also attended the theatre, and bought the quartos of plays which they had seen and enjoyed. The Fortune and Red Bull theatres catered for audiences from the poorer groups of London society, and their repertoire was provided by less well-known playwrights such as Henry Chettle, Richard Hathway and Samuel Rowley. These plays dealt with local topics such as Heywood's *Four Prentices of London* (1600) or Webster and Ford's bloodily prophetic *The Late Murder at Whitechapel* (1624, alas lost), but there were also a surprising number of plays drawn from what we might think of as the elite culture's territory: Chettle, Day and Dekker's *Cupid and Psyche* was put on at the Red Bull in 1600, Hathway and William Rankin's *Hannibal and Scipio* in 1601, and Heywood's *Rape of Lucrece* in 1607. These (and many others) are significant 'cross-over' texts from the learned to the unliterate spheres. Writers and stationers were eager to supply this growing readership of urban artisans and their families, lesser merchants and their wives and daughters, apprentices and their pigsnies [sweethearts], many of them Londoners, and whoever else they might reach in the provinces. Tessa Watt in *Cheap Print and Popular Piety, 1550–1640* concluded:

> it was the late Jacobean and early Carolinian period which first saw the development of a specialist trade in books which were purposefully small, in order to reach a market of potential readers who had been hitherto unlikely to purchase the printed word, except in the form of a broadside ballad.

Paper costs made up three-quarters of the price of a publication, and stationers were quick to exploit the possibility of short and therefore cheap texts. Additionally, books and pamphlets became relatively cheaper in relation to other commodities from 1560 to 1635 (when their prices increased by 40 per cent but were still lower than wage inflation). The growing numbers of conduct books, devotional works, textbooks, translations, pamphlets, ballads, chapbooks (any cheap unbound text sold by itinerant 'chapmen'), jest books, almanacs and (from the 1620s) news-sheets catered for this middle-ground readership which came to literacy during the 'second wave' of educational expansion during the 1630s. The London wood-turner Nehemiah Wallington was a beneficiary of this new popular literacy: partly as a consequence of his tormented religious conscience he kept a continuous spiritual record from 1618 to 1654 in which he wrote over 20,000 pages of meditation and commentary.[2]

But a simple division between 'elite' and 'popular' is unhelpful as a way of characterizing early modern culture, and categories such as 'dominant' and 'mass' culture also seem anachronistic applied to this pre-industrial, largely pre-urban society, not yet driven by large-scale consumption, and which was still for significant numbers of people a society fending off scarcity. Early modern 'mentalities' were such that individuals of significant status might still maintain beliefs or read texts which were also shared by groups of lower social standing. Religious works certainly crossed the degrees in this way, and there were many gentry readers and collectors of ballad-sheets, and the huge numbers of almanacs were enjoyed by a wide range of readers. The godly were quick to deplore the popularity of ballads exactly because of their near-universal appeal. Nicholas Bownde, a Norwich minister with strongly Puritan sympathies, urged:

> You must not only look into the houses of great personages...but also in the shops of artificers, and cottages of poor husbandmen, where you shall sooner see

one of these new Ballads…than any of the Psalms, and may perceive them to be cunninger in singing the one, than the other.

Roger Chartier has argued that 'widely distributed texts and books crossed social boundaries and drew readers from very different social and economic levels. Hence the need for the precaution of not predetermining their sociological level by dubbing them "popular" from the outset.'

We should not be surprised to find that 'educated' people relaxed by reading undemanding or sensational pamphlets. Similarly, significant numbers of new readers among the poorer social groups were motivated by their religious convictions to read beyond the cheapest 'penny godlies' and into much more demanding works of biblical commentary and theology. The fact that the Bible and Foxe's 'Book of Martyrs' can be challenging reading did not discourage many people in all ranks of early modern society from studying them closely. The author of the anonymous pamphlet *The Compassionate Pilgrim* (1644), almost certainly William Walwyn, was alert to the ways in which the educated classes could create difficulties for new readers wanting to read scripture for themselves:

> they being furnished with these Arts and Languages, have a mighty advantage over all such as have them not, & are admirers thereof, (as most men are) so that hereby they become masters of all discourses, and can presently stop the people's mouths, that [and] put them too hard to it, by telling them that it is not for Laymen to be too confident, being no scholars, & ignorant of the Original; That the Original hath it otherwise than our Translations. And thus they keep it all a mystery, that they only may be the Oracles to dispense what, & how they please.[3]

And as always the phenomenon of the commercial theatre in London was exceptional in the way that it could appeal to a wide range of individuals with diverse exposure to education – exceptional, but not unique, since other cultural forms also drew a diverse audience. Metaphors from weaving and sewing provide useful images for the intricate involvement of print with early modern society. Tessa Watt mapped the wide dissemination of cheap print throughout British rural culture by the 1640s, peddled by travelling chapmen from their packs. Print was like '"scotch cloth" or "coarse linen" sold by the yard, to be made into something by the buyer'. This 'weaving' of text into culture spread from the towns to the countryside, and connected social strata that were otherwise separated by income and station. Linda Woodbridge similarly proposed that print culture encouraged a kind of 'patchworking' in early modern thinking and writing, where texts could be 'quilted' together in delicate or startling new combinations.[4] The life and works of John Taylor (1578–1653), arguably England's first self-taught successful author, illustrate the new opportunities which literacy offered to low-status individuals. His pamphlets and poetry draw directly on conventions of the literary elite while addressing the middling sort of urban artisans, and so are a test-case for definitions of 'the popular' in seventeenth-century cultural politics.

'To any Reader He or She, It makes no matter what they be': John Taylor the Water Poet

In 1619 Ben Jonson, aged 47 and increasingly jaundiced about his career in literature, walked to Scotland in order to spend Christmas with William Drummond of Hawthornden, a few miles south of Edinburgh. During two or three weeks they drank (one presumes) and talked freely, and Drummond noted down several pages of Jonson's opinions and literary judgements. The transcript gives an immediate sense of a combative life spent in reading, writing and the theatre. Among many despairing opinions about the current literary scene, Jonson remarked, 'The King said Sir P. Sidney was no poet, neither did he see ever any verses in England [equal] to the Sculler's.' King James, according to Jonson, valued the works of John Taylor the Water Poet above all others.[5] For Jonson, Taylor was a worthless scribbler who pandered to tasteless readers, and he repeated this view in his *Timber, or Discoveries Made upon Men and Matter as They Have Flowed out of His Daily Readings*, compiled during his last years. Reflecting how 'false opinion grows strong against the best men', he wrote,

> The Puppets are seen now in despite of the Players: *Heath's Epigrams*, and the *Sculler's Poems* have their applause. There are [people] never wanting, that dare prefer the worst *Preachers*, the worst *Pleaders*, the worst *Poets*....Nay, if it were put to the question of the Water-rimers works, against *Spenser's*, I doubt not, but that they would find more *Suffrages*...[6]

Jonson equated Taylor's coarse rhyming (as he saw it) with the vulgar pleasure taken by audiences in puppet plays, as opposed to the genuine arts of true poets and skilful actors. He had made the same equation in the hilarious climax to *Bartholomew Fair* in 1614 where John Littlewit, a would-be author, adapts *Hero and Leander* as a puppet show for the common crowds thronging to the three-day Fair. The classical love story becomes an 'ancient modern history' and has to be updated and made 'relevant':

> I have only made it a little easy, and modern for the times sir, that's all. As, for the Hellespont, I imagine our Thames here; and then Leander I make a dyer's son, about Puddle Wharf; and Hero a wench o' the Bankside, who going over to Old Fish Street, Leander spies her land at Trig Stairs, and falls in love with her.

Hero is rowed to Leander across the Thames by a sculler, who is then accused of playing the pander or bawd by the puppet-master. The sculler-puppet knocks him over the head with his oar and rows away shouting insults, leaving the puppet-master to lament, 'there's no talking to these watermen, they will ha' the last word'.

There is one line which must explicitly relate Taylor the Water Poet to Jonson's parody: at the beginning of the show, when he introduces the puppets, one of the audience disparagingly remarks, 'I think one Taylor would go near to beat all this company, with a hand bound behind him.'[7] Three weeks before *Bartholomew Fair* had opened at the Hope Theatre, John Taylor provoked a near-riot on the same stage. Taylor had challenged William Fennor, a successful one-man entertainer, to a 'wit-combat', an early version of stand-up 'impro' comedy, and he hired the Hope Theatre, a low-grade (and therefore popular) venue for the occasion. Taylor distributed a thousand hand-bills advertising his event, and on 7 October he was waiting eagerly on the stage, 'the house being filled with a great Audience, who had all spent their monies extraordinarily: then this Companion [Fennor] for an Ass, ran away and left me for a Fool, amongst thousands of critical Censurers'.[8] The audience became enraged, and Taylor was only rescued by the resident acting company who quickly presented part of their repertoire, anxious to save the theatre – and incidentally Taylor – from the crowd.

Jonson may also have known that Marlowe's *Hero and Leander* was the poem which inspired John Taylor to begin writing his own verses as he plied his trade on the Thames at the end of a day:

> It chanced one evening, on a Reedy bank,
> The Muses sat together in a rank,
> Whilst in my boat I did by water wander,
> Repeating lines of *Hero* and *Leander*,
> The *Triple three* took great delight in that,
> Called me ashore, and caused me sit and chat,
> And in the end, when all our talk was done,
> They gave to me a draught of Helicon,
> Which proved to me a blessing and a curse,
> To fill my pate with verse, and empt my purse.[9]

John Taylor, a Thames waterman, wrote over 150 works during a unique career that bridged 'the golden stirring world'[10] of the Bankside theatres in their heyday of the 1600s, and the bitter sectarian hatreds of the 1640s, ending only with his death in 1653. Taylor produced an extraordinary range of work, usually in the format of the three-sheet quarto or octavo pamphlet selling for three pence. He wrote satires, journalism, sensation pieces, verse miscellanies, devotional tracts, travelogues and travel guides, some disconcertingly modern 'nonsense' verse, and in at least three of these genres he made real innovations. His work has usually been quoted by historians and theatre critics only as a way of providing contexts for more valued writing. The *Dictionary of National Biography* is scathing, describing him as 'a literary bargee...his books – many of them coarse and brutal – are contemptible; but his pieces accurately mirror his age'. However, as serious study of early modern popular culture has developed in the last two decades, Taylor's work has begun to receive more careful attention. He was proud to be known as the 'Water Poet', and he is a quite new phenomenon: a relatively uneducated person who makes a reputation, even occasionally a living, by writing. There may have been aspirations like this in earlier times, but no one could have sustained this career in Britain before the late sixteenth century, relying as it did on publicity and a concentration of urban readers served by a relatively efficient press. Taylor must therefore be one of the earliest examples of an individual from a modest, even poor family who aspired to live by poetry.

The fortunes of poets from similar backgrounds in the eighteenth century mark a clear contrast with Taylor: Stephen Duck (1705–56), a Wiltshire farm labourer, received almost no formal education, but his verses were admired by Lord Macclesfield and he was given a pension by Queen Caroline in 1733; Mary Collier (1689/90–1762?), who may be 'the first published working-class woman poet in England', produced *The Woman's Labour: An Epistle to Mr Stephen Duck* (1739); Mary Leapor (1722–46), a gardener's daughter, devoted herself to writing from the age of 10; Robert Bloomfield (1766–1823), a Suffolk farm labourer, achieved celebrity with *The Farmer's Boy* (1800); and most successful of all, Robert Burns (1759–96), the son of a struggling tenant farmer from Ayrshire.[11] These aspirant writers began in the provinces and were patronized as 'natural' and 'untutored' poets who might make a homespun contribution to the genre of pastoral. By contrast, Taylor's publications depended crucially on London for their content, forms and readership: an artisan-writer could have prospered nowhere else in Britain before 1700.

Taylor was the son of an urban tradesman, born in Gloucester on 24 August 1578; his family was probably of very modest means and there is no other trace of it in the city records. He learned reading and writing at petty school, and did progress briefly to grammar school, but Latin – or circumstances – defeated him. He therefore left formal education in the early 1590s and joined the thousands of young 'economic migrants' who travelled to London each year, where he was apprenticed to a waterman, probably in Southwark. Like many watermen he served in the navy, and took part in the 1596 raid on Cadiz lead by the Earl of Essex, as well as sailing with six other expeditions. Watermen provided the river-taxis of their day and (like cab-drivers the world over) were celebrated – if not notorious – as gossips and raconteurs. Watermen were generally regarded as a rough, drunken crew, and accepting their hire was sometimes more like being taken hostage. They had been incorporated as a Company in 1555, but it was a hard living, with too many scullers chasing too few fares. During the early seventeenth century they were increasingly threatened by rising competition from over 6,000 hackney coaches – road traffic congestion in London had become a serious problem as early as 1601.

The Southwark theatres generated a lot of trade for the river-rowers during the 1590s and well into the first decade of the next century, and John Taylor knew their patrons and companies intimately: 'The Players are men that I generally love, and wish well unto and to their quality, and I do not know any of them but are my friends, and wish as much to me.'[12] An impressive selection of dramatists and actors figure in Taylor's writings as collaborators or friends: Thomas Vincent, prompter at the Globe; Edward Alleyn, actor, manager, founder of Dulwich College; Thomas Heywood, whose *Apology for Actors* (1612) has dedicatory verses from Taylor; and Thomas Dekker, contributing commendatory verses for *Taylor's Urania* (1615) – a copy is inventoried among Edward Alleyn's impressive library left to Dulwich College. Taylor also (improbably) claimed friendship with Ben Jonson, 'a Gentleman to whom I am so much obliged for many undeserved courtesies', the poet George Wither (though after 35 years the Civil Wars divided them), and the translators Joshua Sylvester and Philemon Holland. Taylor had literary associates in common with Shakespeare: John Jackson was a wealthy gentleman-trader and patron for some of Taylor's pamphlets. Jackson, together with John Heminge, one of Shakespeare's 'principal actors', was one of the trustees for Shakespeare's purchase of the Blackfriars Gatehouse on 10 March 1613.[13]

Heminge probably played Falstaff, and in some ways John Taylor would have made a useful study for the role. One of his first pamphlets has the encouraging title *Laugh, and be Fat* (1612) (it was burnt by the public hangman because it was too satirical) and in *Drink and Welcome* (1637) he praised Falstaff's favourite draught: 'our age approves that *Sack* is the best lining or living for a good Poet, and that it enables our modern writers to versify most ingeniously' – though Taylor himself could not tolerate it because it 'hath the power to make me mad'. Taylor used publication to create and promote himself as a celebrity, and he is a very recognizable personality through his writings – Falstaff is by far the most-cited character from Shakespeare throughout the seventeenth century, and Taylor could have been acting to type. He traded on impressing his readers with the personality he created, and there is good reason to think that this projection was close to the life he lived. His pamphlet persona loved ale houses, eating and drinking, and celebrated the ancient virtues of hospitality as if it were vanishing in a new, rapacious age. Like many pamphlet and ballad writers addressing a popular audience, he lamented the decline in 'traditional' celebrations at Christmas. He wrote three pamphlets attacking the new selfishness of farmers and gentry who no longer kept open-house at the season, and he deplored the institutional provision through parish relief which was replacing individual acts of charity. Taylor's nostalgia was a response to widespread changes in customary culture which Peter Burke has identified as 'the reform of popular culture', a Europe-wide shift in values which gained momentum from the early sixteenth century onwards.[14]

Taylor probably articulated the politics and religious beliefs of many middle-ground London artisans, and expresses a familiar kind of English conservatism: mistrusting foreigners, papists, Puritans, nostalgic for an earlier age, resentful of the high and mighty bearing of courtiers and grandees, but paradoxically acknowledging respect for 'true nobility' and the monarch; his writings are also routinely misogynistic. But Taylor's pamphlets can also take contrary, critical positions on most of these issues, and in that sense they articulate complexity as well as sectional prejudice. For example, although he tirelessly reproduces commonplaces of anti-feminist discourse in much of his writing, his own frustrated education probably gave him particular insight into women's resentment of their exclusion from learning. In 1637 two anti-feminist works appeared which provoked a flurry of imitations: Thomas Heywood's *Curtain Lecture* and Joseph Swetnam's *Arraignment of Lewd, Idle, Forward and Unconstant Women* (first published in 1615). Taylor took advantage of this vogue in 1639 by contributing two anti-feminist 'jest books': *A Juniper Lecture. With a description of all sorts of women, good and bad*, and *Divers Crab-tree Lectures*. He published these anonymously, and then, even more opportunistically, in the following year he pretended to reply to his own arguments in *The Women's Sharp Revenge*, 'Performed by Mary Tattle-well and Joan Hit-him-home, spinsters....From our Manor of Make-peace.' Despite the fact that his covert imitation may undercut the point of a genuinely female view, Taylor contrived a cogent and sustained series of arguments against women's subordination, including, according to Simon Shepherd, 'perhaps the best statement of the inequality of education' in the period:

> it hath been the policy of all parents, even from the beginning, to curb us of that benefit [of education], by striving to keep us under and to make us men's mere vassals even unto all posterity. How else comes it to pass that, when a father hath a numerous issue of sons and daughters, the sons forsooth they must be first put to the grammar school, and after perchance sent to the university, and trained up in the liberal arts and sciences, and there (if they prove not block-heads) they may in time be book-learned. And what do they then? Read the poets perhaps, out of which, if they can pick out anything maliciously devised or malignantly divulged by some mad muse, discontented with his coy or disdainful mistress, then in imitation of them he must devise some passionate elegy and pitiful 'ay-me'. And, in the stead of picking out the best poets who have strived to right us, follow the other who do nothing but rail at us.[15]

Today many avenues would be open to John Taylor: tabloid columnist, game and chat show host, prime-time ale taster and connoisseur, 'impro' comedian, pulp fictioneer, but also and more promisingly, documentary reporter and stinging satirist. Bernard Capp noted, '"Honest John" was an epithet applied to Taylor as well as to John Lilburne, the Leveller, and for not dissimilar reasons: each was his own man.'

In 1613 Taylor was taken into the elite among his trade when he was appointed one of the King's Watermen, a select group who manned the royal barge on ceremonial outings, and in early 1614 he was chosen to make representations to the Court on behalf of the Company in a dispute that brought him into direct conflict with the theatres and actors. By this time Bankside was in decline as a place of resort because the theatres had begun to move north of the river, and the watermen were suffering in consequence. Taylor described his petitioning in *The True Cause of the Watermens' Suit concerning the Players* (1614?):

> the Players began to play on the Bank-side and to leave playing in London and Middlesex…then there went such great concourse of people by water, that the final number of watermen remaining at home were not able to carry them, by reason of the Court, the Terms [law courts], the Players and other employments [including a high proportion of bawds and their clients], so that we were enforced and encouraged, hoping that this golden stirring world would have lasted for ever, to take and entertain men and boys.[16]

Taylor's lobbying at Court did nothing to alleviate his Company's difficulties, but it provided new opportunities for him to secure patronage as a writer. He aimed high, dedicating verses to the King and Queen, Prince Charles, Sir Thomas Ridgeway the Lord High Treasurer in Ireland, Oliver St John Lord Deputy in Ireland, as well as to 'the Mirror of Time, the Most Refulgent, Splendidious, Reflecting Court Animal, Don Archibald Armstrong' – this was Archie, King James's official Fool.

Taylor was trying exceedingly hard, and with some notable successes. In 1614 he brought out *Verbum Sempiternum* and *Salvator Mundi*, verse paraphrases of the Old and New Testaments, each in a few hundred lines, works which were reprinted until the early twentieth century. These were tiny 'thumb bibles', measuring only 32 mm by 28 mm, dedicated to the Queen and Prince Charles: 'though the Volume and the Work be small, / Yet it contains the sum of all in ALL.' This was a useful popularizing item but it also impressed even a serious theologian and writer like Joseph Hall, Bishop of Exeter and Norwich, who copied the summaries into his commonplace book. Taylor was attempting to climb the steep gradient of Jacobean social hierarchy, and knew what was at stake. He needed 'good clothes, (for those bear a monstrous sway) because I have occasion to speak with great men, and without good clothes (like a golden sheath to a leaden blade) there is no admittance'. Taylor also used his connections with more established literary figures to secure praise-poems which he then placed as prefaces to his own works, by this time a well-established form of promotional puffery. The high point of the fashion seems to have been the 1650s, when the *Works* of William Cartwright contained no less than 107 pages of commendatory poems, more than a sixth of the entire book.[17]

Despite issuing these and other works and desperately casting about for powerful patrons, Taylor was near to abandoning literature in 1614 because the rewards were so pitiful, but in 1616 he discovered a genre which he would successfully exploit until the end of his career nearly forty years later – the travel narrative as self-promotion. There had been a vogue for these in the 1590s – one intrepid lunatic walked facing-backwards from London to Berwick – but Will Kempe had performed the best-known of these exploits in his *Nine Day's Wonder* (1600), an account of how he danced continuously from London to Norwich, undertaken after he left the Chamberlain's Company at the Globe Theatre. Taylor financed his own journeys by placing bets on the outcome of his increasingly outlandish exploits, hoping to profit both from this sponsorship and the sale of the resulting pamphlets. He first travelled to Germany in 1616, and then followed in the steps of Ben Jonson to Scotland, promoting his trip as a *Penniless Pilgrimage* relying entirely on unsolicited hospitality (Jonson suspected that Taylor was satirizing him). For this journey he recruited over 1,600 backers – Edward Alleyn gave one pound – and attracted wide attention, publishing his account just two weeks after his return, with a dedication to Buckingham. He then found that many of his subscribers would not actually come up with their pledges, and was forced to spend months pursuing them. In the following year Taylor capitalized on his fame by undertaking his most bizarre journey, rowing from Bankside to Queenborough on the Kent coast in a boat made only from brown paper, using no wood or metal in the construction. Thousands watched from the shore or rowed along with the vessel, which rapidly became semi-submerged. By now Taylor had achieved cult status: all he needed were T-shirts and memorabilia, but alas, pamphlets remained his only available outlet. He recorded his paper-boat jape in *The Praise of Hemp Seed*, an unnerving pamphlet discussed below. Taylor undertook what was a more genuinely dangerous journey in August 1620, when he travelled to Prague to observe at first-hand the fateful conflict between the Elector Palatine and the Holy Roman Emperor (see chronology). He completed the trip in six weeks (taking the opportunity to steal a pair of the 1-year old Prince Rupert's baby shoes as souvenir) and immediately brought out *Taylor's Travels*. He was again following trends since newsbooks and corantos were developing at just this moment as a way of meeting public curiosity about international politics.

During the 1620s Taylor produced a mixture of satires, jest books, further travel narratives, and some striking journalism such as *The Fearful Summer*, an account of the London plague outbreak of 1625. The poem illustrates how far Taylor's pamphlets were focused on London readers and antipathetic to country-dwellers:

> The name of *London* now both far and near
> Strikes all the Towns and Villages with fear,
> And to be thought a *Londoner* is worse
> Than one that breaks a house or takes a purse [...]
> Thus Citizens plagued for the City sins
> entertainment in the Country wins [...]
> Poor for why the hob-nailed Boors, inhuman Blocks,
> Uncharitable hounds, hearts hard as Rocks,
> Did suffer people in the field to sink
> Rather than give or sell a draft of drink.[18]

The scale of Taylor's desire to be acknowledged as an author is shown in the collection of sixty-three of his pamphlets which were presented in folio as *All the Works of John Taylor the Water-Poet*, published by James Boler in 1630, 'And that four Printers dwelling far asunder, / Did print this book, pray make the faults no wonder.' With this collection he joined a small and extremely select band of poets whose writings had been published in this way – Sidney, Jonson, Daniel, Shakespeare. Taylor was no less ambitious in his choice of dedicatees – the Marquis of Hamilton, William Herbert, Earl of Pembroke, and Philip Herbert, Earl of Montgomery, the three most powerful office-holders in King Charles's household – the brothers Herbert had also been the dedicatees for Shakespeare's posthumous collected works in 1623. With such a substantial volume Taylor can only have intended to reach a relatively well-off readership, probably among the affluent urban tradesmen and, with luck, the gentry and courtiers (but it may be that some copies were still unsold thirty years later).[19] The collected *Works* appeared mid-way in his career, and he went on to produce at least another ninety titles, writing half of his total output in the final troubled thirteen years of his life. Significantly, after publication of his *Works*, Taylor abandoned the fruitless search for generous patrons and either used no dedications or mocked the convention with ironic addresses. He ceased to rely on the increasingly anachronistic networks of patronage and put himself at the mercy of the market-place.

During the early 1640s Taylor quickly found a new focus for his satire in attacking the excesses of religious sectaries, and as Clerk to the Company of Watermen he also played a key role in opposing attempts by the ordinary membership to democratize the selection of overseers. During the volatile months in late 1642 Taylor had reason to fear for his life since he had become clearly identified as a critic of Parliament through his pamphlets, and in early 1643 he made his way to Oxford. Now in his sixties, he worked closely throughout the war years with George Wharton and John Berkenhead, the editors of the royalist news-sheet *Mercurius Aulicus*, and became one of the most successful royalist propagandists with his pamphleteering. After the King's surrender in 1646 Taylor scraped a living by keeping an alehouse near Covent Garden with his second wife, though he continued to pamphleteer. Taylor's energetic opportunism commands admiration: in 1648 he travelled to the Isle of Wight and visited the King, by then imprisoned in Carisbrooke Castle, since 'I had a great importunate desire to see my gracious sovereign afflicted lord and master', but he was also falling back on his travelogue skills 'with an intent to get some silver in this Iron age'. After Charles's execution in 1649 there is evidence to suggest that Taylor persisted (anonymously) with contributions to royalist news-sheets such as *Mercurius Melancholicus*, and his life was again threatened. He also continued to make journeys by subscription, often raising several thousand pledges, until the year of his death. *John Taylor's Wandering to see the Wonders of the West* (1649) records vivid examples of the destructive events of the Civil Wars. An incident which demonstrates several facets of Taylor's populism is his account of visiting Glastonbury where he was told that the miraculous thorn bush planted by Joseph of Arimathea had been cut down by Parliament troopers 'in pure devotion'. However one of the townspeople had fortunately managed to propagate a cutting from the tree. Taylor took a twig away with him, which he then turned into spills for poking down his pipe tobacco – a touch hypocritical, considering the number of times he had denounced 'filthy tobacco' in his pamphlets.[20]

The Praise of Hemp Seed: Taylor's inversion of all values

In 1642 Taylor made a memorable contribution to the literature of 'social inversion' when he published *Mad Fashions, Odd Fashions, All out of Fashions, or, The Emblems of these Distracted Times*. The text of his pamphlet was not much more than a versified commentary to its striking woodcut, a clear example of the new print culture's reliance on graphic imagery. Taylor's anonymous artist served him well, because his block-cut picture is one of the best known popular images from the period. The pamphlet can only have gained in relevance for Taylor, since, opportunistic as ever, he reissued it during the chaos of 1647 as *The World Turned Upside Down*, locating his text even more firmly in its image.[21]

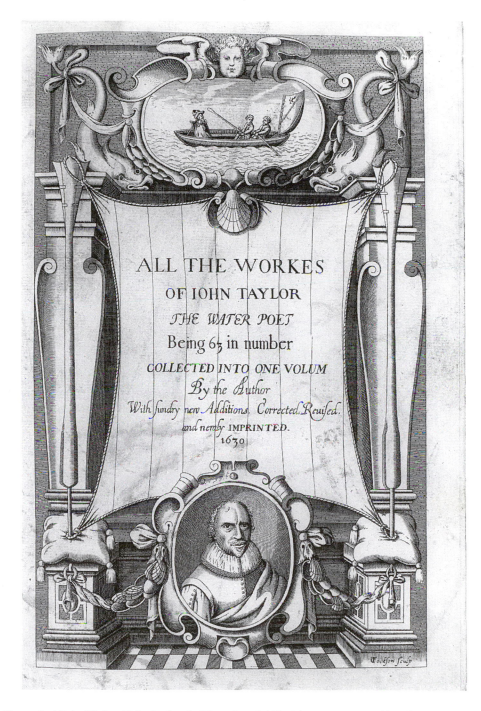

Figure 5 All the Works of John Taylor the Water Poet, 1630, title page, engraved by Thomas Cockson, who unfortunately didn't do the author any favours with his likeness. Printed for J.B. by James Boler. Folio, 30 by 20 cm.

See A. F. Johnson, *Catalogue of Engraved English Title Pages*, Oxford, Oxford University Press, 1934. By permission of the Syndics of Cambridge University Library

Figure 6 Title-page woodcut to *Mad Fashions, Odd Fashions* (1642) and *The World Turned Upside Down* (1647)

By permission of the Syndics of Cambridge University Library

Taylor was again appealing to the popular royalism of the moment because he took his title from a ballad of the previous year, 'The world is turned upside down', which was sung to the tune of Martin Parker's huge success, 'When the King Enjoys His Own Again'. Taylor's couplets gloss the image directly when he describes the kingdom as a 'Transformed Metamorphosis':

> The Church o'erturned (a lamentable show)
> The Candlestick above, the light below,
> The Cony hunts the Dog, the Rat the Cat,
> The Horse doth whip the Cart (I pray mark that)
> The wheelbarrow doth drive the man (oh Base)
> And Eels and Gudgeons fly a mighty Pace.
> And sure this is a Monster of strange fashion,
> That doth surpass all Ovid's Transformation.
> And this is England's case this very day,
> All things are turned the clean contrary way; [...]
> And prating fools brag of the Holy Ghost,

96

> When Ignoramus will his Teacher Teach,
> And Sow-Gelders and Cobblers dare to preach;
> This shows men's wits are monstrously disguised,
> Or that our country is Antipodised.
> For like as on the Poles, the World is Whorled
> So is this land the Bedlam of the World;
> That I amazed and amated am
> To see Great Britain turned to Amsterdam [...]
> For Amsterdam is landed (as I hear)
> At Rye, or Hastings, or at Dover pier [...][22]

'Antipodised' is quite a daring use, not recorded in the *OED*; Amsterdam lands at so many English ports in the form of smuggled tracts from dissenting printers in Holland. Taylor was of course taking over an ancient figure in 'the world inverted', and one which was very current in the 1640s, widely associated with social and psychical madness. But for Taylor this was not a new theme brought on by the Civil Wars because he had explored an intriguing series of radical inversions much more thoroughly in 1620 with his first 'paradoxical encomium', *The Praise of Hemp Seed*. This is a medley of topics threaded about a central conceit: which humble plant unites the ends of the world, levels kings with beggars and promotes lust as the equal of refined theology? This inverting, diverting theme strikes many chords in literature and debates throughout the seventeenth century: Hamlet's king making a progress in the guts of a beggar, or the dust of imperial Caesar patching a wall. Taylor's *Praise of Hemp Seed* makes a particular contribution to this pervasive anxiety about social instability during the period.[23]

In Shakespeare's *The Second Part of King Henry IV*, Mistress Quickly, Hostess of the Boar's Head Tavern, desperately tries to have Falstaff arrested. As the law moves in, Falstaff urges Bardolf to cut off the Sergeant's head and throw Ms Quickly in the gutter. She screams back at him, making one of her characteristic near-malapropisms, 'Ah, thou honeyseed rogue! thou art a honeyseed, a man-queller, and a woman-queller.' Honey has no seed and she means to say 'homicide'. In the fracas Falstaff's page also attacks her, and she beats him off, shouting 'Thou wot, wot thou? thou wot,...thou rogue! do, thou hempseed!' This is partly her word-association with the meaningless 'honey-seed', but the diminutive 'hempseed' drew on quite specific connotations. Here it means a child who will grow up to wear a hempen halter, and be hung. 'Hemp' beaten and spun into coarse cloth often connoted people of low-status, as in the 'hempen homespuns' of *A Midsummer Night's Dream*; otherwise it was a synonym for the noose, as Jack Cade promises Lord Say in *The Second Part of King Henry VI*, 'ye shall have a hempen caudle then'. The phrase is also used in the Marprelate Tracts, by Nashe and elsewhere; a 'hempstring' or a 'stretchhemp' was someone heading for the gallows. Therefore, in singing the praises of hempseed, John Taylor was playing a dangerous game.[24]

Taylor's conceit belongs to the ancient genre of paradoxical encomium, dating back to the origins of formal rhetoric in Athens in the fifth century BC, where unconventional, and so disconcerting, praise is given to a person or object usually thought to be worthless. Influential classical examples included praise of Thersites, Helen of Troy, baldness and flies.[25] In his Dedication Taylor denigrates more authoritative literary genres and offers in their place his celebration of a banal but utilitarian commodity:

I could have sold a greater volume than this with a deal of empty and trivial stuff: as puling Sonnets, whining Elegies, the dog-tricks of Love, toys to mock Apes [Satires], and transform men into Asses [Metamorphoses]....[Rather] I have here of a grain of Hempseed made a mountain greater than the Apennines or Caucasus, and not much lesser than the whole world. Here is Labour, Profit, Clothing, Pleasure, Food, Navigation: Divinity, Poetry, the liberal Arts, Arms, Virtue's defence, Vice's offence, a true man's protection, a Thief's execution. Here is mirth and matter all beaten out of this small Seed.[26]

Taylor from his mechanic perspective celebrates the various uses of hemp – '*Ovid* 'mongst all his *Metamorphosis* / Ne'er knew a transformation like to this' – and justifies the trope in his 'Preamble' by citing authors who have extemporized on trivial items, beginning with the greatest renaissance example, 'Erasmus, that great Clerk of Rotterdam, / In praise of Folly many lines did frame.' He also predictably cites 'Tom Nashe a witty pamphlet did endite / In praise of Herrings, both the red and White', which is *Nashe's Lenten Stuff* (1599), probably the supreme inverted encomium in English Renaissance literature. But rather than praising a red herring, Taylor sings the praises of hempseed because it provides rope, cloth and paper:

> Sweet sacred Muses, my invention raise
> Unto the life, to write great Hempseed's praise.
> This grain grows to a stalk, whose coat or skin
> Good industry doth hatchell [comb], twist and spin,
> And for man's best advantage and avails
> It makes clothes, cordage, halters, ropes and sails.
> From this small Atom, mighty matters springs,
> It is the Art of navigation's wings; [...]
> And therefore Merchants, Mariners, people all
> Of all trades, on your marrowbones down fall:
> For you could neither rise, or bite or sup,
> If noble Hempseed did not hold you up.
>
> (III.63)

Taylor had found a worthwhile 'conceit' in the nature and uses of hemp agrimony, but François Rabelais got there before him. In *Gargantua*, Book Three, Chapters 49–52 (1546), Rabelais described the qualities of 'l'herbe nommée Pantagruelion' in precisely the same ways as Taylor, but at even greater length and with Rabelaisian invention.[27] Even so, the Water Poet deploys his material creditably: hempseed in the form of rope has spread the gospel around the globe, and brings the world's commodities to London; hempseed is an omnipotent solvent which transforms even the elements into goods through commerce and the operations of industry – 'By Hempseed thus, fire, water, air, earth, all / Are chang'd' (III.66). *The Praise of Hemp Seed* articulates a perpetual sense of instability, from status and property, which can be lost to thieves overnight, to the forms of gender: 'A strange change, and yet not stranger than for the women of these times to be turned to the shapes of men.' Hemp is the true defender of law because 'the halter in [thieves'] minds do run' (III.66). Hemp's apotheosis arrives when, as rags and rope-ends, it is turned into paper, again working the most extreme transformation:

> May not the torn shirt of a Lord or King
> Be pashed and beaten in the Paper mill
> And made Pot-paper by the workman's skill?
> May not the linen of a Tyburn slave,
> More honour than a mighty Monarch have? [...]
> And may not dirty socks from off the feet
> From thence be turn'd to a Crown paper sheet?
>
> (III.70)

The collapsing of distinction and value culminates with the elision of theology and bawdy, chastity and immodesty:

> As by desert, by favour and by chance
> Honour may fall, and begg'ry may advance,
> Thus are these tatters allegorical
> Tropes, types, and figures of man's rise or fall.
>   Thus may the relics of sincere Divines
> Be made the ground-work of lascivious lines,
> And the cast smock that chaste *Lucretia* wore
> Bear bawdy lines betwixt a knave and whore.
>   Thus may a *Brownist's* zealous ruff in print
> Be turned to Paper, and a play writ in't,
> Or verses of a May-pole, or at last
> Injunctions for some stomach-hating Fast.
>
> (III.70)

But these fearful instabilities, which extend from the elements themselves through commodity, social degree, gender and morality, are only paradoxically halted on the frail surface of paper, pre-eminently in scripture, but also in the patriarchs, the history of monarchies, and in 'Philosophers, Historians, Chronographers, Poets ancient and modern, the best sort mentioned'.

> In paper many a Poet now survives
> Or else their lines had perish'd with their lives.
> Old Chaucer, Gower, and Sir Thomas More,
> Sir Philip Sidney, who the Laurel wore,
> Spenser, and Shakespeare did in Art excell,
> Sir Edward Dyer, Greene, Nash, Daniel,
> Silvester, Beaumont, Sir John Harington,
> Forgetfulness their works would over-run,
> But that in Paper they immortally
> Do live in spite of Death, and cannot die.
>   And many there are living at this day
> Which do in paper their true worth display:
> As Davis, Drayton, and the learned Donne,
> Jonson, and Chapman, Marston, Middleton,
> With Rowley, Fletcher, Wither, Massinger,

> Heywood, and all the rest where'er they are,
> Must say their lines, but for the paper sheet,
> Had scarcely ground whereon to set their feet.

(III.72)

Written in the summer of 1619, this list reveals the currency of literary reputation in late-Jacobean London, and also shows how quickly Shakespeare's standing had grown in the three years since his death. Taylor knew a number of Shakespeare's plays very well: in the opening paragraph to *Crop-Ear Curried, or Tom Nashe His Ghost* (1640) he quoted or alluded to *Richard III, Julius Caesar, Love's Labours Lost*, and twice to *Hamlet*,[28] and there may be an early echo of Shakespeare in *The Praise of Hemp Seed*. As part of his miscellany describing the shipment of commodities (including 'the black Indians or Newcastle coals' III.66), Taylor adds a digression, 'Striving in verse to show a lively form / Of an imperous gust, or deadly storm.' The ship 'worse than any Drunkard reels', the Master cries 'lower the top-sail, lower', 'Take in the fore-sail, yare, good fellows, yare', 'Clear your main brace'; the mariners take soundings at 'Fathom and a half, three all', then 'There's a plank sprung, something in hold did break'. But they manage to pump out the leak, and the weather fortunately clears. Taylor inserts one of his prose glosses here:

> I think I have spoken Heathen, Greek, Utopian, or Bermudian, to a great many of my readers in the description of this storm, but indeed I wrote it only for the understanding Mariners reading. I did it three years since, and could not find a fitter place than this to insert it, or else it must have lain in silence.

(III.67 [misnumbered '65'])

Taylor had in fact already published the piece in *Fair and Foul Weather: or A Sea and Land Storm* in 1615 as a 'poetical Weatherwork' dedicated to Robert Branthwaite, Gentleman Jailor at the Tower:

> For apprehension must be quick and yare,
> Imagination must be here, and there,
> For if a Tempest be but smoothly read,
> It shows the Reader's Judgement dull and dead
> Or else to seem to make the Welkin split,
> In thundring out a calm shows want of wit.[29]

It may be that watching the opening of Shakespeare's *Tempest* at Blackfriars or the Globe in 1612 gave him some ideas: Shakespeare's Boatswain is not called a 'hempseed', but his 'complexion is perfect gallows', and he is 'born to be hanged'; he also shouts in mariner-jargon close to Taylor's, 'Yare, yare! Take in the topsail' and 'Down with the topmast! Yare! Lower, lower! Bring her to try with main-course.' Gonzalo thinks the Boatswain is destined for hanging even if their ship 'were no stronger than a nutshell and as leaky as an unstanched wench',[30] and this unsavoury simile is also close to Taylor's description of the absurd paper boat in which he rowed from Bankside to Queenborough: 'Our Boat a female vessel gan to leak / Being as female vessels are, most weak' (III.73).

Shakespeare's seamanship in the opening scene of *The Tempest* is apparently more than impressionistic flurry, because 'the right orders are given', but 'He could not have come by this knowledge from books, for there were no works on seamanship in his day.'[31] There were, however, watermen just outside the Globe who knew all about the dangers of being blown on to a lee shore, and John Taylor would have been more than happy to swap sea stories for help with his scansion.

The hydro-poet, sculler-scholar between cultures

Taylor's career and writings usefully illustrate recent critical debates about the nature (and even the existence) of a 'popular literary culture' in early modern England. He energetically seized a new opportunity to live by writing even though he was relatively uneducated. Thomas Nashe (1567–1601) was his model, and Taylor tried to emulate Nashe's bravura satires and miscellanies, his rabid anti-Puritanism, and his habit of conducting vituperative exchanges with other writers. Nashe, however, had the luck and brain to be able to attend St John's College, Cambridge, even if he had to earn his place as a sizar, waiting on his superiors. Looked at in this way, Taylor was a 'wannabe' Elizabethan satirist who found himself living in new, even more deplorable times. The values of Jacobean and Carolean England were to him a steady decline into the sectarian craziness of civil war. Like many satirists, Taylor felt himself to be an anachronism and therefore able to invoke a world of lost and superior values. This conservatism would have struck a chord with many readers during the 1620s and 1630s when there was a widespread feeling that the values of the customary culture were waning and being displaced by a new, narrow moralism.

Taylor wanted to be read along with the celebrated poets of his time, but his education and abilities meant that his writings found a different readership: he did not – could not? – write plays, which was probably a surer way to quick money than turning out three-penny pamphlets. Again this may have been because his status and education counted against him. All the Elizabethan, Jacobean and Carolean playwrights were grammar-school educated and most of them had gone on to university. Taylor never quite escaped from the insecurity he felt over not having mastered Latin, but he was able to take a sceptical view of his own writing; in the personae of the female authors in *The Women's Sharp Revenge* he satirizes his own pretensions very objectively:

> Now concerning your very passionate but most pitiful poetry, a question may be made: whether you be a land laureate or a marine muse; a land poet or a water poet; a scholar or a sculler; of Parnassus or Puddle Dock; of Ionia or Ivy Bridge. But howsoever, it is not in the compass of our reading that Mnemosyne ever lived at Milford Lane, or Terpsichore at Trig Stairs, where they say the devil once took water.[32]

Taylor returns to the same places named by Jonson in his attack on the Water Poet's lumpish pretensions in *Bartholomew Fair*, Puddle Wharf and Trig Stairs transposed. The venerated names of classical Greek culture, mother of the muses, muse of the dance, are sharply counterposed to the banal realities of Taylor's actual environs, and the satire must have had some force because Taylor's authorship was not evident to his readers.

Bernard Capp estimates that in the course of his career Taylor produced around 150 separate titles, printed in over half a million copies, and that his 1618 *Penniless Pilgrimage* alone could have collected pennies to the extent of £480.[33] His income during the 1630s was sufficient to bring him into the Ship Money tax-bracket, so he was by then a citizen of means. As a moderately successful burgess, Taylor was also inescapably a London writer: his most effective satires castigate city vices and he addressed many of his pamphlets to the tradesmen of London. His literary style could be quite demanding, and this also indicates that he was not writing for the least able readers, but addressing people with some reading sophistication and store of reference. He described his 'discourse' in *The World Runs on Wheels*:

> I have embroidered it with mirth, Quilted it with material stuff, Laced it with similitudes, Sowed it with comparisons, and in a word, so played the Tailor with it, that I think it will fit the wearing of any honest man's Reading, attention, and liking.[34]

Taylor had hoped to gain patronage from some of the most powerful courtiers in the land, but he was in fact more intimate with their servants and followers, and this placed him in a difficult position. As an aspiring writer at the fringes of the Court, but with no genuine status, he could easily have become just a figure of fun, along with the court entertainers such as Archy Armstrong, the King's official Fool, or a braggart such as Captain O'Toole, a 'professional Irishman' and one-time soldier. Despite his outlandish promotional stunts and self-advertisement, Taylor made efforts to distinguish himself from the mere entertainers and hangers-on who surrounded King James. He clearly had pretensions for some of his writing and hoped that it would not be dismissed as catch-penny pamphleteering: his extraordinary 1630 folio *Works* demonstrates a real ambition and seriousness about his writing.

Taylor paraded the range of his extensive reading, and also distanced himself from the genuinely popular authors whom he knew, such as Martin Parker, a highly successful ballad writer (and in truth a much more skilful poet), even though his own publisher, Henry Gosson, was a major producer of ballads. He may have been following Ben Jonson's view that 'a poet should detest a balladmaker' as another expression of his desire for purer 'literary' recognition.[35] Here Taylor actually misjudged the readership since, although ballads were the cheapest form of printed stuff at a penny per broadside, they were also appreciated by a wide social range of readers, including the gentry. By the later seventeenth century ballad sheets were being sought out by scholarly collectors such as John Selden and Samuel Pepys: the period's own 'ephemera' were already the object of fascinated study by scholar-antiquarians and amateur archivists.

Taylor's position in the literary markets of his time is therefore intriguing: he wanted to perpetuate the high-satirical mode of Nashe from the 1590s, and he assiduously cultivated monarchs, courtiers, successful authors and dramatists. He was a London author whose pamphlets were distributed through the chapbook network across the country, yet his style was often too demanding for the new low-status readers beginning to buy the cheapest chapbooks, and his extraordinary folio *Works* of 1630 certainly took him beyond the means of the poorest readership. He even contributed to one of the oldest popular genres of all, dating back to the beginning of printing – the life of a saint – when he adapted a Catholic tract as *The Life and Death*

Figure 7 Title page to *The Needle's Excellency*, twelfth edition, 1640 (Oblong quarto, 16 by 20 cm.)

By permission of the Syndics, Cambridge University Library; described in Arthur Mayger Hind, *Engraving in England in the Sixteenth and Seventeenth Centuries*, Cambridge, Cambridge University Press, 1955, pp. 389–90

Taylor's poem 'The Praise of the Needle' prefaces twenty-eight engraved plates of needlework patterns. First published by Taylor in 1631 the title page and patterns are closely copied from Hans Sibmacher, *Neues Modelbuch*, Nürnberg, 1601. Mistresses Wisdom and Industry are busily employed while Folly gossips 'idly'. The manual was clearly a success for Taylor among wives and daughters of the middling sort during the 1630s. In his prefatory poems Taylor opines, 'And for my country's quiet, I should like, / That women-kind should use no other Pike' (fol. Ar). This is followed by praise-poems to illustrous needle-women, including 'The Right Honourable, Vertuous and learned Lady Mary, late Countess of Pembroke' remembered thus: 'a pattern and a patroness she was, / Of vertuous industry and studious learning… / Brave Wilton house in Wiltshire well can show, / Her admirable works in Arras framed' (A3r). So much for Mary Sidney's editing of Philip Sidney's works and her own metrical translations from the Psalms. See Margaret Swain, *Historical Needlework*, London, Barrie and Jenkins, 1970, for the nature and scope of embroidery in the period.

of the Virgin Mary (1620).[36] We might forgive John Taylor his thousands of doggerel lines and his occasionally deplorable attitudes. No other writer bridges such a diverse range of the period's literary cultures, from the Ovidian erotics of *Hero and Leander* to the propaganda wars of the 1640s and Interregnum, and this new writing for common readers deserves better than condescension.

7

'DRESSED UP WITH THE FLOWERS OF A LIBRARY'

Women reading and writing

So far as we know, during the late sixteenth and throughout the seventeenth century, for the first time in Britain significant numbers of women from diverse social ranks were able to read. A small proportion of them also began to write and publish, more than 300 authors producing over 800 first editions.[1] This chapter begins by examining one stark reading-moment experienced in the early 1640s by Dorothy Hazzard during a crisis that was simultaneously religious and domestic. This single instance of reading is then related to a range of issues involved in accurately understanding the scope and nature of early modern female literacy. The final section offers a detailed discussion of Lady Anne Clifford's life in reading and writing, represented by a unique painting which she commissioned in the midst of the Civil Wars. Literacy for both these women was infinitely more important than the characteristic denigration of their time that women's reading was simply the culling of flowers from a library.

Mistress Hazzard's revelation

On a day in 1640 Dorothy Hazzard of Bristol found herself in a great working of conscience and the spirit. She had moved into the parsonage of St Ewins Church the year before with her second husband, the Reverend Matthew Hazzard, and they had begun to establish a godly household, giving shelter to families waiting to make the voyage from Bristol to the Puritan colonies of New England. Mistress Hazzard also provided a birthing chamber for mothers-to-be who wanted to avoid the ceremonies of churching ('purification' after giving birth) and infant baptism in their own parishes; these were two services which gave particular offence to dissenting Christians. Her husband also did what he could to reform worship in his new congregation, but by law he was required to read from the Book of Common Prayer in his services, and this was the cause of his wife's distress. Dorothy Hazzard was a godly woman whose strong conscience had already set her at odds with Archbishop Laud's 'high' church ceremonies. Her reforming spirit would not allow her to sit and listen to the reading of the Prayer Book, even by her own husband, because it seemed to her to be no more than empty ritual. During the later 1630s, when Laud's influence was strongest in the church and country, she had also refused to observe saints' days and holidays as required by the ceremonialist Laudian church. She was then the widow of Anthony Kelly, a moderately successful grocer who had died in 1631, after which she had taken over the business. She so much objected to the observance of 'holy days' that she kept her shop open in Bristol High Street, between the Guilders Inn and High Cross, during 'the day called Christmas', and she sat sewing as a witness for God in the midst of the City, in the face of the sun, and in the sight of all men; even in those very days of darkness, when, as it were, all sorts of people had a reverence of that particular day above all others.

The real sun shone amid metaphorical darkness in the 1630s and 1640s.[2]

Clearly, Dorothy Hazzard was a woman of very strong religious convictions, but even she was torn between her distaste at having to listen to empty recitation of the Book of Common Prayer, as required by law, and the ties of affection and conventional obligation which obliged her to follow her husband, who was, moreover, her parish priest. Some Protestant clerics took their role as the father of their congregation so seriously as to claim that they were a (spiritual) husband to all of their female worshippers, and this again emphasizes the depth of Dorothy Hazzard's disaffection.[3] Her scruple in rejecting the Prayer Book was particularly difficult for her as a woman and wife of the rector, but it was a position being taken in many churches throughout England during 1640 and 1641, as dissenting Christians took strength from Laud's arrest and the collapse of effective press censorship. Katherine Chidley, wife to a tailor and mother of seven children, argued for the absolute duty to separate from the Church of England at this moment in her pamphlet *The Justification of the Independent Churches of Christ*.[4] Even so Dorothy Hazzard found herself nearly immobilized by anxiety, and unable to leave the rectory for St Ewins to hear the service and suffer the distasteful reading.

There remained one authority to consult: she turned back up the staircase and went to her chamber where in desperation she leafed through her old copy of the Bible for guidance (according to contemporary inventories, books are increasingly found in bedrooms during the 1640s, where they migrated from the shared public rooms below). In her state of terrible anxiety, divine providence worked on her behalf, and she found and read exactly the verses that would speak to her, Revelation 14.9–11:

> 'If any man worship the Beast and his image, and receive his mark...he shall be tormented with fire and brimstone...and they have no rest day nor night, who worship the beast and his image, and whosoever receiveth the mark of his name', or print, as she said it was in her old book.
>
> (17)

The text was eloquent because it confirmed her hatred of meaningless ceremonial forms. She had already left one church in the middle of a sermon when the priest had argued that 'pictures and images might be used' in worship: 'when she heard that, away she went forth before them all, and said she would hear him no more, nor never did to this day' (14). Revelation was for many moderate Christians one of the more doubtful books of the Bible, precisely because its highly charged visionary language could be interpreted for individual purposes, and this may be why Dorothy Hazzard turned to the final book of the New Testament. In fact, the text didn't so much comfort her as horrify her, 'striking such terror into her Soul, that she dreaded to go' (17). As a dissenting Protestant, Dorothy Hazzard almost certainly preferred the 1560 Geneva Bible to the 1611 translation commissioned by King James, and this is confirmed by the wording of her text: the 1611 version translates 'karagma' as the *mark* of his name', while the Geneva edition reads 'the *print* of his name' (as do Tyndale's 1534 and Cranmer's 1539 versions).[5]

This was a moment of revelation of a kind recorded by many spiritual autobiographers in the seventeenth century, though the circumstantial details here are unusually precise. Dorothy Hazzard's crisis was also a true Damascus Road conversion, because it gave her the strength and resolve to form an independent congregation, at first with only four other (male) souls, completely 'Separate from the Worship of the World and times they lived in' (18). To remove yourself from the parochial organization of the state church and establish a covenanted meeting in a domestic house was a genuinely radical and potentially dangerous act in 1640: how much more so, when an (older) wife was also taking herself out of her own husband's flock.[6] The five dissenters at first compromised by attending Matthew Hazzard's sermons and omitting the set service, but with the encouragement of John Canne, who had been pastor of the English Independents in Amsterdam since 1630, they finally decided to separate completely from St Ewins. Gossip and innuendo inevitably followed, and people were quick to suggest that since Dorothy Hazzard had abandoned her husband's church she would also soon abandon his bed. The commonplace view in early modern society saw women as sexually voracious by nature and therefore more prone to 'incontinent' behaviour. A double standard regarding sexual morality generally favoured men by overlooking or condoning their infidelities and seductions, whereas women discovered in illicit relationships were more usually arraigned and punished.[7] In the event, Matthew Hazzard continued as priest of St Ewins to 1662 and the couple 'walked blamelessly before the Lord' together (23) until their deaths.

We know of this reading incident and its impact through Edward Terrill, who wrote down Dorothy Hazzard's own account some thirty years later in the 1670s. It was the founding moment of the Broadmead Baptist Church, for the five separatists had soon been joined by an active congregation of some 160 members. Terrill was a scrivener and merchant, who was profiting from the newly established sugar trade with Barbados. Bristol was then the third largest city in the country, after London and Norwich, with 12,000 inhabitants, and Terrill's business partners were keen to establish the Bristol trade securely against London competition. They were also characteristic 'new merchants', exploiting market opportunities which they combined with a powerful commitment to reformed belief, giving material support to the Baptist congregation in the city.[8] Terrill himself only joined the congregation in 1658 so he was not in a position to question Dorothy Hazzard's providential account of the church's foundation. A small group had in fact been meeting since the late 1620s for private prayer and fast days, a very characteristic dissenting activity during the early decades of the seventeenth century. Encouraged by Mr Yeamans, the minister of St Philip's Church, Dorothy and her first husband, Anthony Kelly, had met with Robert Haynes, a writing-schoolmaster, Richard Moone, a farrier, and Goodman Cole, a victualler or butcher, in the houses of fellow tradesmen such as glovers and house-carpenters. They refused to worship through the 'blind devotion' of the kind which they felt was encouraged by the Laudian church, rather 'they did Cry day and night to the Lord to pluck down the Lordly Prelates of the time, and the Superstitions thereof' (8). Their worship could take the form of a study group, where they read over their jottings made from sermons given by visiting preachers, 'Repeating their notes to one another, whetting it on their hearts, and praying it over'. This was an active, studious devotion which would never be satisfied by passively listening to the repeated readings from sanctioned literature such as the Homilies or Book of Common Prayer. As the congregation grew, they attracted more suspicion and ridicule, again of a sexual nature,

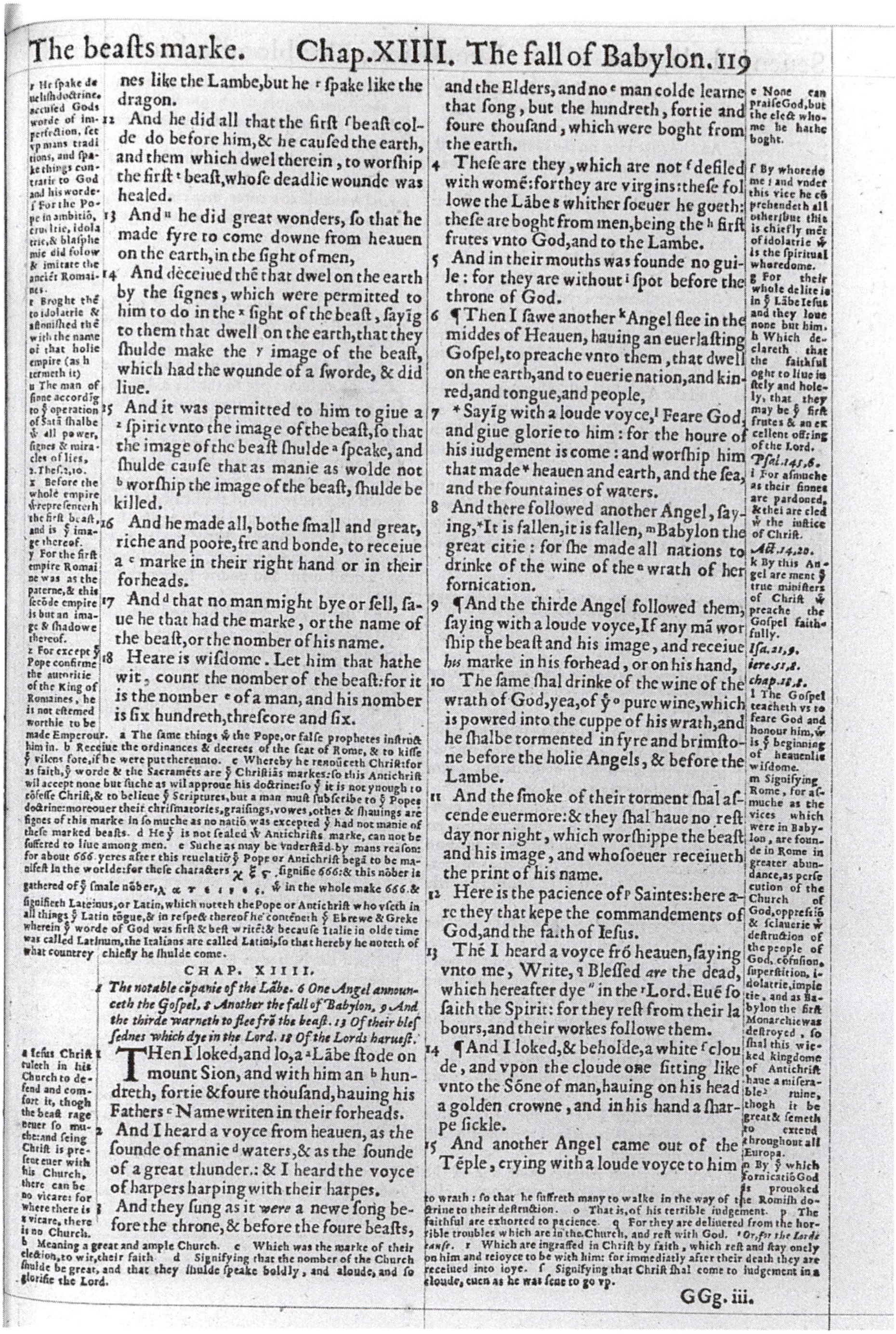

The beasts marke.　Chap.XIIII.　The fall of Babylon. 119

r He spake deuelish doctrine, accused Gods worde of imperfection, set vp mans traditions, and spake things contrarie to God and his worde. *f* For the Pope in ambitiõ, crueltie, idolatrie, & blasphemie did folow & imitate the anciẽt Romaines. *t* Broght thẽ to idolatrie & astonished thẽ with the name of that holie empire (as *h* termeth it) *u* The man of sinne accordĩg to ỹ operation of Satã shalbe wt all power, signes & miracles of lies. 2.Thess.2,10. *x* Before the whole empire wt representeth the first beast, and is ỹ image thereof. *y* For the first empire Romaine was as the paterne, & this secõde empire is but an image & shadowe thereof. *z* For except ỹ Pope confirme the auoritie of the King of Romaines, he is not estemed worthie to be made Emperour.

nes like the Lambe, but he *r* spake like the dragon.

12 And he did all that the first *f* beast colde do before him, & he caused the earth, and them which dwel therein, to worship the first *t* beast, whose deadlie wounde was healed.

13 And *u* he did great wonders, so that he made fyre to come downe from heauen on the earth, in the sight of men,

14 And deceiued thẽ that dwel on the earth by the signes, which were permitted to him to do in the *x* sight of the beast, sayĩg to them that dwell on the earth, that they shulde make the *y* image of the beast, which had the wounde of a sworde, & did liue.

15 And it was permitted to him to giue a *z* spirit vnto the image of the beast, so that the image of the beast shulde *a* speake, and shulde cause that as manie as wolde not *b* worship the image of the beast, shulde be killed.

16 And he made all, bothe small and great, riche and poore, fre and bonde, to receiue a *c* marke in their right hand or in their forheads.

17 And *d* that no man might bye or sell, saue he that had the marke, or the name of the beast, or the nomber of his name.

18 Heare is wisdome. Let him that hathe wit, count the nomber of the beast: for it is the nomber *e* of a man, and his number is six hundreth, thre score and six.

a The same things ỹ the Pope, or false prophetes instruct him in. *b* Receiue the ordinances & decrees of the seat of Rome, & to kisse ỹ vilens fote, if he were put thereunto. *c* Whereby he renoũceth Christ: for as faith, ỹ worde & the Sacramẽts ỹ Christiãs markes: so this Antichrist wil accept none but suche as wil approue his doctrine: so ỹ it is not ynough to cõfesse Christ, & to beleue ỹ Scriptures, but a man must subscribe to ỹ Popes doctrine: moreouer their chrismatories, graisings, vowes, othes & shauings are signes of this marke in so muche as no natiõ was excepted ỹ had not manie of these marked beasts. *d* He ỹ is not sealed wt Antichrists marke, can not be suffered to liue among men. *e* Suche as may be vnderstãd by mans reason: for about 666 yeres after this reuelatiõ ỹ Pope or Antichrist begã to be manifest in the worlde: for these characters χ ξ ς signifie 666: & this nõber is gathered of ỹ smale nũber, α ρ τ ε ι ν ε, wt in the whole make 666.& signifieth Lateinus, or Latin, which noteth the Pope or Antichrist who vseth in all things ỹ Latin togue, & in respect thereof he cõtenẽth ỹ Ebrewe & Greke wherein ỹ worde of God was first & best writẽ: & because Italie in olde time was called Latinum, the Italians are called Latini, so that hereby he noteth of what countrey chiefly he shulde come.

CHAP. XIIII.

1 The notable cõpanie of the Lãbe. *6* One Angel announceth the Gospel. *8* Another the fall of Babylon. *9* And the thirde warneth to flee frõ the beast. *13* Of their blefsednes which dye in the Lord. *18* Of the Lords haruest.

a Iesus Christ ruleth in his Church to defend and comfort it, thogh the beast rage neuer so muche: and seing Christ is present euer with his Church, there can be no vicares for where there is ỹ vicare, there is no Church. *b* Meaning a great and ample Church. *c* Which was the marke of their election, to wit, their faith *d* Signifying that the number of the Church shulde be great, and that they shulde speake boldly, and aloude, and so glorifie the Lord.

THen I loked, and lo, a *a* Lãbe stode on mount Sion, and with him an *b* hundreth, fortie & foure thousand, hauing his Fathers *c* Name writen in their forheads.

2 And I heard a voyce from heauen, as the sounde of manie *d* waters, & as the sounde of a great thunder.: & I heard the voyce of harpers harping with their harpes.

3 And they sung as it were a newe song before the throne, & before the foure beasts, and the Elders, and no *e* man colde learne that song, but the hundreth, fortie and foure thousand, which were boght from the earth.

4 These are they, which are not *f* defiled with womẽ: for they are virgins: these followe the Lãbe *g* whither soeuer he goeth: these are boght from men, being the *h* first frutes vnto God, and to the Lambe.

5 And in their mouths was founde no guile: for they are without *i* spot before the throne of God.

6 ¶ Then I sawe another *k* Angel flee in the middes of Heauen, hauing an euerlasting Gospel, to preache vnto them, that dwell on the earth, and to euerie nation, and kinred, and tongue, and people,

7 * Sayĩg with a loude voyce, *l* Feare God, and giue glorie to him: for the houre of his iudgement is come: and worship him that made *m* heauen and earth, and the sea, and the fountaines of waters.

8 And there followed another Angel, saying, *It is fallen, it is fallen, *m* Babylon the great citie: for she made all *n* nations to drinke of the wine of the *o* wrath of her fornication.

9 ¶ And the thirde Angel followed them, saying with a loude voyce, If any mã worship the beast and his image, and receiue *his* marke in his forhead, or on his hand,

10 The same shal drinke of the wine of the wrath of God, yea, of ỹ *o* pure wine, which is powred into the cuppe of his wrath, and he shalbe tormented in fyre and brimstone before the holie Angels, & before the Lambe.

11 And the smoke of their torment shal ascende euermore: & they shal haue no rest day nor night, which worshippe the beast and his image, and whosoeuer receiueth the print of his name.

12 Here is the patience of *p* Saintes: here are they that kepe the commandements of God, and the faith of Iesus.

13 Thẽ I heard a voyce frõ heauen, saying vnto me, Write, *q* Blessed *are* the dead, which hereafter dye *r* in the *r* Lord. Euẽ so saith the Spirit: for they rest from their labours, and their workes followe them.

14 ¶ And I loked, & beholde, a white *f* cloude, and vpon the cloude one fitting like vnto the Sóne of man, hauing on his head a golden crowne, and in his hand a sharpe sickle.

15 And another Angel came out of the Tẽple, crying with a loude voyce to him

e None can praise God, but the elect whome he hathe boght.
f By whoredome ı and vnder this vice he cõprehendeth all other, but this is chiefly mẽt of idolatrie w is the spiritual whoredome. *g* For their whole desire is in ỹ Lãbe Iesus and they loue none but him. *h* Which declareth that the faithful ought to liue holely and holely, that they may be ỹ first frutes & an exellent offrĩg of the Lord. Psal.145,6. *i* For asmuche as their sinnes are pardoned, & thei are cled wt the iustice of Christ. Act.14,20. *k* By this Angel are mene ỹ true ministers of Christ w preache the Gospel faithfully. Isa.21,9. iere.51,8. chap.18,2. *1* The Gospel teacheth vs to feare God and honour him, w is ỹ beginning of heauenliu wisdome. *m* Signifying Rome, for asmuche as the vices which were in Babylon, are founde in Rome in greater abundance, as persecution of the Church of God, oppressiõ & sclauerie w destruction of the people of God, cõfusion, superstition, idolatrie, impietie, and as Babylon the first Monarchie was destroyed, so shal this wicked kingdome of Antichrist haue a miserable ruine, thogh it be great & semeth to extend throughout all Europa. *n* By ỹ which fornicatiõ God is prouoked

to wrath: so that he suffreth many to walke in the way of the Romish doctrine to their destruction. *o* That is, of his terrible iudgement. *p* The faithful are exhorted to pacience. *q* For they are deliuered from the horrible troubles which are in the Church, and rest with God. *r* Or, for the Lorde cause. *r* Which are ingrafted in Christ by faith, which rest and stay only on him and reioyce to be with him: for immediatly after their death they are receiued into ioye. *f* Signifying that Christ shal come to iudgement in a cloude, euen as he was sent to go vp.

GGg. iii.

Figure 8 'Geneva' Bible, 1560, 'Revelation', Chapter 14, verses 1–15. Printed in Geneva by Rowland Hall

Quarto, 30 cm. By permission of the Syndics of Cambridge University Library

This translation was made and glossed by English Protestant exiles living in Calvinist Geneva. It was a scholarly edition which did not avoid textual difficulties but drew attention to them through 'most profitable annotations upon all the hard places'. It is not surprising that Margaret Hazzard consulted this version in her crisis: it was a Bible intended for ownership by private households rather than for ritual use in churches, and it became the most popular Protestant version until well into the seventeenth century, a text for serious personal study. Its glosses were also incorporated in other translations, including at least eight editions of the 1611 King James Bible. The Geneva Bible was the version which Shakespeare read, it was the Bible taken aboard the Mayflower in 1620, remaining the standard New England text, and a digest of extracts was issued as the Parliamentarian *Soldiers' Pocket Bible* (1643); even William Laud was still quoting from this translation as late as 1629. The Geneva scholars were the first to provide numbered verses in an English translation, following Pierre Robert Olivetan's French edition of 1553. Each verse is set as a separate, capitalized paragraph and the marginal commentary crowds the text; each book and chapter is also preceded by an explanatory 'argument'. Words added to the text for clarity of meaning are set in italic, reminding the reader that this is a mediated version of the divine word. The choice of Roman type rather than black-letter helped legibility and was an aid to lengthy study. This quarto edition of 1560 includes twenty-six engravings, five maps, and a plan of the Garden of Eden, not for decoration, but to explain passages 'so dark that by no description they could be made easy to the simple reader'. The 1539 Great Bible (lacking any contentious notes) remained the official text for use in English churches, replaced by the Bishops' Bible in 1568; this was promoted by Archbishop Matthew Parker, who objected to the 'bitter' notes of the Geneva text. Scotland under John Knox's leadership adopted the Geneva Bible from the early 1560s. However, on Parker's death in 1575 his successor Edmund Grindal supported the Geneva version, and it was printed in more than 120 editions between 1560 and 1611, and a further 60 after that date. If Dorothy Hazzard's Geneva edition was printed after 1599, the book of Revelation would have been glossed by Franciscus Junius's severely anti-Catholic commentary, replacing that of 1560. Forty-two books of the Bible have left resonances in Shakespeare's writing:

> The fact that the Bishops' Bible is the version most heard in the earlier plays and the Geneva Bible is more frequently echoed in the later suggests that it was only in his maturity that Shakespeare owned a Bible and read it at first hand. This is precisely what the general historical picture would lead us to expect.

Patrick Collinson, 'William Shakespeare's religious inheritance and environment', *Elizabethan Essays*, London and Rio Grande, The Hambledon Press, 1994, p. 252; the 1560 edition described in David Norton, *A History of the Bible as Literature*, Cambridge, Cambridge University Press, 1993, pp. 168–71, and Lloyd E. Berry, *The Geneva Bible* (1560), Introduction to the facsimile edition by Lloyd E. Berry, Madison, Milwaukee and London, University of Wisconsin Press, 1969, pp. 1–24.

because the world and wicked men vilified them, saying they met together in the night to be unclean, but the Lord knew their innocency; and would further deride them, as that they had women preachers among them, because there were many good women, that frequented their assembling, that, when they should upon occasion be speaking with the world and about things thereof, in their buying or selling, they would speak very Heavenly.

(11)

Soon enough a 'rude Multitude' attacked the 'Conventicle of Puritans' because it was 'to them…a very strange and unheard of thing for People to meet in a Church with a Chimney in it, as they termed it' (12).

Detractors picked on the 'good many women' in the Broadmead congregation, and it may be that it was predominantly female during its first decades, because the earliest surviving membership list from 1671 indicates that nearly three-quarters of attenders were women; this would be true to the general pattern of membership for congregations in the radical sects during the 1650s. Women had joined the Elizabethan dissenting congregations in large numbers, and this reinforced a well-established prejudice that the gender was particularly susceptible to heresy and 'enthusiasm', in the sense of religious mania.[9]

For sympathizers like Edward Terrill, however, Dorothy Hazzard deserved the highest praise as a leader of her church; he compared her to Ruth ('all the City did know her to be a virtuous woman', Ruth 3.11) and to Deborah, judge and prophetess (Judges 4–5). Terrill also used what might seem to be an unfortunate simile from Jeremiah 50.8 when he wrote that 'she was like a he-goat before the flock' (10), by which he presumably meant to imply that Mistress Hazzard was a leader who took her flock 'out of the midst of Babylon' by practising 'the truth of the Lord (which was then hated and Odious), namely, Separation'. In order properly to take command, the gender of the woman has to be reassigned to the sex which more appropriately gave leadership – even in the metaphorical guise of a beast. The simile also implies that Dorothy Hazzard was an egregious person, in the original sense of 'standing out from the crowd', and she certainly gave further proof of this during a crucial stage of the first Civil War. In July 1643 Bristol was held for Parliament by a reduced garrison under the command of Colonel Nathaniel Fiennes. On the 26th, royalist forces led by Prince Rupert began besieging the city with an attack against the northern perimeter, judging that they would be easily breached because of the shortage of defenders. They quickly overwhelmed the outer works, but were fiercely resisted at the Frome Gate of the old city wall, where they were halted for two hours with heavy losses on both sides. They were opposed by townsmen and soldiers reinforced by about 200 women and girls organized by Joan Batten, who was a leading figure in the defence of the whole city.[10] After Bristol was taken, Nathaniel Fiennes was tried for failing to defend the city effectively, and Dorothy Hazzard gave evidence against him (Fiennes may have capitulated quickly to spare Bristol needless casualties and damage). She had stored three months' provisions for her family and 'a great part of our Estate' in the castle, which was subsequently looted:

this Deponent with divers other women, and maids, with the help of some men, did with Wool-sacks and earth, stop up the Frome gate, to keep out the Enemy from entering into the said city…and when they had so done, they the said women went to the Gunners (this Deponent being one of them) and told them, that if they would stand out and fight, they would stand by them and told them that they should not want for provision.[11]

Prince Rupert's storm-troops held no terrors for the woman who had been spoken to by the Book of Revelation. Some other accounts attribute extreme remarks to Mistress Hazzard:

> [she] then repaired to the Governor, and adjured him to remain firm, assuring him that her Amazons would face the besiegers with their children in their arms 'to keep off the shot from the soldiers if they were afraid'.[12]

No more is heard of her after this, perhaps because of her reduced circumstances, but she 'came to her grave a shock of corn fully ripe' on 14 March 1675 (232). As represented in these different forms of male memoir, Dorothy Hazzard would be an exceptional person in any age, but as a woman of the mid-seventeenth century she broke all the contemporary codes for gendered behaviour. Edward Terrill's account must have shaped her biography to conform to conventions of spiritual narrative; the record of her meeting with Colonel Fiennes, where she is framed as the leader of a fearless band of 'Amazons', summons early modern fears of women breaking free of constraint and behaving with 'unnatural' enthusiasm, apparently willing to sacrifice even their own children. But Dorothy Hazzard frankly contradicted expectations about sex and gender in a culture which enjoined modesty, silence and obedience as the cardinal female virtues. With her example in view, we can now consider some of the central issues and arguments around the study of women's literacy in the early modern period.

Going astray among the Elizabethans: critical problems in early modern female literacy

The 300 female authors who began publishing during the seventeenth century were opposed by a formidable battery of assumptions regarding what was proper and improper to women's conduct. These prejudices were particularly fierce with respect to women writing, and female authors 'almost invariably prefaced their texts with some form of apology for their transgression in speaking with a public voice when silent retirement was proper and becoming to a woman'.[13] The emergence of this new writing-readership from the seventeenth century bears directly on central arguments in feminist-literary and gender studies in four respects:

1   The period is still significantly under-represented by female authors' texts available for routine study, and so is liable to misreading and misrepresentation, all the more so because of the alien social, political and theological belief systems current in early modern Europe. Representative anthologies of women's writing and editions of specific works for the student market have only recently begun to appear, and have not yet been incorporated adequately in feminist accounts of women's literary activities, and certainly not in 'standard' survey literary histories. Early modern women's writing has to be more widely read and discussed before a consensus emerges over the relative literary and social-historical merits of the work – how do we make these kinds of judgement now, if at all? Despite the fact that it was increasing, female publication

in the early years of the century was only 0.5 per cent of total output in England, and only reached 1.2 per cent after 1640; one survey identifies nine published women from 1580 to 1599, and twenty-six from 1600 to 1639, that is 9 per cent of the total number of female authors for the whole period 1580–1720. Kate Aughterson writes that the restricted nature and extent of women's writing during these years makes it difficult to draw balanced conclusions about the material. The temptation is to make every text an extraordinary achievement against the odds, or to ascribe each work's position to 'all women' of the time; both responses distort the actual nature of the writing. The difficulties of understanding this work from what is in strict terms a very small, self-defining minority are comparable to the difficulties encountered in 'subaltern studies' from later periods.[14]

2 The conditions and conventions of early modern literary production are in significant ways so different from those of later periods that they too can be misunderstood if not carefully presented. Sixteenth- and seventeenth-century women's writing is particularly prone to inappropriate readings and misinterpretations, which ignore its diversity and the specific circumstances of its composition and reception. To quote Margaret Ezell, when scholars and students ask why early modern women appear to have been 'silenced' by their culture, 'the answers focus on the means of repression, not the modes of production'. Part of Ezell's response to this misperception is to emphasize the widespread practice of manuscript circulation among semi-formalized correspondence networks, to which women actively contributed in some numbers. Since most accounts of seventeenth-century female writers assume that the transition from a patronage culture to the operation of a literary market-place was the decisive development for all writers in the period, they necessarily focus on the career of Aphra Behn, but ignore the many women authors who wrote for neither publication nor reward:

> The literary profession for a woman has come to represent in our current formation of the canon an escape from social roles and norms, whether the escape is complete, as in the case of Behn, or partial, in the simple attainment of a quiet room. The opportunity to be a *professional* writer in the current canon 'freed' the mind – being an amateur, it appears, did not.[15]

Ezell also argued that many seventeenth-century women wrote in genres that are difficult to claim for a literary canon which is modelled on poetry, drama, fiction and belles lettres, the dominant forms of male literary production. Women contributed significantly to writing on religious topics, prayers and death-bed avowals, as well as to prophecies and books of practical advice. New editions of writing by women and newly discovered works continually modify our knowledge: Lucy Hutchinson's translation of the demanding materialist philosopher Lucretius and a collection of elegies which she wrote late in life are among the most recent additions of this kind. Other scholars, such as Patricia Crawford and Elaine Hobby, considered that a significant amount of anonymous writing at present ascribed to male authors remains to be identified and ascribed to women, in addition to 'invisible' female literary labours such as editing and prefacing men's texts.[16]

3 The remarkable growth in women's literacy during this period was a consequence of – and is therefore inseparable from – the increased opportunities for reading and

writing among the middling and poorer ranks of society. More women and men were simultaneously gaining these skills (though the proportion of women becoming literate was probably growing more rapidly), and therefore the discussion of gender as a defining aspect of early modern cultural life cannot be separated from the material conditions and status conventions which contributed to the 'global' expansion in reading and writing. Simplistic ideas of an all-oppressing patriarchy obscure the ways in which degree and status affected the lives of individuals, irrespective of sex: 'The mere fact of being female created a distinctive experience of literacy, but we cannot be sure that gender-specific differences were more significant than those which can be related to position in the socio-economic hierarchy.'[17]

4   All these differences make the empathetic identification through a common gendered experience with the women – or indeed, the men – of the sixteenth and seventeenth centuries particularly difficult. How many of us can truly understand Dorothy Hazzard's terror when she read Revelation 14.9–11? Or feel as a painful reality her dilemma over not being able to attend her husband's service? This recalcitrance of significant areas of early modern writing and experience actually makes it more worthy of study, and more interesting, rather than less, but it also becomes difficult to draw direct parallels or conclusions from early modern lives, compared with our own, in crucial areas of experience such as religious belief or intimate relations: 'That is the function of subaltern pasts: a necessary penumbra of shadow to the area of the past that the method of history successfully illuminates, they make visible what historicizing does and what it cannot do.'[18]

Dorothy Hazzard's egregious behaviour is only one instance which suggests that individuals' gendered actions in early modern society should not be simply equated with the idealized or stereotyped conventions offered to them in contemporary literature, conduct books or sermons. The gulf between sexuality/gender as represented by the media in our own day and anyone's actual life is perhaps not too far away from the mismatch in early modern society between idealized images of conduct and daily experience – one parallel which may be worth drawing.

But since a central concern in contemporary feminist literary practice has focused on the imaginative reclaiming of a common currency of women's experience and expression, there is particular need to be alert to cultural difference in the work of writers before 1660. Virginia Woolf's argument that 'women's books continue each other' has been the inspiration for so much writing and research over the last twenty-five years, but it is also useful to remember her essay on 'The Strange Elizabethans', where she asked 'why we go further astray in this particular region of English literature than in any other'.[19] Gender codes, no less than the social hierarchy described in Chapter 2, were defensive categories employed to manage or resist social change. Recent research in social, family and education history allows us to appreciate the complexity of specific lives, and the ways in which individual experience often negotiated with or plainly contradicted the oppressive conventional pieties of seventeenth-century society. If Virginia Woolf had taken a degree course in Early Modern Social History she might not have been so perplexed by her 'strange Elizabethans' – but then she might not have written *Orlando* either.

Gendered behaviour in early modern society: conventions and realities

Women were economically, legally and educationally subordinated by the conventions of early modern society, and everyone was routinely reminded of female inferiority. Christianity in all its forms, Catholic, established and dissenting, stressed with only slightly varying emphases the subordination of woman to man as a consequence of original sin. And beyond the church door, 'The core values of popular culture were profoundly misogynistic'.[20] Even in the revolutionary political debates of 1647 instigated by the Levellers, Britain's first genuine political party which articulated sectional grievances and aspirations, there is no sign that women were considered participating individuals in the new franchise or any of the godly reforms that were intended to follow.[21] This was despite the very active contribution of large numbers of women sympathetic to the Leveller programme during the later 1640s. The women's petitions to Parliament at this period framed some of the most audacious claims for equality:

> since we are assured of our Creation in the image of God, and of an interest in Christ, equal unto men, as also of a proportionable share in the Freedoms of this Commonwealth, we cannot but wonder that we should appear so despicable in your eyes, as to be thought unworthy to Petition or represent our grievances to this Honourable House.

But the Petition had little or no impact on attitudes and events.[22]

The models of behaviour constantly enjoined by conduct books and sermons which insisted on the subordination of women to men might be contradicted or renegotiated in marriage and family life, as Dorothy Hazzard seems to have managed, but the legal subordination of women in marriage was inescapable. In English law the woman ceased to exist as an individual after marriage, becoming subsumed as a 'Feme Covert' under her husband's status. A popular legal manual of the time helpfully explained the situation:

> A woman as soon as she is married is called *covert*, in Latin *nupta*, that is, veiled, as it were clouded and over-shadowed....Every Feme Covert is quodammodo [as it were] an infant...even in that which is most her own.

The wife retained possession of any land which she brought to the marriage, but her husband received all profits deriving from it, together with all other monies and goods which she may have contributed as dowry. Numbers of petitions to Parliament framed by or for individual women claiming their rightful share of estates after their husbands' deaths during the Civil Wars testify to the difficulties which unjust property law caused, and we shall see how it dominated Anne Clifford's entire life.[23] The family within its household was the source of all livelihood; marriage was therefore a necessity for most people, and unmarried women had to provide for themselves in a society which rewarded women far less than men. Marriage and the family were the institutions through which the regulation of gendered experience occurred, but even for the 10 per cent who did not marry, it was impossible to escape being overseen. The Statute of Artificers (1563) required that property-less women and men between the ages of 15 and 45 should live and work in a household as servants, and this was enforced for both sexes.

These early modern assumptions about female inequality and subordination were unde-niable reality, but they created contradictions by which individuals might avoid their most oppressive consequences: 'historians have long been familiar with [this] paradox of early modern society'.[24] The same point has been made for the study of women's social posi-tion in all periods:

> documentation and denunciation of women's suppression [seems] virtually
> pointless to many historians and readers unless it is integrated with discussions of
> the resistance, compromises and ambiguities with which women actually negoti-
> ated relations between the sexes.[25]

Therefore, although thought to be weaker, less reliable and more sexually demanding than men, women were also described as more virtuous, less vicious and as equally talented as males. Said to be inferior as a consequence of the burden of original sin, women also undoubtedly had souls which needed to be nurtured and saved – not even John Donne could deny this: 'No author of gravity, of piety, of conversation in the Scriptures could admit that doubt, whether woman were created in the Image of God, that is, in possession of a reasonable and immortal soul.'[26] The fearsome dangers of childbirth were rational-ized as a consequence of original sin, but many husbands' sense of their gender's innate superiority was destroyed when their wife died agonizingly in the course of childbirth. John Taylor the Water Poet was vulnerable to these feelings in his (mock) pro-feminist pamphlet, *The Women's Sharp Revenge*:

> for when children are born into the world, although men feel none of the wifery,
> yet women have a more known sympathy and feeling of one another's pains and
> perils: and therefore, in Christianity and neighbourly love and charity, women do
> meet to visit and comfort the weakness of such as in these dangerous times do
> want it.[27]

Though subordinated within marriage, women were expected to provide significant contributions to domestic economy and give leadership to servants and an example to children. Female apprenticeships were very unusual, occurring during periods of labour shortage in the smaller towns and villages, and later in the seventeenth century as a version of poor relief. Even so the demand for young women as household servants and workers in textiles and nursing 'left considerable scope for independence and initiative during their adolescent and youthful years'. Although not educated to contribute to the running of businesses, wives could benefit from informal training and contribute to family trades, or in the case of widows, sustain their livelihood: 'Between 1600 and 1645 widows in Bristol were engaged in almost all the major occupations in which men could be found as apprentices or masters'[28] – here again Dorothy Hazzard follows a pattern in having taken over her first husband's store in Bristol High Street.

In order to explore the place of literacy among women of the political and cultural elite we can now review some passages in the life of Lady Anne Clifford, Countess of Pembroke, Dorset and Montgomery, which illustrate three central aspects of female iden-tity in the period: inheritance and status, literacy and self-expression among the aristocracy, and the conflicts created by religious belief.

'How careful must you be, To be Your Self': Lady Anne Clifford's Great Picture

For the duration of the first Civil War Lady Anne Clifford did not set foot outside Baynards Castle on Thames' side. From the time of the Battle of Edgehill in October 1642 to the surrender of the King in 1646 she occupied the Castle at the request of her estranged husband, Philip, fourth Earl of Pembroke. He had favoured Parliament while she remained loyal to Charles I, but even so Lady Anne agreed to stay on guard over Pembroke's considerable possessions. Then in the middle of the political chaos and economic disruption of 1646 she commissioned two works which provide one of the most elaborate family histories of their time. The first was a series of 'Books of Record', assembling all available evidence to prove her right to her father's estates in Westmorland. The second was a huge composite portrait representing her parents and (deceased) brothers, a triptych nine feet high and eighteen feet wide, the central panel of which became known as the Great Picture. It is a uniquely elaborate iconography celebrating Anne Clifford's family, and – above all – her pride in their lineage. Beyond this, the Great Picture is also the most comprehensive single account of the reading and intellectual interests of a woman from the early modern social elite, since it identifies a formidable library by author and title.

These books were not just wall-furniture; throughout her life Anne Clifford read widely and deeply, and was able 'to discourse in all Commendable Arts and Sciences…with Virtuosos, Travellers, Scholars, Merchants, Divines, Statesmen, and with Good Housewives in any kind'.[29] She was also a voluminous 'non-professional' writer; from 1617 to 1620 she kept a diary-memoir which began with her recollections of Queen Elizabeth's funeral in 1603, and from January to March 1676 she maintained a day-book until the eve of her death. She also wrote a brief autobiography, biographies of her parents, and commissioned a good deal of architecture and memorial sculpture. These records of her reading life give a sense of the intricate webs of literary patronage woven by the leading families in Elizabethan and Jacobean England. They also demonstrate the singular ways in which women of this rank might pursue a demanding intellectual life, despite the near-total bias of contemporary educational institutions in favour of their male counterparts.

Anne Clifford was born in 1590, the third child and only daughter of Margaret Russell, daughter of the second Earl of Bedford, and George Clifford, third Earl of Cumberland. She was therefore the fortunate child of one of the half-dozen most powerful families in the kingdom, intimately connected to national politics and court faction. Her two brothers died in early childhood, Francis aged 5 in 1589, and Robert aged 6 in 1591. Her father died in 1605 and, in a fateful decision which marked out the rest of his daughter's life, he bequeathed to his brother Francis titles and estates which were arguably due to her. Clifford may have made this decision because of the vast scale of his debts which he felt his brother might resolve better than a juvenile daughter who could become prey to legal wardship. Anne Clifford, however, described her father's decision as one made to favour male inheritance, on account of 'the love he bore his brother, and the advancement of the heirs male of his house'.[30] Lady Margaret immediately began legal proceedings to reclaim the inheritance for her daughter, and supported her unswervingly through later trials.

Anne Clifford had been taught her letters by Mrs Taylor, a pious governess, but in

1598 her mother invited the poet Samuel Daniel to join their household and become her tutor. Daniel was quick to repay this patronage, and dedicated two verse epistles to Lady Margaret and the child. His address 'To the Lady Anne Clifford' emphasizes the extraordinary privilege which she enjoyed, but also her mother's concern 'To make you as highly Good as highly Born, / And set your Virtues Equal to your Kind.' Her education was to be a strenuous training in moral conduct and virtue:

> And young the World appears to a young Conceit,
> Whilst through the unacquainted Faculties
> The late-invested Soul doth rawly view
> Those Objects which on that Discretion wait.[31]

A true education will train the soul to exercise its 'Discretion' via the faculties, and develop a proper bearing in the world, equal to the 'fair Advantage' of birth and abilities which the child already enjoys. Daniel had previously moved in the patronage circles of Mary Sidney and Fulke Greville and his verse has the serious, calvinistic gravity associated with their coteries. Honour is 'the dearest thing on earth', where 'your Nature, Virtue, Happy Birth, / Have therein highly interplaced your Name' (59–60), and therefore, 'how careful must you be, / To be Your Self'. Daniel goes on to warn against flattery and – above all – pride; his conclusion is that this virtuous conduct will perpetuate 'the Honourable Blood / Of *Clifford*, and of *Russell*', 'Since nothing cheers the Heart of Greatness more / Than th'Ancestors' fair Glory gone before' (96–7).

Daniel's poem demonstrates the priorities of a sequestered education designed for a daughter of a powerful and privileged family at the close of the sixteenth century. Moral philosophy is to be drawn from Christianity, classical authors and some contemporary literature to strengthen the virtuous honour of the family's blood-line. Few concessions are made to notions of a weaker sex, or indeed to the youthfulness of the pupil; the course of reading will be demanding and above all ethical, where the bearing of the 'self' is a strenuous and careful activity. The final consequence of this education will be a virtuous death which confirms the status and renown of family name. In Lady Anne's own words, her education consisted in 'true religion and moral virtue and all other qualities befitting her birth', though she 'was not admitted to learn any language, because her father would not permit it; but for all other knowledge fit for her sex none was bred up to greater perfection than she'.[32] (Her father's prohibition of 'language' probably applied specifically to Latin, because she did gain some knowledge of French.) The Clifford Great Picture of 1646 is a complex record of this unique literary life.

In 1609, now one of the most eligible women at the Jacobean Court, Anne married Richard Sackville, third Earl of Dorset, a charming but profligate rake. The first Earl of Dorset had been Lord Treasurer to James I, and was known as 'Sack Fill' because of his avarice. Far from supporting Anne's claim to the Clifford estates, and true to family form, Richard Sackville put considerable pressure on her to renounce the Clifford inheritance in favour of a cash settlement. This would be paid to him since Anne as his wife had the status of 'Feme Covert' (see above). By 1617 the King himself was asked to rule on the dispute, and James predictably confirmed Francis Clifford's right to the inheritance, which however should revert to Anne if Francis's male lineage came to an end. Richard Sackville died in 1624, at the age of 35 (he over-indulged in sweet potatoes, possibly for their aphrodisiac effect, and was fatally weakened by dysentery).[33] Anne was left with two daughters – Margaret born in 1614, and Isabella, born in 1622 – and she had lost three sons in their infancy.

Dorset did provide adequately for his wife and daughters, but he also left huge debts, and in 1630 Lady Anne married one of the most powerful courtiers on the scene – Philip, fourth Earl of Pembroke, son of Mary Sidney and Henry, the second Earl. She may have made this alliance because she was feeling increasingly vulnerable in the continuing legal disputes over the Clifford inheritance and Pembroke's status might have proved useful. As Lord Chamberlain, the Earl of Pembroke occupied the most influential position in the royal household, and he was an efficient and adroit courtier. He was also a contradictory character; as one of Van Dyck's leading patrons he had a sophisticated taste in painting and architecture. With his older brother William, he had been chosen by Heminge and Condell as dedicatee of Shakespeare's folio works in 1623; the King's Men also chose him as dedicatee for the folio edition of Beaumont and Fletcher's works in 1647 – and he was one of John Taylor the Water Poet's patrons for his *Works* of 1630. But Pembroke was also licentious, coarse and, despite his taste and involvement with theatre, said to be barely literate. This was no hindrance to his also being appointed Chancellor of Oxford University. Despite these character flaws in Pembroke, this second marriage placed Lady Anne Clifford at the centre of power: 'a triple countess, the Lord Chamberlain's consort…intimate of the royal family, Anne achieved the pinnacle of her social standing and esteem'.[34]

Unfortunately, this marriage was as unhappy as the first, and she lost two more sons who were born prematurely. The couple lived apart from 1634, though Herbert was helpful in settling income on Anne and waiving some rights in her properties. Anne Clifford's fortunes finally changed in 1643 when both Francis Clifford and his son died in rapid succession, and she inherited her father's lands and titles. For over thirty years she managed the estates imaginatively and prudently, repairing six castles, seven churches and establishing two almshouses in order to leave a good account of her custody.

Her Great Picture, now on display at Appleby Castle, is unsigned, but has been attributed to Jan Van Belcamp (1610–53), a copyist who worked for Van Dyck but of whom very little is known. Remegius Van Lemput has also been suggested, though neither attribution is secure, and some art historians give Peter Lely a hand in the more successful passages. Whoever the artist, it is clear that the content of the painting is the work of Anne Clifford herself, because the details are so consistently organized to display the history and achievements of her family. In one very specific respect, she was the author of the painting: there are over 8,000 words of text carefully inscribed in different areas of the canvas recording the history and genealogy of the family. The writing is minute but legible at very close range, providing a kind of 'text base' or gloss to the pictorial images.

The Great Picture makes an interesting contrast with Van Dyck's group portrait of Anne, Pembroke and his family painted in 1634/5. The Pembroke portrait, installed in the Double Cube Room at Wilton House, is a colourful, dramatically posed composition in which Lady Anne sits to the left of her husband, again dressed in black, and as if detached from her second family. This was the period when, she wrote, 'I gave myself wholly to Retyredness…and made good bookes and vertuous thoughts my companions.' Van Dyck's huge 'uniquely vainglorious picture' is informed by his knowledge of contemporary European art, based in part on Titian's Vendramin family portrait, which he owned. By contrast Anne Clifford's Great Picture, only slightly smaller than Van Dyck's canvas, at first sight appears to be a puzzling medley, a composite picture put together

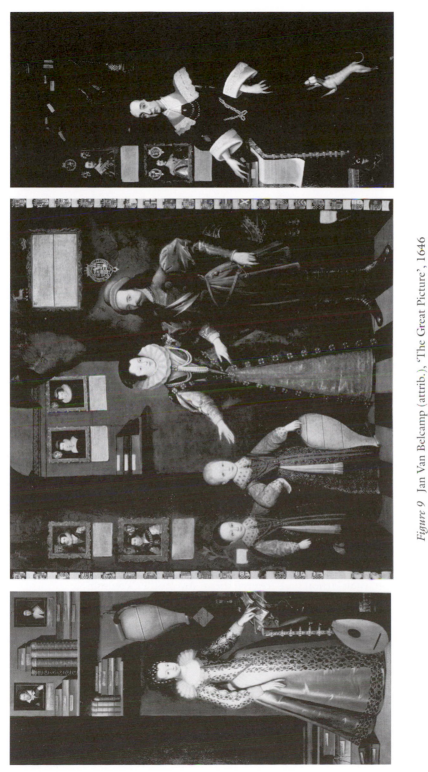

Figure 9 Jan Van Belcamp (attrib.), 'The Great Picture', 1646

Oil on canvas, 270 by 535 cm (approx.). Reproduced by courtesy of Abbot Hall Gallery, Kendal, Cumbria. The 'Great Picture' is displayed in the Great Hall, Appleby Castle, Appleby-in-Westmorland, Cumbria

from several previous works, and harking back to earlier Tudor dynastic images such as 'The Family of Henry VIII: An Allegory of the Tudor Succession', attributed to Lucas de Heere (*c.* 1572), which Anne could have seen in Walsingham's house at Scadbury, Kent. That the presence of books in portraits could carry highly charged meaning is also demonstrated from Gerlach Flicke's supremely accomplished portrait of Archbishop Cranmer, representing the cleric beginning his fifty-seventh year, on 20 July 1545. Cranmer opens a copy of the Pauline Epistles, and has Augustine's *De Fide et Operibus* to hand, ready to reaffirm the predominance of divine grace and human faith over mere works, a fundamental conflict between Cranmer and his temporal lord, Henry VIII.[35]

Pictures might therefore carry profoundly important meanings, and the more one is drawn into the complex narrative encoded in the Cliffords' Great Picture, the more interesting and impressive the painting becomes. Lady Anne is present in each of the three panels (though she is not visible in the central frame). In the left-hand wing she is 15 years old, in 1605, the year in which her father died and when she was deprived of her inheritance. The right-hand panel presents her likeness taken at the time of the picture's composition in 1646, aged 56, having finally come into the patrimony. Anne's mother, Lady Margaret Russell, occupies the central panel as she was certainly the central figure in her daughter's life. A pious, self-possessed woman, 'naturally of an high spirit, though she tempered it well by grace',[36] Lady Margaret holds a psalm book as she gestures with her right hand to her two sons who would not survive to adolescence. Anne Clifford's claim to the legitimacy of her descent is spelled out with complete candour in this panel. The text reads:

> When these originals were drawn did George Clifford, E[arl] of Cumberland, with his worthy Wife, and their two sons lie in the Lo[rd] Phillip Wharton's house, in Channel Row, Westminster, where the said worthy Countess conceived with Child, the first of May, Ano. Dom. 1589, with her only daughter, The Lady Anne Clifford...she afterwards being the only Child of her Parents.[37]

The group portrait from which the panel is copied was painted one month later during June: the embryonic Lady Anne is already present, in close proximity to her mother's book of Psalms. The text scroll explicating this part of the picture ends with the words 'Psalm 139', and this is apt, since that psalm throughout expresses an intense awareness of God's presence governing an entire life, very much in keeping with the piety of Margaret Clifford and her daughter. More than this, verse 13 is graphically apt: 'For thou hast possessed my reins [vitals]: thou hast covered me in my mother's womb.'

Her father George gave Anne Clifford the blood-line of which she was so proud and by which she defined herself. Successively Countess of Dorset and Countess of Pembroke and Montgomery by her marriages, it was her father's name and lineage that she chose to memorialize: 'Viewers would have noted that all the shields in the main sequences were of Anne's male ancestors and relatives. Patriarchalism was upheld.'[38] The Cliffords had been a prominent family since the early thirteenth century, and George Clifford was a daring and successful naval commander. He had fought against the Armada in 1588 and taken many Spanish ships in the West Indies; in 1600 he became one of the founding governors of the East India Company. Queen Elizabeth valued his martial skills and courtly qualities so much that he succeeded Sir Henry Lee as the Queen's Champion in 1590: in this role he was required to represent Elizabeth at the annual Accession Day tournaments. His daughter was clearly proud of his voyages and buccaneering, and particularly of his mathematical skills in navigation. In her memoir on his life she wrote a candid assessment of him:

> But, as good natures through human frailty are oftentimes mislead, so he fell to love a lady of quality, which did by degrees draw and alienate his love and affection from his so virtuous and well deserving wife; so that at the length, for two or three years together before his death, they parted houses.[39]

The Earl is portrayed in the Great Picture wearing his Champion's armour of gold stars on an azure ground, with his helmet and gauntlets on the table in the background. The central panel however belongs to Lady Margaret, who is centre-stage, a more convincingly painted figure, and to the female relations whose portraits hang in the background: Lady Margaret's sisters, Anne Countess of Warwick and Elizabeth Countess of Bath, and George Clifford's sisters, Margaret Countess of Derby and Frances Lady Wharton.

Lady Margaret holds a book of Psalms and on the shelf in an alcove behind her is a Bible, the works of Seneca in English, and a manuscript collection of 'Alchemist Extractions, of Distillations and excellent Medicines' which may well be the collection of 'Receipts' from about 1550, with Lady Margaret's own annotations made in 1598, on deposit in Cumbria Record Office. This is a careful selection of texts, giving spiritual, philosophical and medical succour, Lady Margaret's 'equivalent to her husband's armour'.[40] In his verse epistle Samuel Daniel praised Lady Margaret for her 'Clearness' and her stoical judgement which allowed her to rise above worldly misfortune. There are lines which must glance at her feelings about her husband, from whom she was now estranged:

> [...] Man's Greatness rests but in his Show,
> The best of all whose Days consumed are,
> Either in War, or Peace conceiving War.[41]

The image of Anne Clifford aged 15 in the left-hand panel presents an emblem of her youthful achievements. The likeness may be based on a lost painting from 1615–20 because the silver and sea-green embroidered silk dress is characteristic of that period rather than of 1605, and it has been compared to the more sophisticated portrait of Lady Mary Wroth at Penshurst, attributed to Marcus Gheeraerts, from 1620. The girl is leafing through a music manuscript, possibly a lute primer, and an instrument is propped in front of her (again, a slight anachronism, this particular lute was popular in the 1640s). During this period, she recorded, 'I used to wear my Hair color'd velvet every day & learned to sing & play on the Bass Viol of Jack Jenkins my Aunt's Boy.' This Jack was John Jenkins, born in 1592, who went on to compose viol consorts and sonatas that became popular during the Civil Wars.[42] Also on the table is a sample of the girl's embroidery, and an hour-glass indicating the brevity of youth since the sands have run into the lower glass. Where the central and right-hand wings include portraits of immediate relations and Lady Anne's two husbands, the left-hand panel in an extraordinary act of homage displays portraits of her teachers: Mrs Anne Taylor, her governess, 'a religious and good woman', and Samuel Daniel, her tutor.

Daniel had a good knowledge of Latin, Italian and French, and read widely in history,

Figure 10 Jan Van Belcamp (attrib.), 'The Great Picture', 1646, the left-hand panel, detail.
270 by 77 cm (approx.). Reproduced by courtesy of Abbot Hall Gallery, Kendal, Cumbria

which became one of Anne Clifford's favourite subjects. Daniel's *Delia* was one of the most successful sonnet sequences of the 1590s and Jonathan Bate speculates that Daniel may have been the 'rival poet' in Shakespeare's sonnet sequence, written at the same period (Daniel did write a praise poem to the Earl of Southampton, Shakespeare's patron).[43] The volumes neatly ranged above the girl's head and lying on the rush matting are a fascinating glimpse of a reading life from the first decades of the seventeenth century. One group of books is particularly poignant: on the floor is a copy of 'The Feigned History of Don Quixote', not in fact translated until 1612, but the latest word in leisure reading. On top of this is a sceptical rebuttal of all worldly learning, Agrippa's *Vanity of Arts and Sciences*, and then behind these is Abraham Ortelius's best-selling *Maps of the World*, against which is propped a pair of compasses: had Anne been charting her father's voyages in the atlas? Camden's *Britannia* lies behind Ortelius, useful for checking the extent of her Clifford patrimony. The complete collection of books from the left-hand panel can be grouped in four categories:

Scripture and theology: the Bible; St Augustine, *City of God*, (tr. 1610); John Downham, *The Christian Warfare* (1604); Eusebius, *History of the Church* (tr. 1577); Joseph Hall, *Works* (1621)

Classical philosophy and literature: Boethius, *Consolation of Philosophy* (tr. 1556, 1609); Epictetus, *Encheiridion* (tr. 1567); Ovid, *Metamorphoses* (tr. 1565)

English literature and instructional works: William Camden, *Britannia* (1586, tr. 1610); Chaucer, *Works* (1561); Samuel Daniel, *Works* and *The Chronicle of England* (1612); John Gerard, *Herbal* (1597); Sidney, *Arcadia* (1593); Spenser, *Works* (1609)

Continental literature, philosophy and instructional works: Cornelius Agrippa, *The Vanity of the Arts and Sciences* (tr. 1575); Baldassare Castiglione, *The Book of the Courtier* (tr. 1561); Cervantes, '*The Feigned History of Don Quixote*' (tr. 1612); Pierre De La Primaudaye, *The French Academy* (tr. 1586); Guillaume Du Bartas, *Divine Weeks and Works* (tr. 1605, 1620); Abraham Ortelius, *The Theatre of the Whole World* (tr. 1603); Montaigne, *Essays* (tr. 1603); Tasso, *Godfrey of Bulloigne* (tr. 1600); Louis Le Roy, *The Interchangeable Course of Things* (tr. 1594).

The right-hand panel depicts Anne Clifford painted from life, aged 56. She might be mistaken for a widow in her black satin dress, but she was still married to Pembroke, who puts in a proxy appearance as a portrait to the left of the Countess, below that of Sackville, her first husband. While the background to the extreme left of the youthful Lady Anne is a panelled wall leading into a book alcove, the area to the extreme right of the elderly person is much darker, a sombre exit. Her only companions now are a fawning whippet and a self-possessed, owlish cat. A puzzling, naturalistic feature of the right-hand panel is the disorderly jumble of books and the untidy statecloth in the background: they may indicate a 'working' library, and a growing disdain for worldly goods. The books also seem to be out of reach, perhaps discarded in favour of the only text that finally mattered, the Bible, on which rests a single philosophical commentary, Pierre Charron's *Book of Wisdom* (1612), in serious contrast to the lute primer of her youth. The selection of works has predictably become more grave. The categories are now:

Scripture and theology: the Bible; William Austin, *Meditations* (1635); Henry Cuffe, *The Difference in the Ages of Man's Life* (1603); John Donne, *Sermons* (1640); G.

Figure 11 Jan Van Belcamp (attrib.), 'The Great Picture', 1646, the right-hand panel, detail.
270 by 77 cm (approx.). Reproduced by courtesy of Abbot Hall Gallery, Kendal, Cumbria

Hakewill, *Apology of the Power and Providence of God* (1618); John King, *Sermons* (1606); John Moore, *A Map of Man's Mortality* (1617); George Sandys, *Paraphrase upon the Psalms of David* (1636); G. Strode, *Anatomy of Mortality* (1618)

Classical history and philosophy: Marcus Aurelius Antoninus, *Meditations* (tr. 1557, Casaubon, 1635); Ammianus Marcellinus, *Roman History* (tr. 1609); Plutarch, *Lives* (in French?); Plutarch, *Moralia* (in French?)

English literature and instructional works: John Donne, *Poems* (1633); Fulke Greville, *Works* (1633); George Herbert, *The Temple* (1633); Ben Jonson, *Works* (1616); Sir Henry Wootton, *The Elements of Architecture* (1624)

Scots Latin romance: John Barclay, *Argenis* (1621, tr, 1625)

Continental history and philosophy: Pierre Charron, *Book of Wisdom* (1601, tr. 1612); Philippe de Commines, *History* (tr. 1596); Francesco Guicciardini *History* (French, tr. from Italian, 1568).

This selection of titles in the ideal library of the Great Picture must have been carefully considered because reading and quotation formed a central part of Anne Clifford's mental life. She would excerpt 'sententiae' [memorable remarks] from the works which she valued and

> with these her Walls, her Bed, her Hangings, and Furniture must be adorned; causing her Servants to write them in Papers, and her Maids to pin them up, that she, or they, in the time of their dressing, or as occasion served, might remember, and make their descants on them. So that, though she had not many Books in her Chamber, yet it was dressed up with the flowers of a Library.[44]

The scrupulous record of this library serves two functions: first, the volumes are a central part of the memorial and record of the Clifford dynasty, a visible sign of the family's active networks of patronage and literary connection. Second, the books suggest a map of the religious, philosophical and literary interests of such a family across half a century, where the webs of patronage demonstrate the close connections of prominent authors with the social elite.

As leading courtiers in the 1580s, Anne's parents knew Sir Philip Sidney and Fulke Greville. William Camden and Edmund Spenser frequented the Court, and Spenser dedicated poems to George Clifford. George Sandys, translator of the *Metamorphoses* and paraphraser of the Psalms, was Clifford's godson. Anne Clifford must have derived a good deal of her intellectual curiosity from her mother, who, 'though she had no language but her own, yet was there few books of worth translated into English but she read them'. Lady Margaret was also a 'private' writer, having composed a reflective memoir in a letter to her chaplain in 1589. The magus John Dee was a close friend, and Lady Margaret herself practised alchemy and physic – Gerard's *Herbal* was a key reference work for her prescriptions. She was dedicatee in Robert Greene's *Penelope's Web* (1587), Thomas Lodge's *Prosopopeia* (1596), Spenser's *Four Hymns* (1596), Daniel's *Poetical Essays* (1599) and *Whole Works* (1601, 1604, 1607), and Aemilia Lanyer's *Salve Deus Rex Judeorum* (1611).[45] Both Margaret and Anne were invoked as patrons by Lanyer in very direct ways. She wrote of Anne in her 'Description of Cookham',

> Unconstant Fortune, thou art most too blame,[...]
> Where our great friends we cannot dayly see,
> So great a diffrence is there in degree.

But despite her best efforts, Lanyer's book is not among those represented in the Great Picture.[46] In addition to these literary collections, no less than twelve works of divinity were dedicated to Lady Margaret, including the influential *Works* (1600) by the Calvinist William Perkins.

Augustine's *City of God*, in many ways a sympathetic book for Calvinist readers, was dedicated to William, Earl of Pembroke, Anne's brother-in-law by her second marriage. It had been translated by J[ohn] H[ealey] and published by Thomas Thorpe in 1610 (who had brought out Shakespeare's *Sonnets* the year before). Montaigne's *Essays* were translated by John Florio, Samuel Daniel's brother-in-law. Daniel's own works are well represented in the Great Picture, as are those of his poetic mentors, Sidney, Spenser and Fulke Greville. Lady Anne became so attached to Spenser's poetry that she commissioned his monument from the sculptor Nicholas Stone for Westminster Abbey, twenty years after the poet's death. At Court in the first decade of the new century, she had danced as one of Queen Anne's attendants in Jonson's *Masque of Beauty*, as Berenice of Egypt in the *Masque of Queens* and as the river Ayr in her tutor Daniel's *Tethys Festival*.[47] Perhaps Jonson's *Works* of 1616 were a reminder of those happier years. In 1620 Joshua Sylvester dedicated his translation of Du Bartas's *Divine Weeks and Works* to Anne, and in 1624 Sir Henry Wotton, a relation, published his *Elements of Architecture*; designs from the book may have contributed to the rebuilding of Pembroke's Wilton House in the 1630s. John Donne had been a rector at Sevenoaks, near Knole house, and had stayed with Anne Clifford and her first husband for a week in 1617, also sending copies of his poems to Sackville. George Herbert was of course a relation of Pembroke, Anne's second husband, and may have acted as their chaplain. Yet despite this complex matrix of patronage and writing, Anne Clifford did not follow her mother's example as an active patron for circles of writers, perhaps preferring to memorialize her self and family in more direct ways.

The grouping of works around Daniel's portrait in the Great Picture is fascinating: Sidney's *Arcadia* is stacked on Spenser's *Works* which in turn lies on Ovid's 'Metamorphosis', all displayed horizontally with fore-edge to the viewer. The titles are written on slips folded down over each volume's fore-edge, recalling a method for shelving and labelling books in the medieval period, by 1646 rather old-fashioned. Next to these is a Bible in both Testaments, shelved vertically, bound in black with elaborate gilding on the spine. This proximity of Scripture to the major English poets and Ovid's influential pagan miscellany is daringly eclectic, but in a way true to the syncretic interests of both Spenser and Sidney. Another notable inclusion on this shelf is a copy of Chaucer's *Works* which were not widely read in early modern England, though they were important for Spenser and Daniel. Anne Clifford was also an enthusiastic reader of Chaucer. In 1649, having finally taken possession of her northern estates, and meeting resistance from her tenants, she wrote to the Dowager Countess of Kent,

> if I had not excellent Chaucer's book here to comfort me I were in a pitiful case, having so many troubles as I have, but when I read in that I scorn and make light of them all, and a little part of his divine spirit infuses itself in me.[48]

As Barbara Lewalski points out, this is partly a quotation from *The Faerie Qveene* where Spenser invoked Chaucer 'Through infusion sweet / Of thine own spirit' (6.36.6–7). Contemporary European literature and philosophy are also well represented in Castiglione's *Courtier*, standard treatise for cultured behaviour, Tasso's romance and

Cervantes's *Quixote*. Florio translated Montaigne's *Essays* in 1603 with a preface by Daniel, and Montaigne's study decorated with *sententiae* may have inspired Anne Clifford's selected quotations pinned around her chamber. De La Primaudaye's *Academy* and Du Bartas's *Divine Weeks* provided encyclopaedic surveys of God's creation, stressing its inherent mutability and corruption.

The theological works in the Great Picture reveal a piety characteristic of Anne Clifford's family allegiance, generation – and gender. Unlike Dorothy Hazzard, she approved the Elizabethan 'middle way' in doctrine and forms, accepting the rule of bishops and the Prayer Book, but also following a moderate Calvinist perspective. Again like many of her contemporaries, she set great store by Paul's Epistle to the Romans, Chapter 8, reciting it each Sunday. This was a forthright statement on key articles of belief on the relation between salvation and faith, the Pauline argument developed by Luther, Tyndale, and Calvin. Anne Clifford was therefore neither Puritan nor Laudian, but a devout adherent of the established Church with Calvinist sympathies. Again her mother must have been the dominant influence; Margaret Cavendish was dedicatee for a number of Puritan theologians, and her personal tribulations inclined her to a kind of Christian stoicism. The loss of her two sons in the 1590s and her deteriorating marriage encouraged her to take solace in the Bible, from which time 'the Book of Job was her daily companion'. Theological works in the 1605 panel confirm this kind of sober puritanism, passed from mother to daughter: Downham's influential *Christian Warfare* and the *Works* of the Anglican Neostoic, Joseph Hall, 'our English Seneca'. Two widely read works of classical stoicism served similar purposes: Epictetus and Boethius's *Book of Philosophical Comfort* (which was read as an early Christian work during the middle ages and renaissance).[49]

The selection of books in the right-hand panel demonstrates a continuing interest in poetry, adding three important collections from 1633, each of them bringing links of patronage or kinship to the Clifford, Dorset and Pembroke families: Fulke Greville's *Works*, John Donne's *Poems* and George Herbert's *Poems*, in addition to Jonson's *Works* of 1616. Classical stoic writings continued to provide comfort and reflection, including Plutarch, Seneca and Marcus Aurelius's *Meditations*. The 1646 library is however dominated by grave theology which must have been added during the middle period of Anne Clifford's life. The years 1617–19 were peculiarly difficult. Dorset was conducting a public affair at Court with Lady Penistone, and Lady Anne was left to her own devices at Knole. The pressures on her to renounce her claim to the Westmorland estates were intense, including confrontations with King James himself, and she fell into melancholy. The brief journal notes that she made during this period offer fascinating glimpses of a privileged life under extreme duress. On 15 February 1616 she played Glecko – a popular card game – with Lady Elizabeth Gray and Frances Carr, Countess of Somerset, and lost £15 at a sitting – the equivalent of a year's income for many families at the time. On 19 April (while Shakespeare lay on his deathbed in Stratford) she recorded,

> About this time I used to rise early in the Morning & go to the Standing in the garden, & taking my Prayer Book with me beseech God to be merciful to me in this & to help me as He always hath done.

'This' was the dispute over her inheritance. In May, Dorset took away their daughter Margaret, then 2 years old, and threatened complete separation:

Saued by hope.   Chap.viij.   Predeſtination.

9 But ye are not in the fleſh, but in the ſpirit, if ſo be that the ſpirit of God dwell in you. Now if any man haue not the ſpirit of Chriſt, he is none of his.

10 And if Chriſt be in you, the body is dead becauſe of ſinne : but the ſpirit is life, becauſe of righteouſneſſe.

11 But if the ſpirit of him that raiſed vp Ieſus from the dead, dwell in you : he that raiſed vp Chriſt from the dead, ſhall alſo quicken your moꝛtall bodies, ‖by his ſpirit that dwelleth in you.

12 Therefoꝛe brethren, we are detters, not to the fleſh, to liue after the fleſh.

13 Foꝛ if ye liue after the fleſh, ye ſhall die : but if ye through the ſpirit doe moꝛtifie the deeds of the body, ye ſhall liue.

14 Foꝛ as many as are led by the ſpirit of God, they are the ſonnes of God.

15 Foꝛ ye haue not receiued the ſpirit of bondage againe to feare : but ye haue receiued the ſpirit of adoption, whereby we cry, Abba, father.

16 The ſpirit it ſelfe beareth witnes with our ſpirit, that we are the childꝛen of God.

17 And if childꝛen, then heires, heires of God, and ioynt heires with Chriſt : if ſo be that we ſuffer with him, that wee may be alſo gloꝛified together.

18 Foꝛ I reckon, that the ſufferings of this pꝛeſent time, are not woꝛthy to be compared with the gloꝛy which ſhall be reuealed in vs.

19 Foꝛ the earneſt expectation of the creature, waiteth foꝛ the manifeſtation of the ſonnes of God.

20 Foꝛ the creature was made ſubiect to vanitie, not willingly, but by reaſon of him who hath ſubiected the ſame in hope :

21 Becauſe the creature it ſelfe alſo ſhall bee deliuered from the bondage of coꝛruption, into the gloꝛious libertie of the childꝛen of God.

22 Foꝛ wee know that ‖the whole creation groaneth, and trauaileth in paine together vntill now.

23 And not only they, but our ſelues alſo which haue the firſt fruites of the ſpirit, euen we our ſelues groane within our ſelues, waiting foꝛ the adoption, to wit, the*redemption of our body.

24 Foꝛ wee are ſaued by hope : but hope that is ſeene, is not hope : foꝛ what a man ſeeth, why doth he yet hope foꝛ?

25 But if wee hope foꝛ that wee ſee not, then doe wee with patience waite foꝛ it.

26 Likewiſe the ſpirit alſo helpeth our infirmities : foꝛ we know not what wee ſhould pray foꝛ as wee ought : but the ſpirit it ſelfe maketh interceſſion foꝛ vs with groanings, which cannot bee vttered.

27 And he that ſearcheth the hearts, knoweth what is the minde of the ſpirit, ‖becauſe he maketh interceſſion foꝛ the Saints, accoꝛding to the will of God.

28 And wee know that all things woꝛke together foꝛ good, to them that loue God, to them who are the called accoꝛding to his purpoſe.

29 Foꝛ whom he did foꝛeknow, he alſo did pꝛedeſtinate to be confoꝛmed to the image of his ſonne, that hee might bee the firſt boꝛne amongſt many brethren.

30 Moꝛeouer, whom he did pꝛedeſtinate, them he alſo called : and whom he called, them he alſo iuſtified : and whom he iuſtified, them he alſo gloꝛified.

31 What ſhall wee then ſay to theſe things? If God be foꝛ vs, who can bee againſt vs?

32 He that ſpared not his owne ſon, but deliuered him vp foꝛ vs all : how ſhall hee not with him alſo freely giue vs all things?

33 Who ſhall lay any thing to the charge of Gods elect? It is God that iuſtifieth :

34 Who is he that condemneth? It is Chriſt that died, yea rather that is riſen againe, who is euen at the right hand of God, who alſo maketh interceſſion foꝛ vs.

35 Who ſhall ſeparate vs from the loue of Chriſt? ſhall tribulation, oꝛ diſtreſſe, oꝛ perſecution, oꝛ famine, oꝛ nakedneſſe, oꝛ perill, oꝛ ſwoꝛd?

36 (As it is written,*foꝛ thy ſake we are killed all the day long, wee are accounted as ſheepe foꝛ the ſlaughter.)

37 Nay in all theſe things wee are moꝛe then conquerours, thꝛough him that loued vs.

38 Foꝛ I am perſwaded, that neither death, noꝛ life, noꝛ angels, noꝛ pꝛincipalities, noꝛ powers, noꝛ things pꝛeſent, noꝛ things to come,

39 Noꝛ height, noꝛ depth, noꝛ any other creature, ſhalbe able to ſeparate vs from the loue of God, which is in Chriſt Ieſus our Loꝛd.

CHAP. IX.

1 Paul is ſory for the Iewes. 7 All the ſeed of Abraham

Marginal notes:
‖Or, becauſe of his ſpirit.
‖Or, euery creature.
*Luke 21. 28.
*Pſal. 44. 22.
‖Or, that

Figure 12 King James Bible, 1611, 'The Epistle of Paul the Apostle to the Romans', Chapter 8, verses 9–39, Robert Barker

Folio, 43 cm. By permission of the Syndics of Cambridge University Library

This is the translation which, with some modifications, was most widely read in the Church of England until the 1960s, and is the version of the Bible for which many people today have a special affection. Often called the 'Authorized Version', it was actually never officially 'authorized', although described as such from 1620. In 1611 this was a contentious translation, and remained so until the late eighteenth century when it began to be valued as a 'literary monument'. The new edition was commissioned by James VI and I in 1604 as a result of petitioning by moderate Puritans within the Church of England who resented some aspects of liturgical language and ritual practised under Elizabeth. The terms on which the translation was to be made were very limiting. The copy text was to be the already unsatisfactory Bishops' Bible of 1568, and only errors were to be altered; Tyndale and Coverdale, and the Matthew, Great Bible, and Geneva versions might be consulted where the Bishops' Bible was faulty. Marginal glosses are discarded, first introduced into printed bibles by Luther with his 1522 New Testament, and continued by Tyndale; only cross-references or notes on literal and alternative senses are retained, and no distinction is made in the text between poetry and prose. Richard Bancroft, as acting Archbishop of Canterbury, selected 54 scholars drawn from Westminster College, Oxford and Cambridge; they were divided into six Companies each with specific selections of Books to complete and the final version was to be agreed by all the scholars involved. The King James Bible replaced the Geneva translation from 1644 only because the King's Printer and Cambridge University Press asserted their monopoly to print the 1611 text, despite the fact that the Geneva version was more helpful (and therefore more popular) and better produced in versions manufactured in Amsterdam. Appreciation of the 'literary' qualities of the King James Bible is largely a nineteenth-century phenomenon. During the seventeenth century the text was often criticized for its supposed inaccuracies. Hugh Broughton (1549–1612), the leading Hebrew scholar of the period, was forthright: 'Tell his Majesty that I had rather be rent in pieces with wild horses than any such translation by my consent should be urged upon poor Churches' (Norton 1993: 161). The 1611 Bible was designed to be read in public from a lectern and the main text is printed in black letter, by then a font used either as a display type on status documents such as decrees, proclamations and statutes, or in the cheapest balladsheets. Chapter summaries, page headings, and words added to the original text are in roman. The massive scale of the first edition presents the book as an item of 'church architecture' and the double-column boxes give the appearance of 'the text in corsets' (Norton 1993: 174). We do not know that this is the translation which Anne Clifford used, but reading Chapter 8 of Paul's Epistle to the Romans each Sunday would have confirmed the importance of a convinced spiritual life for her, and it may also have sustained her 'earnest expectation' which spent decades waiting for the 'manifestation' of God's judgement in the matter of her birthright inheritance.

Quotations from David Norton, *A History of the Bible as Literature*, Cambridge, Cambridge University Press, 1993, and for a more enthusiastic assessment of 1611, see *The Bible. Authorized King James Version*, with an introduction and notes by Robert Carroll and Stephen Prickett, Oxford, Oxford University Press, 1997, pp. xxiv–xxix.

> All this time my Lord was in London where he had all and infinite great resort coming to him. He went much abroad to Cocking, to Bowling Alleys, to Plays and Horse Races, & [was] commended by all the World. I stayed in the Countrey having many times a sorrowful & heavy Heart & being condemned by most folks because I would not consent to the Agreement, so as I may truly say, I am like an Owl in the Desert.[50]

But a mainstay was listening to readings from the Old Testament and theology. Works which may have been added to Anne Clifford's library at this time include Moore's *Map of Man's Mortality*, Hakewill's *Apology of the Power and Providence of God*, and Strode's *Anatomy of Mortality*.

There are interesting omissions from the Great Picture's library: no drama other than Jonson, no Milton (antipathetic politics?) and no Shakespeare, who may have been a deliberate omission: John, the thirteenth Baron Clifford (1435–61) was called 'The Butcher' because he was said to have mercilessly stabbed to death the 18-year-old Edmund, son of the Duke of York. This was a revenge killing, since York had killed John Clifford's father at the first battle of St Albans in the Wars of the Roses. In the penultimate scene of *The Second Part of King Henry VI*, Shakespeare portrayed 'Butcher' Clifford as a vengeful monster typifying the anarchy into which the nation was descending:

> Henceforth I will not have to do with pity:
> Meet I an infant of the house of York,
> Into as many gobbets will I cut it
> As wild Medea young Absytris did;
> In cruelty will I seek out my fame.[51]

Anne Clifford always denied that her ancestor was a dishonourable murderer, and this representation of her family was probably enough to disqualify Shakespeare's works from appearing in her dynastic portrait.

Both Dorset and Pembroke frequented the plays while Lady Anne was left to her own devices at home, and the players sought out Pembroke's patronage. Her sincere Calvinist faith may also have hardened her against the seductions of theatre (though not against Glecko). This might suggest that women of her status distinguished between participating in the pleasures of Court masque and attending the quite different drama of the professional players who were invited to perform at Court. There may also be an indication here of a significant distinction by gender among the Court hierarchy: husbands followed the theatre and cultivated artists while some wives found consolation in divinity, reading that could create strange potential alliances.[52]

Graham Parry points out a remarkable overlap between Anne Clifford's reading and that of the Leveller leader, William Walwyn, recorded at the same moment. In his pamphlet *Walwyn's Just Defence* (1649), the Leveller politician described a conversation which he shared after walking out of a feeble, irrelevant sermon. The weak ministry promoted thoughts about 'the wisdom of the heathen, how wise and able they were in those things unto which their knowledge did extend; and what pains they took to make men wise, virtuous, and good common-wealth's men'. Walwyn then described how he read judiciously in 'humane' (classical) authors:

but I used them always in their due place; being very studious all that time in the Scriptures, and other divine authors, as some of Mr Perkins' works, Mr Downham's divinity [which] I had, as it were, without book [by memory]. Also Doctor Hall's meditations, and vows, and his heaven upon earth, and those pieces annexed to Mr Hooker's *Ecclesiastical Polity*, hearing, and reading continually; using Seneca, Plutarch's *Lives*, and Charron *Of Human Wisdom*, as things of recreation, wherein I was both pleased, and profited.[53]

Reading could make strange links in the 1640s. While Anne Clifford guarded Pembroke's collections in Baynards Castle, Walwyn's (anonymous) tract *The Power of Love* was calling on its readers in the streets outside the castle to look about on the 'thousands of miserable, distressed, starved, imprisoned Christians', and compare them with the 'gallant bravery of multitudes of men and women abounding in all things that can be imagined'.[54] Yet the Leveller and the triple Countess had in common an appreciation of this entire range of theological and philosophical reading. Careful attention to the constituencies created by patronage, and to the reading preferences of individuals from very diverse, even opposed, ranks in mid-seventeenth century England reveals complex alliances of belief which would otherwise be difficult to comprehend. On matters that really touched her heart Anne Clifford may have shared more with Walwyn the Leveller than ever she did with her two Earl husbands.

8

'THE POWER OF SELF AT SUCH OVER-FLOWING TIMES'

The politics of literacy

'I never read it in any book, nor received it from any mouth': writing and revolt 1450–1650

Marlowe's Envy portrayed a resentment that was powerless and ignorant, but Shakespeare soon created a much more dangerous figure whose anti-intellectualism combined with outright sedition. In the turbulent fourth act of *King Henry VI Part 2* the Kentish revolutionary Jack Cade menaces London and threatens all established hierarchy. Shakespeare's Cade enters the stage accompanied by Dick the butcher, Smith the weaver, a sawyer and 'infinite numbers'. Addressing the 'good people' he offers a radical programme and articulates grievances that were widespread in the 1590s, a decade troubled by bad harvests, urban insurrection and food riots. Cade promises to cut inflation immediately, slashing the price of staple commodities – bread and beer – by more than a third. He will introduce comprehensive land reform by abolishing hated enclosures so that 'all the realm shall be in common'. But Cade's commonwealth will also be a monarchy, with himself king in a Land of Cockaigne: 'There shall be no money, all shall eat and drink on my score.' At this point, Cade's associates bring a schoolmaster before him, one who 'can write and read, and cast accompt' [is numerate]. Cade affects to be appalled by the clerk's skills:

CADE: O monstrous.
SMITH: We took him setting of boys' copies [devising pen exercises].
CADE: Here's a villain!
SMITH: H'as a book in his pocket with red letters in't.
CADE: Nay then, he is a conjurer.
DICK: Nay, he can make obligations and write court-hand.
CADE: I am sorry for't. The man is a proper man, of mine honour: unless I find him guilty, he shall not die. Come hither, sirrah, I must examine thee […] Dost thou use to write thy name? Or hast thou a mark to thyself, like an honest plain-dealing man?
CLERK: Sir, I thank God, I have been so well brought up that I can write my name.
ALL: He hath confessed: away with him! He's a villain and a traitor.
CADE: Away with him I say! Hang him with his pen and inkhorn about his neck.[1]

This calculated bigotry is depressingly familiar: Stalin's purge of the intellectuals, scholars forced to carry typewriters slung around their necks in the Maoist 'Cultural' Revolution, Cambodia's Khmer Rouge killing anyone who happened to wear glasses at Year Zero. This Cade exploits the resentment of men who feel themselves disadvantaged by their ignorance and he easily turns their suspicion of learning to violent hatred. Entering London he orders the destruction of every significant building – London Bridge, the Tower, the Inns of Court, and the burning of 'all the records of the realm'; if Broadcasting Centre had been there, he would have taken it first. These dangerous scenes inevitably catch the attention of the Master of the Revels and, perhaps anticipating his reaction, Cade's megalomania is consistently undercut by asides from some of his more sceptical followers who are perfectly capable of seeing through his pretensions. In a line that Brecht would have applauded, Smith the weaver observes that if the law is only to be what Cade pronounces, then it 'will be stinking law, for his breath stinks with eating toasted cheese'.

Yet for Cade the attack on feudal privilege, legitimized by the play's emphasis on popular grievances, is also an attack on the means of knowledge itself. Arriving in London, the rebels arrest Lord Say, the Chancellor, and bring him before Cade, who declares himself to be 'the besom [broom] that must sweep the court clean of such filth as thou art'. Cade begins his prosecution with Say's part in the loss of England's territories in France, but then his diatribe escalates unsettlingly:

> Thou hast most traitorously corrupted the youth of the realm in erecting a grammar school: and whereas, before, our forefathers had no other books but the score and the tally, thou hast caused printing to be used, and, contrary to the king, his crown, and dignity, thou hast built a paper-mill. It will be proved to thy face that thou has men about thee that usually talk of a noun and a verb, and such abominable words as no Christian ear can endure to hear. Thou hast appointed justices of peace, to call poor men before them about matters they were not able to answer. Moreover, thou hast put them in prison; and, because they could not read, thou hast hanged them; when indeed, only for that cause, they have been most worthy to live.[2]

Cade's speech is simultaneously absurd and terrifying, a delirious crescendo which assaults the material bases of all knowledge – schools, paper, print, grammar itself (he is also visionary, or anachronistic: printing and paper production were not to be established in England for several decades). How could this speech be used in performance? There is almost certainly some joking turned against playwrights and the intellectual free-booters in the audience, a sardonic humour which mocks the means of its own advancement: the grammar schools and universities were already producing 'superfluous men' educated 'above' themselves and their station. But there are other, darker elements. Shakespeare seems to have combined accounts of the earlier 'Peasants' Revolt' of 1381 with Cade's rebellion of 1450 so that more representation is given to the grievances of the commons, and on stage the scenes have been produced to elicit this sympathy, and even present Cade's radical opportunism in a favourable light. But Cade's populism is surely sinister, appealing to a dim-witted nostalgia for simpler times when robust men were not betrayed by sophisticated exploitation. His emphasis that specifically 'Christian' ears are offended by 'abominable words' such as 'noun' and 'verb' aligns his hate-speech with all the outraged rhetoric aimed at the Jews who, throughout the Renaissance, were routinely portrayed as the epitome of super-subtle exploitation and the antithesis of Christian values. Yet his tirade is mixed with genuine grievance: men have been hanged simply because of their illiteracy, that is to say because they could not gain 'Benefit of Clergy' by reading the 'neck verse', Psalm 51, verse one (see above, Chapter 2). The judge passing sentence on two men arrested for breaking into the Earl of Sussex's house in 1613 made just this fatal discrimination, 'The said Paul reads, to be branded; the said William does not read, to be hanged.' Cade's example of the power of literacy to revoke execution could not be a clearer demonstration of his general case that the ability to read had become a matter of life and death.

There are multiple levels of dissimulation and irony at work in the scene. Cade is in fact the creature of the Duke of York in Shakespeare's narrative, promoted as part of the Duke's own insurrection against the King; the commons are being co-opted into a larger power game which is just as merciless and self-seeking as their own, but much more effective. And even as some of the commoners see through Cade's posturing, he himself has to act out his role against his better nature: Say's plea for mercy does touch him, but Cade tells himself that Say 'shall die, [if only for] pleading so well for his life'.[3] Can we imagine the relevance of this strange, obsessive material for Elizabethan play-goers? It may be that Cade's attack on the engines of literacy and the persuasive effect of noble rhetoric strengthened the London audience's growing awareness that literacy was now inextricably woven into the social fabric at every level, a potential for each individual and for every act of administration. Two-thirds of the population could not read or write in 1590, and for another century this might not be a serious disadvantage, but the future certainly lay in talk of nouns and verbs.

Shakespeare's stage-revolutionary struck attitudes against books and learning, but the political radicals of the 1640s were committed to literacy and utterly alert to its potency: printed argument and propaganda would contribute vitally to every future revolutionary moment, in 1642 and even more so in 1776 and 1789. Gerrard Winstanley (1609–76), a leader of the Digger movement, made a heroic attempt to deliver Cade's promise that 'all the realm shall be in common'. Winstanley came from a dissenting Lancashire family of the middling sort and was apprenticed to the London cloth trade in 1630, but by 1643 he had been 'beaten out of both estate and trade' by the disrupted times and was reduced to working as a hired farm labourer. Radicalized by the Civil Wars and his dissenting faith, in 1648 he began publishing anti-clerical pamphlets which argued for the right of anyone to preach, regardless of their education or status. On Sunday 1 April 1649 Winstanley was one of the leading spirits in the occupation of St George's Hill, Walton-on-Thames, by a collective of Diggers who began to cultivate the parish common in a symbolic protest against private ownership of the land. The Digger community on St George's Hill only survived on its eleven acres for a year but it had expressed nation-wide resentments and aspirations for the landless majority. The Diggers intended to uproot tithes, lawyers' fees and prisons, and plant 'the pleasant fruit trees of freedom in the room [place] of that cursed thornbush, the power of the murdering sword'. Their labour of levelling and digging was to be physical and metaphorical, the tending of crops and simultaneously the nurture of social freedoms.

On 20 December 1649, in the middle of the occupation, when 'those diggers that remain have made little hutches to lie in like calf-cribs, and are cheerful', Winstanley described his relationship to writing and the sources of his inspiration:

Sometimes my heart hath been full of deadness and uncomfortableness, wading like a man in the dark and slabby weather; and within a little time I have been filled with such peace, light, life and fulness, that if I had had two pair of hands, I had matter enough revealed to have kept them writing a long time....Then I took the opportunity of the spirit and writ, and the power of self at such over-flowing times was so prevalent in me, that I forsook my ordinary food whole days together, and if my household-friends would persuade me to come to meat, I have been forced with that inward fulness of the power of life to rise up from the table and leave them to God, to write. Thus I have been called in from my ordinary labour, and the society of friends sometimes hath been a burden to me, and best I was when I was alone. I was so filled with that love and delight in the life-within that I have sat writing whole winter days from morning till night and the cold never offended me, though when I have risen I was so stark with cold that I was forced to rise by degrees and hold by the table, till strength and heat came into my legs, and I have been secretly sorry when night came, which forced me to rise. The joy of that sweet anointing was so precious and satisfactory within my spirit that I could truly say, 'O that I had a tabernacle builded here, That I might never know or seek any other frame of spirit.'[4]

Winstanley's inspiration begins in a divine ecstasy of light and flowing, a sense of plenitude which informs writing itself as a joy, but this is swiftly de-coupled from its merely sacred source. More compelling than cold, hunger and the claims of society, Winstanley's involvement in his composition is only brought to an end by darkness, and his lack of means to continue. In mid-seventeenth century passages such as this, writing and self-possession seem to be removing themselves from the religious ground in which they began, in order to construct new possibilities for the 'frame of the spirit' by turning from the ecstasy of composition to the social world. Not long before setting down this passage, Winstanley had confirmed his revolutionary motive, utterly at odds with early modern assumptions about the conventional sources of knowledge and authority: 'all that I have writ concerning the matter of digging, I never read it in any book, nor received it from any mouth'.[5] No boy was taught such offensive attitudes in any early modern schoolroom, this dangerous enthusiasm of the sectary who turns his rapture from God to the world. 'Digging' is the sowing of crops, the overthrow of oppressive law, and the self-confidence of an unemployed farm labourer to write, against the entire weight of his culture's conventions.

'Mob' (1691): 'The common mass of people; the lower orders; the uncultured or illiterate as a class; the populace, the masses'

The developments in education and the growth of a print culture between 1590 and 1700 were crucial aspects of more general economic change and were in turn promoted by the fundamentally religious ethos of the period. This burgeoning literacy broadly affected English society in three ways. First, the political and economic male elite increasingly shared similar cultural values through studying at grammar school, university and Inns of Court, a knowledge generally regarded as refined accomplishment rather than professional competence. Mid-sixteenth-century participation in higher education among the male gentry was around 50 per cent, but 100 years later had increased to over 80 per cent. These cultural assumptions were then gradually domesticated: the Grand Tour of Europe, sometimes lasting several years, became an obligatory part of any cultivated person's education – Milton's travels, mostly in Italy from 1637 to 1639, were not untypical. The number of private libraries in gentry households grew, with religious works predominating in the collections; individual men (and some women) began to make significant contributions to learning as antiquaries and 'virtuosi', following scientific development, debating constitutional issues, and participating in the world of polite letters. And from the mid-seventeenth century families of the 'middling sort' also began to aspire to these new manners of their immediate superiors and sought to distance themselves via 'refinement' from what they considered to be the coarser attitudes and beliefs of people 'below' them. The rate of publication increased dramatically and the categories of book diversified to meet new reading interests and fulfil aspirations.[6]

Second, while education consolidated the culture of the nobility and gentry, and created fresh aspirations in the towns, literacy began to spread beyond the middling sort to urban artisans and then into the villages and hamlets, bringing other developments. Town-dwellers were much more likely to be readers and writers than were the majority of the population living in the countryside, and urban women may have been the group which most dramatically increased its literacy, but there was now a significant minority of rural workers – copyholders, day labourers, both men and women – who participated in the culture of print, generally more often as readers than writers. At this level of society the stories, songs and sayings which formerly circulated as oral, customary culture were transformed: from the 1620s onwards stationers catered for this new and growing readership with ballads, romances, chapbooks, almanacs, jest books and prints in tens of thousands of cheap copies. The conventions of customary, semi-literate culture (which were already to an extent informed by materials from printed text) were further recast in the form of literary genres to produce the beginnings of a print-based common culture in a host of different guises, with devotional works continuing as a significant proportion of the materials.

Third, while the population expanded and society as a whole grew in prosperity and became more economically integrated, there was a widening of the wealth-gap between those whom opportunity favoured and others who were falling victim to the new times; inevitably the unliterate were among the most vulnerable. Some historians argue that the customs and beliefs characteristic of preliterate society were denigrated and marginalized by people seeking respectability, and from the late seventeenth century the more familiar outlines of an urban, class-based society began to emerge, displacing the world of rank and degree described in Chapter 2. The vigorous policing of urban vice by the religiously motivated 'Societies for the Reformation of Manners' that sprang up in London and other cities from the mid-1680s was one response to this moral panic over the behaviour of the destitute and desperate urban poor. The Societies were a new incarnation of the moral oversight of the lower orders that had previously been exercised by the Church Courts and godly magistrates of the pre-Civil War towns and burghs, but they were responding to what was perceived to be a new challenge.[7] The slow but inexorable spread of literacy was a crucial element in this growing complexity of English society, enabling some, disadvantaging others. Literacy as such is value-free, but through its medium many individuals in those classes now discovering reading and writing found a friend, a true glass and a power of self for their over-flowing times.

9

A CONSTANT REGISTER OF PUBLIC FACTS 1589–1662

Compilation of genealogies, biographies and curiosities was a feature of the period, as in the proposal of 1626 made by a group of courtiers and antiquaries for 'A Constant Register' which would enshrine 'the history of our country' in a 'grave and free authentic text' (Portal 1916). This 'chronology' (first recorded word-use 1593) provides a skeleton narrative of significant political and constitutional developments, followed by a selection of publications, performances and choice details for each year from 1589 to 1662. The year is given from 1 January, rather than from 25 March, Lady Day, which was the practice in the period; authors are listed alphabetically by surname and work(s). Entries for drama rely largely on Alfred Harbage, *Annals of English Drama 975–1700* (1989). Nearly all dates for composition and performance of plays are conjectural – the precise chronology of Shakespeare's work for example is very much open to debate; we might assume that he was contracted to write two plays each year.

1589   Government issues Proclamation against seditious printers in response to the Martin Marprelate tracts, vigorous satires attacking the bishops. Probably written by the Warwickshire MP Job Throckmorton, their publishers arrested and tortured.

Jane Anger [pseudonym?], *Her Protection for Women*. Richard Hakluyt, *The Principal Voyages*. Thomas Kyd, *The Spanish Tragedy*. Christopher Marlowe, *The Jew of Malta*. George Puttenham, *The Art of English Poesy*. Shakespeare probably writes *The Two Gentlemen of Verona*.

1590   Anti-Puritan campaign continues vigorously.

Shakespeare, *I, II Henry VI*. Sir Philip Sidney, *The Countess of Pembroke's Arcadia* (unauthorized edition). Edmund Spenser, *The Faerie Queene* I–III. Births: Lady Anne Clifford.

1591   Thomas Cartwright and other leading Puritans brought before Star Chamber, committed to prison for eighteen months. Commissioners appointed to search for recusant (Catholic) priests in all shires.

Anon. (Thomas Kyd?), *Arden of Faversham*. Byrd, *Cantiones sacrae* II. Shakespeare, *III Henry VI*, *King John*. William Perkins, *The Golden Chain*, reprinted twelve times by 1600. Sidney, *Astrophil and Stella*. Births: Robert Herrick.

1592   Plague endemic in many areas until 1594. Scottish witchcraft trials. Approximately 2,000 individuals were tried in England 1560–1706, many fewer than in Scotland or

Europe; the suspects were 93 per cent female, generally labourers' wives from the poorest level of society, of whom 300 were executed.

Samuel Daniel, *Delia*. Marlowe, *Dr Faustus*, *Edward II*. Thomas Nashe, *Pierce Penniless*, *Summer's Last Will and Testament*. Shakespeare, *The Comedy of Errors*, *Richard III*, *The Taming of the Shrew*, *Henry VI, Part One*, *Titus Andronicus*. Mary Sidney, Countess of Pembroke, translates *Antonius* by Robert Garnier, and *A Discourse of Life and Death* by Philippe de Mornay. Elizabeth incorporates Trinity College, Dublin as centre of Protestant learning. Summer closure of theatres because of apprentice riots. Plague kills 15,000 in London: an estimated 660,000 deaths in Britain from plague 1570–1670.

1593 Successive harvest failures until 1598. Act against recusants confines them to within five miles of their residence: 123 Jesuit missionary priests are executed during Elizabeth's reign by hanging, drawing and quartering.

John Donne 'Satires' circulating in ms(?). Michael Drayton, *Idea*. Richard Hooker, *The Laws of Ecclesiastical Polity*. Marlowe, *The Massacre at Paris*. Thomas Nashe, *The Terrors of the Night*, *The Choice of Valentines* (?). Shakespeare, *The Two Gentlemen of Verona*; publication of *Venus and Adonis*, dedicated to Henry Wriothesley, the third Earl of Southampton; fifteen more editions by 1640, 'over ten thousand copies in a decade, which would make it the best-selling poem of the Elizabethan age' (Bate 1997: 20): beginning of the composition of the *Sonnets*? Authorized folio edition of Sidney's *Arcadia*. *The Phoenix Nest* (anthology). Births: George Herbert, Nicolas Poussin, Izaak Walton. Deaths: Marlowe, stabbed 30 May in Deptford.

1594 Nine Years' War in Ireland begins with Tyrone-Tyrconnell rebellion.

Thomas Nashe, *The Unfortunate Traveller* and Shakespeare, *The Rape of Lucrece*, both dedicated to Earl of Southampton.

1595 Food riots and apprentice disorders in London provoke martial law. Eight Spanish galleys burn Penzance and locality. English force defeated by Tyrone at Clontibret.

George Chapman, *Ovid's Banquet of Sense*. Anthony Munday, Thomas Dekker, Henry Chettle and Shakespeare (?), *Sir Thomas More*, censored by Edmund Tilney, Master of the Revels, revised by Shakespeare (?). Shakespeare, *Love's Labours Lost*, *Richard II*. Deaths: Thomas Kyd (?), Robert Southwell tortured and executed, Torquato Tasso.

1596 October: an invasion fleet of 100 ships and 16,000 men leave Ferrol, but is dispersed by storms. Spain captures Calais, Cadiz is sacked by the English.

Thomas Nashe, *Have With You to Saffron Walden*. Shakespeare, *The Merchant of Venice*, *A Midsummer Night's Dream*, *Romeo and Juliet*. Spenser, *Four Hymns* (dedicated to Margaret Russell Clifford, mother of Anne Clifford). Gresham College founded. Births: René Descartes. Deaths: Hamnet Shakespeare, age 11 years 6 months, twin to Judith (died 1662).

1597 October: invasion fleet of 136 ships and 9,000 men sailing from Ferrol again dispersed by storms. Continuing conflict in Ireland. A wet summer and another poor harvest.

Francis Bacon, *Essays*. Joseph Hall, *Virgidemiarum sex libri* [*Six Books of Lashes*], part of the season of satires (see 1599). James VI of Scotland, *Demonology*. Ben Jonson and

Thomas Nashe, *The Isle of Dogs*, now lost, but probably a satire on the court, provokes closure of the theatres late July to October. Shakespeare, *I & II Henry IV*, *The Merry Wives of Windsor*, *Richard II* printed omitting the deposition scene.

1598 4 August: death of William Cecil, Lord Burghley, Elizabeth's most trusted minister from her accession in 1558.

Chapman, *Seven Books of Homer's Illiad*. John Florio, *A World of Words*. James VI of Scotland, *The True Law of Free Monarchies*. Ben Jonson, *Every Man in his Humour* (Shakespeare in the cast). Marlowe, *Hero and Leander*. Shakespeare, *Much Ado about Nothing*. Sidney, *Works* in folio, a precedent for substantial editions of contemporary literary authors.

1599 The Earl of Essex heads the largest army to have left the country in Elizabeth's reign –16,000 foot soldiers and 1,300 cavalry – to Ireland, but his pacification campaign fails and he returns in disgrace.

James VI of Scotland, *Basilikon Doron* [*The King's Gift*]. Jonson, *Every Man out of his Humour*. Shakespeare, *As You Like It*, *Henry V*, *Julius Caesar*. June: Archbishop Whitgift issues injunctions forbidding further printing of satires, part of the government's efforts to protect Essex. The censorship is ineffective and satires reappear within two years.

1600 London now embraces 130 parishes, 250,000 people, one-twentieth of the population. Extensive fighting in Munster lead by the Earl of Tyrone. Formation of the East India Company.

William Gilbert, *De Magnete*. Will Kemp dances from London to Norwich. William Adams is the first known Englishman to reach Japan. Births: Charles, second son of James VI and Anne of Denmark.

1601 Commons vociferously demand the reform of the sale of monopolies during Elizabeth's final Parliament; growing disenchantment with the administration's failure to reform finances. Spanish troops land at Kinsale, Ireland and are defeated. February: Earl of Essex and 200 followers attempt to raise London against the Queen. Execution of Essex.

Jonson, *Poetaster*. Thomas Morley, *Triumphs of Oriana*. Shakespeare, *Hamlet*, *Twelfth Night, or What You Will*.

1602

Shakespeare *Troilus and Cressida*.

1603 24 March: death of Elizabeth, age 70, having ruled 44 years. Accession of James I (James VI of Scotland), age 37. Presentation of Millenary Petition (signed by 1,000 ministers) to James by disaffected Puritan clergy, objecting to pluralism, non-residence and ministers' failure to preach. Capitulation of Tyrone in Ireland.

Irish Gaelic New Testament, *Tiomna Nuadh ár Dtighearna* published in Dublin, commissioned by Elizabeth in the mid-1560s. Michel de Montaigne, *The Essays Or Moral, Politic and Military Discourses* translated by John Florio. Shakespeare, *All's Well That Ends Well*. Deaths: Gráinne O'Malley.

1604 January, Hampton Court conference between the bishops and Puritan clergy seeking reform, presided over by James. James presses his case for the union of his two kingdoms as 'Great Britain', resisted by the Commons. Peace signed with Spain after twenty years' hostilities. Increasing Scottish settlement of north-east Ireland.

Elizabeth Carey, *Mariam, the Fair Queen of Jewry*, a Senecan closet tragedy. Daniel, *Vision of the Twelve Goddesses* at Court, Queen Anne playing Pallas Athena, encouraging female participation in masques. Elizabeth Grymeston, *Miscelanea* (the first of six mother's advice books in the period). Marston, *The Malcontent*. Middleton, *The Black Book*. Shakespeare, *Measure for Measure, Othello*.

1605 November: the Catholic Gunpowder Plot attempts to destroy Parliament at the opening of the new session.

Francis Bacon, *Advancement of Learning*. Jonson, *The Masque of Blackness*. Middleton, *A Trick to Catch the Old One*. Shakespeare, *The Tragedy of King Lear*. Miguel de Cervantes begins *Don Quixote*, completed 1615.

1606 Severe anti-Catholic legislation in response to the Gunpowder Plot.

Jonson, *Hymenaei, Volpone*. Middleton, *A Mad World, My Masters*. Shakespeare, *Macbeth*. Middleton?, *The Revenger's Tragedy*. Births: William Davenant (who claimed to be Shakespeare's illegitimate son).

1607 September: the 'Flight of the Earls' Hugh O'Donnell of Tyrconnell and Hugh O'Neill of Tyrone from Ireland to avoid arrest, followed by increasing exodus of Irish Catholic elite to Europe. Agrarian unrest in English Midlands, the first references to 'Levellers' and 'Diggers'.

Beaumont *The Woman Hater*, (with John Fletcher?) *The Knight of the Burning Pestle*. Shakespeare, *Antony and Cleopatra, Timon of Athens* (not acted?).

1608 Royal finances in crisis with estimated annual deficit of £75,000. Bate's Case finds in favour of the monarch being able to tax trade at his prerogative.

Jonson, *The Masque of Beauty*. Shakespeare, *Coriolanus*, (and as reviser) *Pericles*.

1609 Beginning of mass colonization of Ulster by 40,000 English and Scottish settlers, London livery companies heavily involved. Derry renamed Londonderry.

Jonson, *Epicoene, The Masque of Queens*. Shakespeare, *Cymbeline*.

1610 Lord Treasurer Salisbury proposes the Great Contract, a comprehensive attempt to solve the deficit in royal finances, resisted by both Commons and factions in Court. Plantations – settlements – established in Leinster and Leitrim.

Beaumont and Fletcher, *The Maid's Tragedy*. Jonson, *The Alchemist*. Shakespeare, *The Winter's Tale*.

1611 After failure of the Great Contract, Salisbury extends sources of royal revenue through sale of titles, rationalization of land rents, and other resented innovations.

Dekker and Middleton, *The Roaring Girl*. Jonson, *Catiline*. Shakespeare, *The Tempest*. Spenser, *Works* in folio.

1612   Death of Prince Henry from typhoid aged 18.
   John Taylor the 'Water Poet', *The Sculler,* the first of more than 150 pamphlets and chapbooks to 1653. Webster, *The White Devil.*

1613   Marriage of Princess Elizabeth to Frederick Elector Palatine of the Rhine, leader of the German Protestant Union.
   Middleton, *A Chaste Maid in Cheapside, The Witch.* Shakespeare (and Fletcher?), *Henry VIII (All Is True).* Shakespeare, Fletcher (and Beaumont?), *The Two Noble Kinsmen.*

1614   The Addled Parliament fails to resolve tensions between Commons and James.
   Jonson, *Bartholomew Fair.* Sir Thomas Overbury, *Characters.* Sir Walter Ralegh, *History of the World.* Webster, *The Duchess of Malfi.*

1615
   Jonson, *The Golden Age Restored.* Births: Richard Baxter, John Denham.

1616   George Villiers created Duke of Buckingham, James's final favourite. Trial of Frances Howard and the Earl of Somerset for the murder of Sir Thomas Overbury.
   Cervantes, *Don Quixote* (1605, 1615, trans. Thomas Shelton). Chapman, *The Whole Works of Homer.* Jonson, *The Devil Is an Ass, Works* in folio. Construction of Inigo Jones's Queen's House, Greenwich (to 1618). Deaths: Francis Beaumont, Hugh O'Neill Earl of Tyrone, William Shakespeare.

1617   Villiers promoted to Earl and then Marquis of Buckingham.
   Rachel Speght, *A Mouzell for Melastomus.* Ben Jonson created Poet Laureate, though the position is only made official in 1668 with Dryden's nomination.

1618   Royal debt of £900,000, the greatest ever in peace time; further revelations of high corruption at court. Outbreak of the Thirty Years' War in Europe precipitated by James's son-in-law Frederick accepting the crown of Bohemia in defiance of the Holy Roman Emperor Ferdinand. Execution of Ralegh as part of James's overtures to Spain. James issues the *Book of Sports,* authorizing named entertainments after Sunday service (see 1633).
   Anon., *Swetnam the Woman-Hater Arraigned by Women.*

1619   First slave shipments to Virginia.
   Johannes Kepler, *Harmony of the World.* Inigo Jones begins construction of Banqueting House, Whitehall (to 1622).

1620   The collapse of the European Protestant cause after the defeat of Frederick by Spanish and Austrian Catholic forces led by the Holy Roman Emperor at the Battle of White Mountain. Widespread (anti-Catholic) feeling against the court in the country. The Mayflower sails for America.
   Anon., *Hic Mulier* and *Haec-Vir,* pamphlets attacking and defending a current fashion for women to dress as men. Bacon, *Novum Organum.*

1621 England enters the severest economic depression of the century. James's third Parliament is called to raise revenue for war preparations. The Commons mounts a sustained campaign against the abuse of monopolies and patents, and calls for the ending of negotiations with Spain over Prince Charles's marriage. James dissolves Parliament in a fury.

Robert Burton, *The Anatomy of Melancholy*. Middleton, *Women Beware Women* (?). Lady Mary Wroth, *The Countess of Montgomery's Urania*, including as an appendix *Pamphilia to Amphilanthus*, the first extended sonnet sequence written by a woman in English. 24 September: the first 'newspaper' printed in England.

1622 Intense anti-Catholic sentiments in the country. Proclamation forbids discussion of all contentious matters in religion. Economic depression is intensified by harvest failures and famine in the north-west.

Drayton, *Poly-Olbion*. Middleton and Rowley, *The Changeling*.

1623 Prince Charles and the Duke of Buckingham quixotically leave for Spain (as 'the Smith brothers') in an attempt to resolve marriage negotiations.

Mr William Shakespeare's Comedies, Histories, & Tragedies. Published according to the True Original Copies, the First Folio. Births: Margaret Cavendish, Duchess of Newcastle. Deaths: William Byrd, William Camden, Mrs Anne Shakespeare.

1624 James's fourth Parliament. In exchange for Parliament's support of a military expedition against Spain, the Statute of Monopolies is passed.

Donne, *Devotions upon Emergent Occasions*. Middleton's *A Game at Chess* satirizes Prince Charles's failed marriage negotiations in Spain; the play is a sensation, banned by Privy Council. A royal Proclamation forbids the printing or importation of books discussing religion or politics without approval. Captain John Smith, *The General History of Virginia*. Formation of a syndicate within the Stationers' Company to control the ownership of the lucrative ballad stock: the burgeoning country-wide market in chapbooks is distributed through their network of itinerant peddlars (chapmen).

1625 27 March: death of James, accession of Charles I, who 'must rank among the most inept of English kings' (Hirst 1986: 137). He marries Princess Henrietta Maria, daughter of Henry IV of France, and sister of Louis XIII, and grants extensive liberties of worship to Catholics; the Queen is allowed to continue a Catholic and bring up her children in the faith. The Commons refuse to vote Charles adequate subsidy for the war with Spain; from this point the division over religious differences increases sharply.

Massinger, *A New Way to Pay Old Debts*. John Milton admitted to Christ's College. Nicholas Ferrar establishes an Anglican community at Little Gidding, Huntingdonshire.

1626 Charles's second Parliament. Demand for the impeachment of Lord Admiral Buckingham. In response Charles dissolves Parliament and raises a forced loan to finance the war effort. William Laud emerges as Charles's closest adviser in church politics. Beginning of 'Western Rising' to 1632, resistance by poor cottagers against royal sales of woodlands.

Francis Bacon, *New Atlantis*. Jonson, *The Staple of News*. The Dutch West India Company buys the island of Manhattan from native chiefs for the equivalent of $24.

1627   The Five Knights' Case is brought against individuals refusing to pay Charles's forced loan: the judiciary endorse the monarch's right to imprison without showing reasons and to raise finance without Parliament's agreement. The loan is financially successful. Charles makes over the last significant area of Crown lands to the City in exchange for cancellation of his debts. 'He thereby ended the traditional role of land as a major source of royal revenue, and with it, it might be said, the medieval monarchy' (Hirst 1986: 148). Eighteen hundred persons are employed by Charles as members of the Royal Household, consuming over 40 per cent of total expenditure.

   Bacon, *Sylva Sylvarum, New Atlantis.*

1628   Charles's third Parliament. June: the Commons presents the Petition of Right which declares the arbitrary imposition of taxes and imprisonment without good cause to be illegal. August: the assassination of Buckingham, and the beginning of the eleven years of Charles's 'personal rule', exercised largely through William Laud (Archbishop of Canterbury 1633) and Sir Thomas Wentworth (Earl of Strafford 1640). A mounting sense of division between the court versus the City and country.

   William Harvey, *Exercitatio Anatomica de Motu Cordis* (Frankfurt) establishes the principle of circulation of the blood. Significant increase in manuscript copies of major parliamentary speeches circulating among the minor gentry in the country.

1629   Peace with France after a pointless and expensive conflict.

   Lancelot Andrewes, *XCVI Sermons.* Richard Brome, *The Northern Lass.* Jonson, *The New Inn.*

1630   Socio-economic crisis and plague. The Great Migration to Massachusetts begins – nearly 16,000 individuals by 1640 – and the consistent development of colonial enterprises in New England and the West Indies. Queen Henrietta Maria becomes the single greatest influence on the King. Masque is institutionalized as favourite court entertainment.

   Richard Brome, *The City Wit.* Diana Primrose, *A Chain of Pearl.* Boston, New England, founded.

1631   Lord Chief Justice drafts a Book of Orders, regularizing the work of JPs in the localities, one aspect of Charles's ordering and centralizing of administration in response to the disorders of 1629–30.

   Philip Massinger, *Believe As You List.* Shirley, *The Traitor.*

1632   Wentworth created Lord Deputy of Ireland, where he comes to be known as 'Black Tom Tyrant', resented by the New English, Old English and indigenous Irish alike for his policy of 'Thorough', a slogan he shares with Laud.

   T. E., *The Law's Resolution of Women's Rights.* Jonson, *The Magnetic Lady.* William Montagu, *The Shepherd's Paradise*, masque in which Henrietta Maria participates. William Prynne, *Histrio-Mastix.* Shirley, *Hyde Park.* Van Dyck appointed 'principal Painter to their majesties'. Proliferation of print shops in London, catering for growing demand for engravings among the urban middling sort. October: the Privy Council in Star Chamber forbids the publication of all news-books to prevent the reporting of the victories of Gustavus Adolphus. The Second Folio of Shakespeare's works, including 'An Epitaph on the admirable Dramatic Poet', generally thought to be one of Milton's earliest poems: two reissues, perhaps made as late as 1640.

1633   Charles nominates Laud as Archbishop of Canterbury. Laud works for a major reversal of Reformation theology and practices, valuing the place of the sacraments above the giving of sermons, favouring the altar above the pulpit, and reverence rather than godly fervour. He concerns himself with 'the beauties of holiness' and so appeals to the 'ceremonialist' aspect of Charles's character. Charles re-issues his father's 1618 Proclamation authorizing specific entertainments after Sunday services, an attempt to strengthen the Laudian ideal of a dignified Church tied to customary culture of seasonal festivals, which were in fact in gradual decline (Hutton 1994: 198–201).
   Donne, *Poems*. George Herbert, *The Temple*. Milton, *Arcades*. Spenser, *A View of the Present State of Ireland*, completed in 1596, is published.

1634   Charles exercises his right to raise Ship Money, a tax on coastal towns and counties for protection against sea raiders and pirates, now troublesome. The collection is efficient and legitimately committed to naval expenses.
   Michaelmas Night, Ludlow Castle, *A Masque...presented...Before the Earl of Bridgewater*, Milton's *Comus*, with music written by Henry Lawes. Thomas Carew *Coelum Britannicum*. Star Chamber fines William Prynne £5,000 for *Histrio-Mastix* and imprisons him for life. Privy Council requires licensing of all almanacs.

1635   Ship Money is extended to inland regions and becomes a notorious example of the ways in which the King increased his rights over taxation. Monopolies are extended to include salt, starch, bricks. Annual royal income now greater than expenditure.
   Brome, *The New Academy, or The New Exchange*. Francis Quarles, *Emblems Divine and Moral*. The maypole at Cerne Abbas is chopped down and used to construct a ladder, one instance of the struggle over seasonal festivities in the localities (Hutton 1994: 198).

1636   The Ship Money levy continues to be widely complied with. 'About that time, abundance of the Godly Transported themselves into...America, for Conscience' sake, to enjoy the Gospel...without the imposition of men' (Edward Terrill). Plague summer.
   Sir Thomas Browne, *Religio Medici*.

1637   John Hampden and Lord Saye and Sele bring a case to test the legality of Ship Money, and the judges find narrowly by seven to five in favour of the tax. But by 1640 the collection effectively collapses. Charles attempts to impose a new form of the Prayer Book in Edinburgh churches.
   René Descartes, *Discours de la Méthode* (Leyden). Milton, *A Masque* (*Comus*) published. Sir John Suckling *Aglaura*. 24 January: *Hamlet* given at Hampton Court. Rubens paints the ceilings of the Banqueting House, Whitehall. Prompted by Laud, Star Chamber limits the number of printers to twenty-three and type founders to four throughout the country. The Act loses its force when the Star Chamber is abolished in 1641.

1638   Nearly universal refusal of payment of Ship Money. In Scotland almost one-third of the clergy and nobility sign the National Covenant which commits them to defending their church against Laud and Charles.

Charles plans a huge palace at Whitehall under the direction of Inigo Jones, intended to be the envy of Europe. Milton travels in Europe, 'Lycidas' published.

1639 March: First Scottish (Bishops') War; Charles has again to reach accommodation with the Covenanters and is obliged to capitulate in the Pacification of Berwick treaty.

August: Milton returns to England and writes 'Epitaphium Damonis', his last poem for a number of years.

1640 April: the Short Parliament meets for three weeks, united against the King, and is dissolved. Apprentice riots break out in London against Laudian churches. August: the Second Bishops' War: Charles's disorderly army is routed by the Covenanters, who take Newcastle and occupy the borders. The City refuses all loans to the King. October: peace is signed on terms humiliating to Charles.

> Events and aspirations in Scotland and Ireland, two polities much less committed to polite assumptions of consensus, imposed their own momentum, to more devastating effect than had the European struggles of the 1620s. The outlying kingdoms at last took their revenge for decades of subordination.
>
> (Hirst 1986: 188)

3 November: the Long Parliament, sitting until 1660.

21 January: Inigo Jones and Davenant, *Salmacida Spolia*, the final, and most elaborate of the Court masques given at Whitehall. Donne, *LXXX Sermons*. 3 November: Star Chamber is abolished, leading (temporarily) to a free trade in printing; existing rights in publications everywhere infringed.

1641 16 February: the Triennial Act, the first reforming statute of the Long Parliament, requiring the automatic assembly and election of Parliament every three years. Bills to abolish Star Chamber, the Court of High Commission, the Council of the North and the episcopacy are prepared. 3 May: the Army Plot attempts to free Strafford from the Tower: in response the Commons issues the Protestation Oath, to be signed throughout the country by all males aged 18 and above, pledging in effect to resist any form of coup. Charles fears for his family's safety as huge crowds demonstrate outside Whitehall palace. 12 May: Strafford executed. June–July: in a series of measures which form a constitutional revolution, severe limits are placed upon royal powers and prerogatives, including the abolition of Ship Money, knighthood fines, and the further extension of forest rights. Charles attempts to organize the second Army Plot. August–September: Parliament effectively governs in the King's absence while he travels north to join his army and treat with the Covenanters. Severe polarization between radicals and conservatives in the Commons; the parliamentary leaders are caught between the two groups; feverish, disorderly months in London. October: the Grand Remonstrance, an extensive denunciation and indictment of Charles and his advisers. Fearful of a Puritan government in England, a Catholic uprising in Ireland (with significant leadership from Old English rebels) attempts to capture Dublin Castle and attacks New English and Scottish settlers in Ulster; reciprocal atrocities follow, provoking anti-Catholic hysteria in England and the Commons. December: political revolution through municipal elections installing a radical majority in London.

Brome, *A Jovial Crew*, (comedy, Beeston's Boys: playing when the theatres were closed). Katherine Chidley, *The Justification of the Independent Churches of Christ*. Milton, *Of Reformation*. John Amos Comenius arrives in England, invited by a group of supporters of Parliament to encourage reform of education.

1642   4 January: Charles, plotting a coup, attempts to arrest the five leading opposition members: Pym, Hampden, Haselrig, Holles and Strode. 10 January: fearing mob assault, he leaves Whitehall, not returning until 1648 for trial and execution. Serious disturbances in London: 'roundhead', 'prickears' (for parliamentarians) and 'rattlehead' (for cavaliers) are now common forms of abuse. 'Everywhere men sought an escape into neutralism' (Hirst 1986: 223). 22 August: the King raises his standard at Nottingham. 23 October: Battle of Edgehill, decisive for neither side. 12 November: Prince Rupert is prevented from taking London at Turnham Green. The royalist party occupies Oxford as their head-quarters. The north is secured for the King by the Marquis of Newcastle, and the south-west by Ralph Hopton. The Earl of Essex is appointed to lead the parliamentary armies.

The theatres are closed, re-opening at the Restoration in 1660, but clandestine and private ('closet') performances continue in various venues.

1643   During the early part of the year the royalists maintain the military initiative owing to their greater number of professional soldiers and an initial advantage in resources: royalist forces dominate in Wales, the midlands and the north. Pym begins to establish a fiscal basis for Parliament's campaigns. 20 September: battle of Newbury, another indecisive major engagement. The autumn is a defining moment when London is finally secured for Parliament, and the Scots army of 20,000 joins with Parliament through the Solemn League and Covenant.

Anon., *Tyrannical Government Anatomized* (political allegory: closet). Eleanor Douglas, *Amend, Amend*, one of seventy known works by this author from the 1640s. Milton, Divorce pamphlets. Martin Parker, 'When the King Enjoys His Own Again', an instant ballad success, sung on London streets until the nineteenth century. January: *Mercurius Aulicus* the first royalist answer to parliamentary news-books, published from Oxford until 1646: Parliament replies with *Mercurius Britannicus* and re-establishes censorship, appointing Henry Walley, Clerk to the Stationers' Company, as Licenser.

1644   February: the Committee of Both Kingdoms is formed by Parliament and the Covenanters to direct the war efforts. 2 July: Marston Moor won by the combined forces of Scotland, Yorkshire and the Eastern Association, where Cromwell's cavalry is decisive. Parliament gains control of the north, occupying York, but is defeated 2 September at Lostwithiel and 27 October at the second battle of Newbury.

Milton, *Of Education*, and *Areopagitica*. Parliament orders the removal and destruction of all church organs.

1645   10 January: execution of William Laud. The Committee of Both Kingdoms recommends the raising of a permanent army of 22,000 men, the New Model, which delivers a decisive victory at Naseby, 14 June, leading to Charles's surrender one year later.

Jane Cavendish and Elizabeth Brackley, *The Concealed Fancies* (closet comedy written at Welbeck Abbey under siege and occupation by parliamentary forces). *Poems of Mr. John*

Milton: literary publication falls off from 1643 to 1645. A parliamentary Ordinance confirms the monopoly of the Stationers' Company in overseeing all publications.

1646 Episcopacy is abolished and all bishops' lands sold off. Charles surrenders to the Scots army at Southwell. The end of the first Civil War. Two dominant groupings emerge among parliamentarians: a Presbyterian majority, which proposes to disband the army without payment and redeploy a new force in Ireland; and the Independents who gain more support from the army and dominate the government from 1649 until the Restoration. Widespread military disorder and mutiny. At £120,000 per month, Parliament's yearly demand for revenue exceeds pre-war levels. Poor harvests until the end of the decade; plague outbreak.

Sir Thomas Browne, *Pseudodoxia Epidemica*. Richard Crashaw, *Steps to the Temple*. Henry More, *Philosophical Poems*. Shirley, *The Triumph of Beauty* (masque, privately acted). Three widely read attacks on sectaries: Daniel Featley, *The Dippers Dipt*, Ephraim Pagitt, *Heresiography* and Thomas Edwards, *Gangraena*.

1647 Steep rises in the price of food together with new high levels of taxation: widespread refusal of payment. April: the army moves towards becoming a politicized group when regiments elect 'agitators' – agents – to voice their grievances over non-payment of wages and proposed redeployments. 14 June: the *Representation*, articulating Leveller ideas, attacks parliamentary corruption, demanding toleration of religious dissent and fixed-term Parliaments. The Levellers are 'the first political party...(that) exposed a nerve which looks remarkably like class hostility' (Hirst 1986: 274). 28 October: army 'grandees', agitators and Levellers meet in Putney Church to debate the Levellers' (first) *Agreement of the People*, arguing for a new constitutional arrangement. The discussions are inconclusive and forcibly disbanded by Cromwell.

Beaumont and Fletcher, *Comedies and Tragedies* in folio. 30 September: An ordinance against unlicensed printing of scandalous pamphlets and for a better regulation of printing, aimed at the numbers of news-books which had proliferated to meet the appetite for news of the war. All actors to be branded as rogues, theatres raided and broken up, attenders fined 5 shillings. Ferrar's 'Arminian Nunnery' at Little Gidding dissolved by Parliament.

1648 Increasing revolts against Parliament through non-payment of tax, deep resentments against the army, and the ejection of low-church ministers in favour of Anglican clergy. March: outbreaks of resistance on behalf of Charles. April: open revolt in South Wales; numerous petitions are compiled calling for a settlement with the King. Extensive fighting in Essex and Kent, royalist forces threatening London. 8 July: the Duke of Hamilton invades England with an army of 9,000. August: Cromwell destroys the Scots army at the Battle of Preston. 6 December: Colonel Pride's Purge to ensure the King's trial: musketeers block the entry to Parliament, excluding some 110 MPs.

Anon., *Crafty Cromwell, or Oliver Ordering Our New State* (closet political dialogue, ten others recorded). Anon., *The Mournful Cries of Many Thousand Poor Tradesmen*: 'Necessity dissolves all laws and government, and hunger will break through stone walls.' Anon., *The Light Shining in Buckinghamshire*, a Leveller tract calling for the equal distribution of property. Robert Herrick, *Hesperides*. Henry and William Lawes, *Choice Psalms Put into Music for Three Voices*. Elizabeth Poole, *An Alarum of War*. There is evidence of some 300 women who spoke out or wrote as prophets during the 1640s and 1650s. The Peace of Westphalia concludes the Thirty Years' War in Europe.

1649 30 January: the execution of Charles at Whitehall:

> His bearing at the trial, and then in the cold on the scaffold...was undoubtedly the most dignified of his career....He did far more for the cause of kingship than he had ever achieved during his lifetime...
>
> (Hirst 1986: 287)

5 February: Charles II proclaimed King at Edinburgh. 15 March: Cromwell is nominated Lord Lieutenant and Commander-in-Chief in Ireland. 17 March: monarchy is abolished, 19 March: the House of Lords is abolished. 1 April: embracing the folly of April Fool's Day some forty persons settle on St George's Hill, Walton-on-Thames, and establish a community; under the leadership of Gerrard Winstanley they are identified as the Digger movement. Other communities are begun at Barnett, Iver, Wellingborough, Enfield and Bosworth. May: England is declared 'a commonwealth and free state'. 14 May: mutinous Leveller regiments are suppressed by Cromwell at Burford. July: Cromwell leads an expeditionary force to Ireland, massacring the garrisons and some civilians at Drogheda and Wexford. December: deepening financial crisis for the Commonwealth. A higher proportion of unmarried men emigrate to the colonies during the 1650s than at any period until the 1880s.

Eikon Basilike. The Portraiture of His Sacred Majesty in His Solitudes and Sufferings is published the day after the King's execution, purportedly the testament of Charles I, though ghost-written by John Gauden, Bishop of Worcester. It runs to 36 editions during 1650. Anon., *Tyranipocrit Discovered*, an attack on Parliament for failing to establish true equality, printed in the Netherlands. Joanna Cartwright, *The Petition of the Jewes*. Abiezer Coppe, *A Fiery Flying Roll*. Gerrard Winstanley, *A Watch-Word to the City of London*, *The True Levellers Standard Advanced*. Numbers of news-books suppressed, ballad singing forbidden and street singers flogged. Parliament orders the dispersal of Charles's collection of paintings. Milton is appointed Secretary of State for Foreign Tongues to defend regicide against European opinion, and publishes *The Tenure of Kings and Magistrates*.

1650 April: the Rump passes acts for the observance of the Sabbath, against adultery, fornication, swearing and blasphemy, and re-imposes the censorship which fell in 1641; the numbers of pamphlets published gradually decreases during the decade. Charles Stuart raises an army in Scotland, but is defeated by Cromwell after a difficult campaign, 3 September at Dunbar.

Richard Baxter, *The Saint's Everlasting Rest*. Anne Bradstreet, *The Tenth Muse Lately Sprung Up in America*. Davenant, *Gondibert* (Paris). Marvell, 'An Horatian Ode upon Cromwell's Return from Ireland': compare with Dáibhídh Ó Bruadair, 'Créacht do dháil mé im arthrach galair' ['A wound has made of me an ailing vessel']. Henry Vaughan, *Silex Scintillans*. Milton, now completely blind, publishes *Defence of the English People*.

1651 Charles Stuart marches south, hoping to inflame opposition against the Rump, but only 2,000 join his colours, and he is defeated at Worcester on 3 September and flees to France.

Thomas Hobbes, *Leviathan*. Hobbes and John Evelyn return to England.

1652   Act for the settlement of Ireland. The First Dutch War. The Republic drifts closer to bankruptcy. Army dissatisfaction against the Rump continues, and coups are plotted.

Anon., *Eliza's Babes: or The Virgins-Offering*. Richard Crashaw, *Carmen Deo Nostro* (Paris). Winstanley, *The Law of Freedom*.

1653   20 April: Cromwell forcibly dissolves the Rump, and as Lord General of the Army is now chief power-broker in the country. July: the Barebones Parliament draws on members from Ireland and Scotland, and so can be viewed as the first British assembly, passing over thirty acts in five months, including legislation for civil marriage. Levellers active again, agitating for all legal legislation to be condensed to 'the bigness of a pocket book'. 12 December: Barebones Parliament dissolved and power is vested in the army, through the person of the Lord General. The Instrument of Government establishes Cromwell as Lord Protector. The franchise is re-organized. 'The inauguration of the protectorate has strong claims to be a turning point, as England retraced its steps towards the safely monarchical order of the Restoration' (Hirst 1986: 317). The government determines to settle all remaining Catholic Irish landowners 'in hell or Connaght', in order to clear the mainland for Protestant possession: several thousand are relocated during the following two years. Royalist revolt continues sporadically in the Scottish Highlands until 1655.

Margaret Cavendish, *Philosophical Fancies, Poems and Fancies*. An Collins, *Divine Songs and Meditations*. Robert Cox, as author or adaptor, stages drolls and pastorals (illegally) at the Red Bull Theatre. Izaak Walton, *The Complete Angler*.

1654   Widespread confiscation of Catholic territories throughout Ireland until the end of the decade, often resettled by former parliamentarian soldiers: the displaced Catholics forcibly moved to marginal lands in Connacht, Galway and Clare.

The major defences of the Protectorate: *The True State of the Case of the Commonwealth* and Milton's *Second Defence of the English People*. Anna Trapnel, *The Cry of a Stone*.

1655   22 January: Cromwell dissolves Parliament and orders taxes to be collected in a style reminiscent of the royal absolutisms of the 1630s. Major-Generals are appointed to twelve military districts throughout the country in response to abortive royalist uprisings, remaining until January 1657.

Hester Biddle, *Woe to Thee Town of Cambridge, Woe to Thee City of Oxford*. Margaret Cavendish, *The Philosophical and Physical Opinions, The World's Olio*. John Denham, *Cooper's Hill*. Jews are 'readmitted' to England; Moses Maimonides, *Porta Mosis*, the first Arabic text in Hebrew type, printed at Oxford.

1656   The second Parliament of the Protectorate.

Margaret Cavendish, *Nature's Pictures drawn by Fancy's Pencil to the Life*, the first autobiography (other than spiritual journals) by an English woman (removed from the second edition, 1671). Abraham Cowley, *Poems*. Davenant, *The Siege of Rhodes*, the first English opera, music by Henry Lawes. Margaret Fell, *A Testimony of the Touch-Stone*. George Fox, *The Woman Learning in Silence*. James Harrington, *The Commonwealth of Oceana*, robust pro-republican argument.

1657 The Humble Petition and Advice, a revision of the constitution of 1654/5, in effect a reversion to the pre-revolutionary constitution. Under pressure from the army, Cromwell refuses the title of King, and continues as plain Lord Protector. Poor harvests until 1661.

Henry King, *Poems, Elegies, Paradoxes and Sonnets*. The completion of Brian Walton's Polyglot Bible, a major achievement of scholarship and printing.

1658 January: the third Parliament of the Protectorate, dissolved after sixteen days. 3 September: the death of Cromwell.

Sir Thomas Browne, *Hydriotaphia* and *Garden of Cyrus*. Margaret Cavendish, 13 plays written during the Interregnum, including *The Female Academy*, published in folio 1662. Sarah Jinner, *An Almanack*, 'You may wonder to see one of our Sex in print, especially in the Celestial Sciences.' Milton: probably the period of sustained composition of *Paradise Lost*.

1659 22 April: Parliament attempts to dictate terms to the army and is dissolved. 5 May: the generals restore the Rump Parliament, Richard Cromwell, having been nominated as successor by his father, retires into oblivion. October: Parliament again dissolved.

Anna Maria van Schurman, *The Learned Maid; or, Whether a Maid may be a Scholar?*

1660 3 February: General Monck enters London, surrenders to the City and so brings down the Parliament. 25 April: a new Parliament is elected with a significant proportion of Royalist members; the House of Lords is restored. Parliament accepts Charles II's Declaration made at Breda, which offers liberty of conscience and settlement of debts to the Army, subject to Parliament's agreement. 25 May: Charles II lands at Dover, restoration of monarchy. An Act of 13 September restores ejected ministers to their parishes, displacing about 695 'intruded' priests. The Militia Act establishes a standing army under the monarch's control.

Cowley, *A Proposition for the Advancement of Experimental Philosophy*. April: the Stationers' Company is given general search warrants to seek out unlicensed pamphlets attacking Parliament. Following the Restoration the Company hunts down anti-monarchical publications. Milton is under threat for some months as a traitor and regicide, but is finally included in the Act of Oblivion. The King's, the Duke's and the Theatre Royal re-open. Samuel Pepys begins keeping a diary (to 1669).

1661 January: Venner's Rising, an abortive revolt of Millenarians in London, confirms feelings against religious enthusiasm which is increasingly blamed for the excesses of the Commonwealth period. 8 May: the Cavalier or Pensioner Parliament meets until 1679.

24 August: Pepys attends a performance of *Hamlet*, the first recorded since 1637. Francis Kirkman, one of the leading London publisher-booksellers, opens the first commercial lending library.

1662 Women take female roles on the public stage. Royal Society established by charter, its *Philosophical Transactions* appearing from 1665. Licensing Act for 'preventing the frequent abuses in printing seditious, treasonable and unlicensed books and pamphlets': master type-founders reduced to four, master printers to twenty, the Act continuing to 1695.

Coda: 1666

The sad and never to be forgotten Judgement by the fire which upon the 2nd, 3d, 4th and 5th days of September destroyed the greatest part of this City, and in the common calamity our Hall, Warehouses and stock of Books and other goods therein.

(Blagden 1960: 216)

BIBLIOGRAPHY

Bate, Jonathan (1993) *Shakespeare and Ovid*, Oxford, Clarendon Press.

Blagden, Cyprian (1960) *The Stationers' Company. A History, 1403–1959*, London, George Allen and Unwin.

Harbage, Alfred (1989) *Annals of English Drama 975–1700*, revised by S. Schoenbaum, third edition revised by Sylvia Stoler Wagonheim, London, Routledge.

Hirst, Derek (1986) *Authority and Conflict. England 1603–1658*, London, Edward Arnold.

Hutton, Ronald (1994) *The Rise and Fall of Merry England. The Ritual Year 1400–1700*, Oxford, Oxford University Press.

Portal, Ethel M., 'The Academ Roial of King James I', *Proceedings of the British Academy*, 1916, vol. VII, pp. 189–208.

FURTHER READING

1 'Paper I make my Friend and mind's true Glass'

The Reading Experience Database (RED), launched in 1996, seeks documented examples of specific 'reading experiences' in the British Isles, and for people born in the British Isles, from 1450 to 1914, in order to develop a searchable archive for the historical study of reading. Records note the text, reader or listener and source of the example, as well as genre, form of text and details of the reader/listener, such as age, gender, ethnic origin, socio-economic group, religion, and date/time/place of experience. Graphic representations of readers and reading are also collected by RED, as are 'observations on the act of reading', revealing assumptions brought to literacy in past times. Information and record forms are available from www.open.ac.uk OU Academic Arts RED. To explore the wealth of Renaissance Studies via the Internet, begin at Voice of the Shuttle: English Literature: Renaissance, or the Centre for Reformation and Renaissance Studies. James Raven, Helen Small and Naomi Taylor (eds), *The Practice and Representation of Reading in England*, Cambridge, Cambridge University Press, 1996, is an excellent resource for exploring new scholarship on the history of reading.

Stephen Greenblatt, *Renaissance Self-Fashioning: From More to Shakespeare*, Chicago and London, University of Chicago Press, 1980, established the key concerns of new historicist criticism, which he redefined as 'cultural poetics' in *Shakespearean Negotiations: The Circulation of Social Energy in Renaissance England*, Oxford, Oxford University Press, 1988. Jean E. Howard, 'The new historicism in renaissance studies', *English Literary Renaissance*, 1986, vol. 16, pp. 13–43, defined issues clearly. Jonathan Dollimore's introduction to the second edition of *Radical Tragedy. Religion, Ideology and Power in the Drama of Shakespeare and his Contemporaries*, New York, London, Toronto, Sydney, Tokyo, Harvester Wheatsheaf, 1989 (first published 1984) argued 'the procedures and aims of a materialist criticism' (xiv) and reviewed debates over new historicist and cultural materialist practice. Jonathan Dollimore and Alan Sinfield (eds), *Political Shakespeare. New Essays in Cultural Materialism*, Manchester, Manchester University Press, 1994, also updated the first edition of 1985 which launched cultural materialist work in the UK. Richard Wilson, *Will Power. Essays on Shakespearean Authority*, New York, London, Toronto, Sydney, Tokyo, Harvester Wheatsheaf, 1993, and Lisa Jardine, *Reading Shakespeare Historically*, London and New York, Routledge, 1996, debated and extended the uses of historical combined with theoretical approaches. Both new historical and cultural materialist critical practices were evaluated in Jean E. Howard and Marion F. O'Connor (eds), *Shakespeare Reproduced. The Text in History and Ideology*, New York and

London, Methuen, 1987. More recent overviews and collections are Aram H. Veeser (ed.), *The New Historicism*, London and New York, Routledge, 1989 and *The New Historicism Reader*, London and New York, Routledge, 1994; Kiernan Ryan (ed.), *New Historicism and Cultural Materialism: A Reader*, London, Arnold, 1996, and John Brannigan, *New Historicism and Cultural Materialism*, London, Macmillan, 1998. Martin Elsky, *Authorizing Words. Speech, Writing, and Print in the English Renaissance*, Ithaca and London, Cornell University Press, 1989, considers early modern literacies from 'deconstructive' perspectives.

2 Status and literacy

Keith Wrightson, *English Society 1580–1680*, London, Unwin Hyman, 1982, is essential, and can be supplemented with J. A. Sharpe, *Early Modern England. A Social History 1550–1760*, Part II: 'The social hierarchy and social change', London, Edward Arnold, 1987, Barry Coward, *Social Change and Continuity in Early Modern England 1550–1750*, London and New York, Longman, 1988, and Mark Kishlansky, *A Monarchy Transformed. Britain 1603–1714*, 1 'The Social World', Harmondsworth, Allen Lane, The Penguin Press, 1996. Steve Rappaport, *Worlds Within Worlds: Structures of Life in Sixteenth-Century London*, Cambridge, Cambridge University Press, 1989, is a 'reconstitution of the careers of one thousand men who lived in Tudor London' (21). A great deal of fascinating research on families is contained in Ralph Houlbrooke, *The English Family, 1450–1700*, London and New York, Longman, 1984, *English Family Life, 1576–1716*, Oxford, Oxford University Press, 1989, and Mary Abbott, *Life Cycles in England 1560–1720*, London and New York, Routledge, 1996. Useful journals are *Past and Present, Continuity and Change, The Historical Journal, History* and *The Journal of British Studies*.

3 'Towardness'

Lawrence Stone's 'optimist' articles began current debates on early modern literacy: 'The educational revolution in England, 1560–1640', *Past and Present*, 1964, vol. 28, pp. 41–80 and 'Literacy and education in England, 1640–1900', *Past and Present*, 1969, vol. 42, pp. 69–139. David Cressy, *Literacy and the Social Order*, Cambridge, Cambridge University Press, 1980, remains standard but increasingly qualified by local studies. Regional detail is given in R. A. Houston, *Scottish Literacy and the Scottish Identity. Illiteracy and Society in Scotland and Northern England 1600–1800*, Cambridge, Cambridge University Press, 1985. Of all the scholarship surveyed in *Writing and Society*, the history of early modern education is probably the area which has received least attention in the past two decades. Classic studies are T. W. Baldwin's *William Shakespere's Petty School* and *William Shakespere's Smalle Latine & Lesse Greeke*, two vols, Urbana, University of Illinois Press, 1943 and 1944. Joan Simon, *Education and Society in Tudor England*, Cambridge, Cambridge University Press, 1966, and Rosemary O'Day, *Education and Society 1500–1800. The Social Foundations of Education in Early Modern Britain*, London and New York, Longman, 1982, are valuable overviews. Only the first stages of education are dealt with in this chapter; for discussion of the universities, see O'Day, Chapters 5, 6 and 7. For popular literacy, see reading recommended for Chapter 6.

4 'Mechanics in the Suburbs of Literature'

Lucien Febvre and Henri-Jean Martin, *The Coming of the Book. The Impact of Printing 1450–1800* (1958), translated by David Gerard, edited by Geoffrey Nowell-Smith and David Wootton, London, Verso, 1984 is a ground-breaking and influential survey from the 'Annales' school of cultural historians, which can be supplemented by Elizabeth L. Eisenstein, *The Printing Press as an Agent of Change*, two vols, Cambridge, Cambridge University Press, 1979. S. H. Steinberg, *Five Hundred Years of Printing*, new edition, revised by John Trevitt, London, The British Library and Oak Knoll Press, 1996, is a well-illustrated conspectus. Cyprian Blagden, *The Stationers' Company. A History, 1403–1959*, London, George Allen and Unwin, 1960 and John Feather, *A History of British Publishing*, London, Routledge, 1988, are standard accounts. Steve Rappaport, *Worlds Within Worlds: Structures of Life in Sixteenth-Century London*, Cambridge, Cambridge University Press, 1989, contextualizes the Companies within the City and society. John Sutherland, 'Production and reception of the literary book', in Martin Coyle, Peter Garside, Malcolm Kelsall and John Peck (eds), *Encyclopedia of Literature and Criticism*, London, Routledge, 1990, pp. 809–24, John Feather 'The printed book', pp. 825–36, and 'Publishing before 1800', pp. 848–61, are concise overviews. Tessa Watt, *Cheap Print and Popular Piety 1550–1640*, Cambridge, Cambridge University Press, 1991, explores the burgeoning popular market. Cyndia Susan Clegg, *Press Censorship in Elizabethan England*, Cambridge, Cambridge University Press, 1997, revises many older assumptions about the rigour of early modern censorship. Philip Gaskell, *A New Introduction to Bibliography*, Oxford, Clarendon Press, 1972, is a standard work of reference. See also reading recommended for Chapters 4 and 5.

The *History of the Book in Britain* project, published by Cambridge University Press, is forthcoming: John Barnard and D. F. McKenzie edit vol. IV, '1557–1695'; data accumulated in the course of research for the project is available through the History of the Book-On-Demand Series (HOBODS), details in *Publishing History* (devoted to 'The social, economic and literary history of book, newspaper and magazine publishing'). The Society for the History of Authorship, Reading and Publishing (SHARP) was established to provide a forum for exchange of research and ideas between social historians, literary historians and book historians on every aspect of the history of the book; for information, see SHARP: http://www.indiana.edu/~sharp/intro.html.

5 Censorship and state formation

The main issues in the debate over early modern censorship presented here can be followed through: Christopher Hill, 'Censorship and English literature', in *Writing and Revolution in Seventeenth-Century England*, Brighton, Harvester Wheatsheaf, 1985, pp. 32–71; Margot Heinemann, *Puritanism and Theatre: Thomas Middleton and Opposition Drama under the Early Stuarts*, Cambridge, Cambridge University Press, 1980; Gerald

Eades Bentley, 'Regulation and censorship', *The Profession of Dramatist in Shakespeare's Time, 1590–1642*, Princeton, Princeton University Press, 1971, pp. 145–96; Jonathan Dollimore, 'Censorship', *Radical Tragedy. Religion, Ideology and Power in the Drama of Shakespeare and his Contemporaries*, New York, London, Toronto, Sydney, Tokyo, Harvester Wheatsheaf, 1989, pp. 22–5; Annabel Patterson, *Censorship and Interpretation. The Conditions of Writing and Reading in Early Modern England*, Madison, University of Wisconsin Press, 1984, and *Fables of Power. Aesopian Writing and Political History*, Durham and London, Duke University Press, 1991; A. B. Worden, 'Literature and political censorship in early modern England', in A. C. Duke and C. A. Tamse (eds), *Too Mighty To Be Free. Censorship and the Press in Britain and the Netherlands*, 'Britain and the Netherlands', vol. IX, Zutphen, De Walburg Pers, 1987; Janet Clare, *'Art made tongue-tied by authority': Elizabethan and Jacobean Dramatic Censorship*, Manchester and New York, Manchester University Press, 1990, reviewed by Jill Levenson, *Studies in English Literature*, 1991, vol. 31, p. 394; Paul Yachnin, 'The powerless theatre', *English Literary Renaissance*, 1991, vol. 21, pp. 49–74; Cyndia Susan Clegg, *Press Censorship in Elizabethan England*, Cambridge, Cambridge University Press, 1997; Janet Clare, 'Historicism and the question of censorship in the renaissance', *English Literary Renaissance*, 1997, vol. 27/2, pp. 155–76; Sheila Lambert, 'State control of the press in theory and practice: the role of the Stationers' Company before 1640', in Robin Myers and Michael Harris (eds), *Censorship and the Control of Print in England and France 1600–1910*, Winchester, St Paul's Bibliographies, 1992, pp. 1–32. Charles Nicholl's *The Reckoning. The Murder of Christopher Marlowe*, Chicago, University of Chicago Press, 1992, is a compelling and utterly persuasive reconstruction of Elizabethan state surveillance and espionage.

For early modern Irish literary culture, Edmund Spenser, *A View of the Present State of Ireland*, W. L. Renwick (ed.), Oxford, Clarendon Press, 1970, is salutary reading. It is very difficult to gain a sense of the power and beauty of early modern Gaelic poetry as it would have been sung, and nearly everything must be lost in translation. Some editions with précis are: *Irish Bardic Poetry*, texts and translations by Osborn Bergin, Dublin, Dublin Institute for Advanced Studies, 1970, J. Carmichael Watson (ed.), *Gaelic Songs of Mary MacLeod*, Edinburgh, Oliver and Boyd for the Scottish Gaelic Texts Society, 1982, and the series throughout. Derick Thomson, *An Introduction to Gaelic Poetry*, Edinburgh, Edinburgh University Press, 1989, for the Scottish poets, contains many translations and explains the difficulties in transposition. David Norbrook and H. R. Woudhuysen's *Penguin Book of Renaissance Verse*, Harmondsworth, Penguin, 1992, contextualizes Ireland, Wales and Scotland helpfully, pp. 26–8, and includes Gaelic authors. Catherine Kerrigan's *An Anthology of Scottish Women Poets*, Edinburgh, Edinburgh University Press, 1991, has a wide selection of Gaelic verse in translation. Perhaps the best way of gaining some sense of what the Gaelic oral tradition was like at its most powerful is to read – and better still listen to recorded performances by – great current practitioners: the finest was Somhairle MacGill-Eain [Sorley MacLean], *O Choille gu Bearradh* [*From Wood to Ridge*], Collected Poems in Gaelic and English, (translated by the poet), Manchester, Carcanet, 1990; there are essays on seventeenth- and eighteenth-century Gaelic poetry in his *Ris a' Bhruthaich* [*The Criticism and Prose Writings*], edited by William Gillies, Stornoway, Acair, 1985. T. W. Moody, F. X. Martin, F. J. Byrne (eds), *A New History of Ireland*, vol. III, *Early Modern Ireland 1534–1691*, Oxford, Clarendon Press, 1976, corr. repr. 1991, is encyclopaedic. For recent scholarship, see Brendan Bradshaw, Andrew Hadfield and Willy Maley (eds), *Representing Ireland: Literature and the Origins of Conflict, 1534–1660*, Cambridge, Cambridge University Press, 1993. For Wales, see G. Williams, *Recovery, Reorientation and Reformation: Wales c. 1415–1642*, Oxford, Oxford University Press, 1987, and R. Geraint Gruffydd (ed.), *A Guide to Welsh Literature*, vol. III, 'c. 1530–1700', Cardiff, University of Wales Press, 1997.

6 'Penny merriments, penny godlinesses'

Tim Harris (ed.), *Popular Culture in England, c. 1500–1850*, London, Macmillan, 1995, is a recent overview; see especially Harris, 'Problematising popular culture', Susan Amussen 'The gendering of popular culture in early modern England' and Jonathan Barry 'Literacy and literature in popular culture: reading and writing in historical perspective'. Among older work, Louis B. Wright, *Middle-Class Culture in Elizabethan England*, 1935, Ithaca, New York, Cornell University Press, 1958, despite its anachronistic description of class, is full of materials on literacy and popular taste. Keith Thomas, *Religion and the Decline of Magic*, London, Weidenfeld and Nicolson, 1971, is an outstanding reconstruction of 'popular' beliefs. A major work of synthesis is Peter Burke, *Popular Culture in Early Modern Europe*, particularly Part 3: 'Changes in popular culture', pp. 205–86, Aldershot, Scolar Press, 1994, second revised edition. Bernard Capp, 'Popular literature', pp. 198–243 in Barry Reay (ed.), *Popular Culture in Seventeenth-Century England*, London and Sydney, Croom Helm, 1985, is a valuable survey; see also his *Astrology and the Popular Press: English Almanacs 1500–1800*, London, Faber and Faber, 1979. Margaret Spufford set the standard for work on popular literacy with *Small Books and Pleasant Histories. Popular Fiction and its Readership in Seventeenth-Century England*, London, Methuen, 1981. Tessa Watt, *Cheap Print and Popular Piety 1550–1640*, Cambridge, Cambridge University Press, 1991, is the best account of the ballad and chapbook trade and its readership. An attempt to reconstruct ballad composition and reading is Adam Fox, 'Popular verses and their readership in the early seventeenth century', in James Raven, Helen Small and Naomi Tadmor (eds), *The Practice and Representation of Reading in England*, Cambridge, Cambridge University Press, 1996, pp. 125–37. Bob Scribner, 'Is a history of popular culture possible?' in *History of European Ideas*, 1989, vol. 10/2, pp. 175–91, is a useful overview of the debates on definitions of 'the popular' in the period. John Taylor's works are difficult to find as books outside major libraries, but many are available via the Chadwyck-Healey Literature Online database. *All the Works of John Taylor the Water Poet* (1630) was issued in facsimile with an Introductory note by Victor Neuburg, Menstone, The Scolar Press, 1973 – the volume is not through-numbered but divided into three separately numbered sections, perhaps because it was distributed among four printers: references below are by gathering and page, for example 'II.55', preceded by the date of first publication. Many of Taylor's other works were reprinted by the Spenser Society, vols 7, 14, 19, 21, and 25 [no editor], also not through-numbered (Manchester, 1870–8, reprinted New York, Burt Franklin, 1967). Bernard Capp's *The World of John Taylor the Water-Poet 1578–1653*, Oxford, Clarendon Press, 1994, is invaluable, and this chapter depends heavily on his researches.

7 'Dressed up with the flowers of a Library'

Recent anthologies are Randall Martin (ed.), *Women Writers in Renaissance England*, London, Longman, 1997; James Fitzmaurice (general editor), Josephine A. Roberts (textual editor), *Major Women Writers of Seventeenth-Century England*, Ann Arbor, The University of Michigan Press, 1997; S. P. Cerasano and Marion Wynne-Davies (eds), *Renaissance Drama by Women. Texts and Documents*, London and New York, Routledge, 1996; Kate Aughterson (ed.), *Renaissance Woman. Constructions of Femininity in England*, London and New York, Routledge, 1995; N. H. Keeble (ed.), *The Cultural Identity of Seventeenth-Century Woman. A Reader*, London and New York, Routledge, 1994. Maureen Bell, George Parfitt and Simon Shepherd (eds), *A Biographical Dictionary of English Women Writers 1580–1720*, New York and London, Harvester Wheatsheaf, 1990, reviews many issues in 'Critical appendices', pp. 245–98; see also Hilda L. Smith and Susan Cardinale (eds), *Women and the Literature of the Seventeenth Century*, New York, Westport Connecticut, London, Greenwood Press, 1990. A useful overview is Helen Wilcox (ed.), *Women and Literature in Britain 1500–1700*, Cambridge, Cambridge University Press, 1996. Online resources include: The Brown University Women Writers Project; The Perdita Project: Early Modern Women's Manuscript Compilations; Society for the Study of Early Modern Women.

For Lady Anne Clifford and her 'Great Picture', the standard life is George C. Williamson, *Lady Anne Clifford, Countess of Dorset, Pembroke and Montgomery, 1590–1676. Her Life, Letters and Work*, (1922), second edition, Wakefield, S. R. Publishers Ltd, 1967. D. J. H. Clifford edited and introduced *The Diaries of Lady Anne Clifford*, Thrupp, Sutton Publishing Ltd, 1992. Barbara Kiefer Lewalski gives a reading of the life as 'an instance of sustained public opposition to patriarchal authority and property settlements' in Chapter 5, 'Claiming patrimony and constructing a self: Anne Clifford and her *Diary*', in *Writing Women in Jacobean England*, Cambridge, MA, London, England, Harvard University Press, 1993, pp. 125–152. Richard T. Spence provides the most recent account of the life through archival records in *Lady Anne Clifford Countess of Pembroke, Dorset and Montgomery (1590–1676)*, Thrupp, Sutton Publishing Ltd, 1997, and numerous articles. Graham Parry gives an art-historical perspective in 'The Great Picture of Lady Anne Clifford', in David Howarth (ed.), *Art and Patronage in the Caroline Courts. Essays in Honour of Sir Oliver Millar*, Cambridge, Cambridge University Press, 1993, pp. 202–19.

NOTES

1 'PAPER I MAKE MY FRIEND AND MIND'S TRUE GLASS'

1 'Paper I make my Friend and mind's true Glass', line 16 from Hester Wyat, 'A Poem Made by a Friend of Mine in Answer to One Who Asked Why She Wrote', 1640?, (Bod. MS Rawl.d.360, fol. 53), in Germaine Greer, Susan Hastings, Jeslyn Medoff and Melinda Sansome (eds), *Kissing the Rod: An Anthology of Seventeenth-Century Verse*, London, Virago, 1988, pp. 5–6; 'I am Envy', *Doctor Faustus*, in David Bevington and Eric Rasmussen (eds), *Tamburlaine, Parts I and II, Doctor Faustus, A- and B-texts, The Jew of Malta, Edward II*, Oxford, Clarendon Press, 1995, 2.3.127–32, p. 160.

2 Morton W. Bloomfield, *The Seven Deadly Sins. An Introduction to the History of a Religious Concept, with Special Reference to Medieval English Literature*, Michigan State College Press, 1952; 'fishwife' and 'oysterwife' as abuse, in Maureen Bell, George Parfitt and Simon Shepherd (eds), *A Biographical Dictionary of English Women Writers 1580–1720*, New York, London, Harvester Wheatsheaf, 1990, p. 263. Chaucer, 'For in oure dayes', 'The Former Age', in Larry D. Benson, general editor, *The Riverside Chaucer*, Boston, Houghton Mifflin Company, 1987, p. 651.

3 A. C. Hamilton (ed.), *The Faerie Queene*, Book I, Canto IV, stanza 32.6–8, London and New York, Longman, 1977.

4 On 'productions not of the world of Cicero', Alan K. Bowman, 'The Roman imperial army: letters and literacy on the northern frontier', in Alan K. Bowman and Greg Woolf (eds), *Literacy and Power in the Ancient World*, Cambridge, Cambridge University Press, 1994, p. 116; Claudia Severa's invitation, Alan K. Bowman and J. David Thomas with contributions by J. N. Adams, *The Vindolanda Writing-Tablets (Tabulae Vindolandenses II)*, London, British Museum Press, 1994, p. 257; 'the earliest known examples', p. 257; Michael T. Clanchy, *From Memory to Written Record. England 1066–1307*, Oxford, Oxford University Press, 1993; and for the complexities involved in assessing medieval literacy rates, Clanchy, 'Literate and illiterate; hearing and seeing: England 1066–1307', in Harvey J. Graff (ed.), *Literacy and Social Development in the West: A Reader*, Cambridge, Cambridge University Press, 1981, pp. 14–45; William V. Harris, 'Levels of Greek and Roman literacy', in *Ancient Literacy*, Cambridge, MA and London, Harvard University Press, 1989, pp. 3–24; and Bowman, 'Technology and education', in 'The Roman imperial army', *Literacy and Power*, pp. 111–12.

5 Literacy estimates 1500/1680, David Cressy, 'Literacy in context: meaning and measurement in early modern England', in John Brewer and Roy Porter (eds), *Consumption and the World of Goods*, London and New York, Routledge, 1993, p. 305; Julia Boffey, 'Women authors and women's literacy in fourteenth and fifteenth-century England', in Carol M. Meale (ed.), *Women and Literature in Britain, 1150–1500*, Cambridge, Cambridge University Press, 1993, pp. 159–82; nuns' literacy, R. A. Houston, *Scottish Literacy and the Scottish Identity. Illiteracy and Society in Scotland and Northern England 1600–1800*, Cambridge, Cambridge University Press, 1985, p. 57.

6 'Peruse it th[o]roughly', *Doctor Faustus*, 2.3.162–3, p. 161; 'The iterating of these lines', 2.1.158–60, p. 155, 'Come not, Lucifer', 5.2.114–5, p. 182; 'Remember/First', *The Tempest*, Stephen Orgel (ed.), Oxford, Oxford University Press, 1987, 3.2.89–92, p. 160.

7 Maureen Bell and John Barnard, 'Provisional count of *STC* titles 1475–1640', *Publishing History*, 1992, vol. XXXI, pp. 48–64, based on *A Short-Title Catalogue of Books Printed in England, Scotland and Ireland and of English Books Printed Abroad, 1475–1640*, first compiled by A. W. Pollard and G. R. Redgrave, 2 vols, second edition revised and enlarged, begun by W. A. Jackson and F. S. Ferguson, completed by Katharine F. Pantzer, London, The Bibliographical Society, 1976–91; for the new 'popular' readership of the 1620s, Tessa Watt, *Cheap Print and Popular Piety 1550–1640*, Cambridge, Cambridge University Press, 1991.

8 John Aubrey, *'Brief Lives,' chiefly of Contemporaries, set down by John Aubrey, between the Years 1669 & 1696*, two vols, edited by Andrew Clark, Oxford, Clarendon Press, 1898, vol. 2, p. 244; 'stark natural elements', Zirka Zaremba Filipczak, 'Reflections on motifs in Van Dyck's portraits', in Arthur K. Wheelock, Jr, Susan J. Barnes, Julius S. Held (eds), *Anthony Van Dyck*, National Gallery of Art, Washington, 1990, p. 59; Thomas Clayton, 'An historical study of the portrait of Sir John Suckling', *Journal of the Warburg and Courtauld Institutes*, 1960, vol. XXIII, pp. 106–26; Malcolm Rogers, 'The meaning of Van Dyck's portrait of Sir John Suckling', *Burlington Magazine*, 1978, vol. 120, pp. 741–5; the portrait discussed in Thomas Clayton (ed.), *The Works of Sir John Suckling. The Non-Dramatic Works*, Oxford, Clarendon Press, 1971, vol. 1, pp. lxii–lxiii, and *Aglaura* in L. A. Beaurline (ed.), *The Plays*, vol. 2, pp. 33–119, commentary pp. 253–74; Dryden, 'The First Satire of Persius', line 19.

9 Prynne, 'To the Christian Reader', *Histrio-Mastix. The Players' Scourge, or Actors' Tragedy...* (1633) collated reprint with preface by Arthur Freeman, New York and London, Garland Publishing, 1974, fol. 1v, shoulder-note c; Milton, *Eikonoklastes. In Answer To a Book Entitled 'Eikon Basilike'...*, edited with preface and notes by Merritt Y. Hughes, in the *Complete Prose Works of John Milton*, vol. III, *1648–1649*, New Haven and Yale, Yale University Press, 1962, p. 361; Henrietta Maria at Stratford, Alison Plowden, *Women All On Fire. The Women of the English Civil War*, Thrupp, Sutton Publishing Ltd, 1998, p. 29; 'Witty above her sex', tombstone inscription, chancel, Holy Trinity, Stratford, for 'Susanna wife to John Hall, gent; the daughter of William Shakespeare, gent...deceased July 1649, aged 66.'

10 On 'the first pictorial reference', Rogers, 'The meaning of Van Dyck's portrait', p. 742; Christopher Brown proposed that the critical argument implied by the portrait would almost certainly have been devised by Suckling since Van Dyck did not frequent literary coteries, *Van Dyck*, Oxford, Phaidon, p. 214; 'sweetest Shakespeare', 'L'Allegro', 133–4; 'the first writer', Jonathan Bate, *The Genius of Shakespeare*, London, Picador, 1997, p. 161.

11 See further reading for Chapter 1 for key works of new historicist and cultural materialist criticism, and further reading for Chapter 7 for feminist and gender studies research.

12 Foucault defined the notion of 'discursive formations' in *The Archaeology of Knowledge* (1969) translated by A. M. Sheridan Smith, London, Tavistock/Routledge, 1972. Critiques of Foucault are, Charles Taylor, 'Foucault on freedom and truth', in David Hoy (ed.), *Foucault: A Critical Reader*, Oxford, Blackwell, 1986, and J. G. Merquior, *Foucault*, London, Fontana, 1991; David Simpson reviewed literary critical appropriations of Derrida, Foucault and Macherey in 'Literary criticism and the return to "history"', *Critical Inquiry*, 1988, vol. 14, pp. 721–47.

13 Assessments of new historicist and cultural materialist practice are Carolyn Porter, 'Are we being historical yet?', *The South Atlantic Quarterly*, 1988, vol. 87, pp. 743–86, Alan Liu, 'The power of formalism: the new historicism', *English Literary History*, 1989, vol. 59, pp. 721–71, and Porter, 'History and literature: after the new historicism', *New Literary History*, 1990, vol. 20, pp. 253–72; a definition and defence of the 'historicist enterprise' in relation to new historicism is Robert D. Hume, 'Texts within contexts: notes towards a historical method', *Philological Quarterly*, 1992, vol. 71, pp. 69–100; David Cressy drew on the 'new social history' to critique some versions of the 'new cultural history' in 'Foucault, Stone, Shakespeare and social history', *English Literary Renaissance*, 1991, vol. 21, pp. 121–33, and 'Gender trouble and cross-dressing in early modern England', *Journal of British Studies*, 1996, vol. 35, pp. 438–65.

14 See the further reading for Chapters 3 and 6 for key works of the 'new social history' on early modern hierarchy, status, literacy and popular culture. Chapter 5's further reading gives

indicative bibliography on the 'Four Kingdoms' debate and recent work on early modern Celtic literary cultures.

15 Roger Chartier, 'History between narrative and knowledge', *On the Edge of the Cliff*, Baltimore, Johns Hopkins University Press, 1996; for 'microstoria', Carlo Ginzburg, *The Cheese and the Worms: The Cosmos of a Sixteenth-Century Miller* (1976) translated by Anne and John Tedeschi, London, Routledge and Kegan Paul, 1980; Giovanni Levi, 'Les usages de la biographie', *Annales: Economies, Sociétés, Civilisations*, 1989, pp. 1325–36.

16 Chartier, 'History', p. 369; Merquior, *Foucault*, p. 143; 'a rhetorical personification', Porter, 'Are we being historical yet?', p. 758, discussing Greenblatt, 'Invisible bullets: Renaissance authority and its subversion, *Henry IV* and *Henry V*', in Jonathan Dollimore and Alan Sinfield (eds), *Political Shakespeare. New Essays in Cultural Materialism*, Manchester, Manchester University Press, 1994, pp. 18–47.

17 Roger Chartier, Introduction and Part I: Debate and Interpretations, in *Cultural History: Between Practices and Representation* (1985) translated by Lydia G. Cochrane, Cambridge and Oxford, Polity Press in association with Blackwell Publishers, 1988; see further reading for Chapter 4 for key works on publishing history; Simpson, 'Literary criticism and the return to "history"', pp. 741–7; Lynn Hunt, 'Introduction: history, culture and text' and Roger Chartier, 'Texts, printing, readings', in Lynn Hunt (ed.), *The New Cultural History*, Berkeley, University of California Press, 1989, pp. 154–75; Chartier (ed.), *The Culture of Print. Power and the Uses of Print in Early Modern Europe* (1987) translated by Lydia G. Cochrane, Cambridge, Polity Press, 1989; Jerome J. McGann, 'How to read a book', in *The Textual Condition*, Princeton, Princeton University Press, 1991, pp. 101–28; Jonathan Rose, 'Rereading the English common reader: a preface to a history of audiences', *Journal of the History of Ideas*, 1992, vol. 53, pp. 47–70. For a sceptical account of the convergence, John Sutherland, 'Publishing history: a hole at the centre of literary sociology', *Critical Inquiry*, 1988, vol. 14, pp. 574–89; 'Language in history: that full field', Raymond Williams, 'Cambridge English, past and present', in *Writing in Society*, London, Verso, [n.d.; lecture given 25 April 1983], p. 189.

18 For example, Jonathan Dollimore, *Radical Tragedy. Religion, Ideology and Power in the Drama of Shakespeare and his Contemporaries*, New York, London, Toronto, Sydney, Tokyo, Harvester Wheatsheaf, 1989 (first published 1984), pp. 89–90, on E. M. W. Tillyard.

19 Janet Clare, 'Historicism and the question of censorship in the Renaissance', *English Literary Renaissance*, 1997, vol. 27, pp. 155–76; Cyndia Susan Clegg, *Press Censorship in Elizabethan England*, Cambridge, Cambridge University Press, 1997.

20 Text and translation from Bowman and Thomas with contributions by J. N. Adams, *The Vindolanda Writing-Tablets*, p. 257, fragments of two other letters from Claudia to Severa, pp. 259–63; for 'women's literacy in the western provinces', Harris, *Ancient Literacy*, pp. 270–1; the 'emotive and regular position', Bowman and Thomas, 'New texts from Vindolanda', *Britannia*, 1987, vol. XVIII, p. 139; for Severa's 'elaborate and elegant expression' contrasting with her 'hesitant, ugly and unpractised hand', see Bowman, 'The Roman imperial army', in *Literacy and Power*, p. 124. With thanks to Dr Bowman for these references.

21 Bod. MS Rawl.d.360, fol. 53, in Greer *et al.*, *Kissing the Rod*, pp. 5–6.

2 STATUS AND LITERACY

1 The best-known surveys are: William Harrison, *The Description of England* (1577) quotations from which are taken from Frederick J. Furnivall's edition of the Second and Third Books, London, N. Trübner and Co., 1877, also referenced to George Edelen's edition, New York, Dover Publications, 1994; Sir Thomas Smith, *De Republica Anglorum* (1583), largely cribbed from Harrison; Sir Thomas Wilson, *The State of England Anno Dom. 1600 by Thomas Wilson*, F. J. Fisher (ed.), Camden Miscellany, 1936, vol. XVI, Camden Society, 3rd series; John Graunt's *Natural and Political Observations Made upon the Bills of Mortality* (1662), which broke with all previous commentaries and 'is moreover universally recognised as a work of genius, and most competent authorities attribute to it the origin of statistics and of demography': Peter Laslett, Introduction, in *The Earliest Classics*, 'Pioneers of Demography' series, n. p., Gregg International Publishers, 1973, p. [5]. See also Sir William Petty, *Political Arithmetic*,

or a Discourse Concerning the Extent and Value of Lands, People, Buildings...of Great Britain (1690). See also David Cressy, 'Describing the social order of Elizabethan and Stuart England', *Literature and History*, 1976, vol. 3, pp. 29–44; Wrightson, 'Degrees of people', in *English Society*, and '"Sorts of People" in Tudor and Stuart England', in Jonathan Barry and Christopher Brooks (eds), *The Middling Sort of People. Culture, Society and Politics in England, 1550–1800*, London, Macmillan, 1994, pp. 28–52.

2 Status-gender hierarchies in Susan Dwyer Amussen, *An Ordered Society. Gender and Class in Early Modern Britain*, Oxford, Blackwell, 1988, p. 3. And see below, Chapter 7.

3 On 'nothing is more constant in England', 'Of Apparel', Furnivall p. 170, Edelen p. 147; John Williams, *A Sermon of Apparell*, 1620, p. 24.

4 Thomas Wilson, *The State of England*, p. 19; 'Quinquennial English population totals', Table 7.8 in E. A. Wrigley and R. S. Schofield, with contributions from Ronald Lee and Jim Oeppen, *The Population History of England 1541–1871: a Reconstruction*, Cambridge, Cambridge University Press, 1981, 1989, pp. [208–9]; 'the City repairs its loss', Graunt, *Observations*, p. 39; Bishop Goodman quoted by Paul Griffiths, *Youth and Authority. Formative Experiences in England 1560–1640*, Oxford, Clarendon Press, 1996, p. 5; on family structure, 'Marital status by age and sex', Table 1.4 in Peter Laslett, *Family Life and Illicit Love in Earlier Generations*, Cambridge, Cambridge University Press, 1977, pp. 26–7, and 'Enduring patterns and forces of change', Houlbrooke, *The English Family*, pp. 18–38.

5 The Protestation Oath in David Cressy, *Literacy and the Social Order*, Cambridge, Cambridge University Press, 1980, p. 65; nineteenth-century proportions of readers to writers in Jonathan Barry, 'Literacy and literature in popular culture: reading and writing in historical perspective', in Tim Harris (ed.), *Popular Culture in England, c. 1500–1850*, London, Macmillan, 1995, p. 78; London female literacy in Peter Earle, 'The female labour market in London in the late seventeenth and early eighteenth centuries', *The Economic History Review*, 1989, 2nd series, vol. xlii, pp. 334–6; reading-only abilities in Tessa Watt, *Cheap Print and Popular Piety 1550–1640*, Cambridge, Cambridge University Press, 1991, p. 7; Keith Thomas, 'The meaning of literacy in early modern England', in Gerd Baumann (ed.), *The Written Word. Literacy in Transition*, Oxford, Clarendon Press, 1986, pp. 97–131; Margaret Spufford, *Small Books and Pleasant Histories: Popular Fiction and its Readership in Seventeenth-Century England*, London, Methuen, 1981, p. 35, quoted in Margaret W. Ferguson, 'Renaissance concepts of the "woman writer"', in Helen Wilcox (ed.), *Women and Literature in Britain, 1500–1700*, Cambridge, Cambridge University Press, 1996, p. 148.

6 Knights, Harrison, Furnivall, p. 114, Edelen, p. 94; Smith, *De Republica Anglorum*, pp. 64–77; Sir Henry Wotton, *The Elements of Architecture Collected...from the best Authors and Examples*, 1624, p. 82; James's jewellery, Mark Kishlansky, *A Monarchy Transformed. Britain 1603–1714*, 1 'The Social World', Harmondsworth, Allen Lane, The Penguin Press, 1996, p. 83; Henry Peacham, learning and nobility, in *The Complete Gentleman, The Truth of Our Times, and The Art of Living in London*, Virgil B. Heltzel (ed.), Ithaca, New York, Cornell University Press, 1962, p. 28.

7 *Hamlet*, Harold Jenkins (ed.), London, Methuen, 1982, 5.2.31–6, pp. 395–6.

8 *Measure for Measure*, N. W. Bawcutt (ed.), Oxford, Oxford University Press, 1991, 4.3.64, p. 194; execution of the Earl of Orkney, Peter D. Anderson, *Black Patie. The Life and Times of Patrick Stewart, Earl of Orkney, Lord of Shetland*, Edinburgh, John Donald Publishers, 1992, pp. 17, 139; Houston, *Scottish Literacy*, pp. 73, 160; anti-clan legislation in Derick Thomson, 'Clan and politics', *An Introduction to Gaelic Poetry*, Edinburgh, Edinburgh University Press, 1989, pp. 116–17; the Statutes of Icolmkill (Iona) in *The Register of the Privy Council of Scotland*, edited and abridged by David Masson, Edinburgh, H. M. General Register House, 1889, vol. IX, 'A.D. 1610–1613', pp. 26–30, on Lowland English education, p. 29; thanks to Mrs Sheila MacDonald of Inverness for this reference.

9 W. P. Griffith, *Learning, Law and Religion. Higher Education and Welsh Society c. 1540–1640*, Cardiff, University of Wales Press, 1996, pp. 108–9; Rosemary O'Day, *Education and Society 1500–1800*, London and New York, Longman, 1982, p. 39.

10 O'Day, *Education*, p. 35.

11 Female status in the Irish elite in Ciaran Brady, 'Political women and reform in Tudor Ireland', in Margaret MacCurtain and Mary O'Dowd (eds), *Women in Early Modern Ireland*, Edinburgh, Edinburgh University Press, 1991, p. 77, and Granuaile in Margaret MacCurtain, 'Women, education and learning in early modern Ireland', MacCurtain and O'Dowd, p. 166 n. 23; O'Malley's petition to Elizabeth in Anne Chambers, *Granuaile. The Life and Times of Grace O'Malley, c. 1530–1603*, Portmarnock, Wolfhound, 1979, pp. 133–52; Countess of Argyle in William J. Watson (ed.), *Scottish Verse from the Book of the Dean of Lismore*, Edinburgh, Oliver and Boyd for the Scottish Gaelic Texts Society, 1937, pp. 307–8; two courtly lyrics by her in Catherine Kerrigan (ed.), *An Anthology of Scottish Women Poets*, Edinburgh, Edinburgh University Press, 1991, p. 61; for 'the first Elizabethan woman to achieve public acclaim as a literary figure', see Margaret P. Hannay *et al.* (eds), *The Collected Works of Mary Sidney Herbert Countess of Pembroke*, vol. I, 'Poems, Translations, and Correspondence', vol. II, 'The Psalmes of David', Oxford, Clarendon Press, 1998, vol. I, p. [1].

12 Wrightson, *English Society*, p. 24; 'few noblemen', Derek Hirst, *Authority and Conflict. England 1603–1658*, London, Melbourne, Auckland, Edward Arnold, 1986, p. 228.

13 Harrison, 'Of Degrees', Furnivall, pp. 128–9, Edelen, pp. 113–4.

14 Charles Brenner, *Commercial Change, Political Conflict, and London's Overseas Traders, 1550–1635*, Cambridge, Cambridge University Press, 1993, p. 40.

15 Peacham, *The Complete Gentleman*, 'To My Reader', p. 8.

16 *A Bawd*, in *All the Works of John Taylor the Water-Poet*, 1630, [vol. 2], p. 98.

17 Houston, *Scottish Literacy*, p. 60.

18 Richard Boyle's children in Nicholas Canny, *The Upstart Earl. A Study of the Social and Mental World of Richard Boyle first Earl of Cork 1566–1643*, Cambridge, Cambridge University Press, 1982, pp. 102, 82.

19 A. J. Winnington-Ingram, 'Hereford and the English Bible', *Transactions of the Woolhope Naturalists' Field Club*, 1958–60. vol. XXXVI, pp. 297–305.

20 Anthony [à] Wood, *Athenae Oxonienses. An Exact History of all the Writers and Bishops who have had their Education in…Oxford*, 1721, vol. 1, '1691–2', col. 490.

21 Michael Talbot, in Houston, *Scottish Literacy*, p. 31; Gregory King, *Natural and Political Observations* in *The Earliest Classics*, pp. 34–5; 'Citizens and burgesses' in Harrison, Furnivall, p. 130, Edelen, p. 115; Peacham, *The Complete Gentleman*, p. 22; 'magisterial cliques' in Peter Clark, *English Provincial Society from the Reformation to the Revolution: Religion, Politics and Society in Kent 1500–1640*, Hassocks, The Harvester Press, 1977, p. 141, Brian Manning, 'The middle and poorer sort of people', *The English People and the English Revolution*, Harmondsworth, Penguin, 1978, p. 162, and Steve Rappaport, *Worlds Within Worlds: Structures of Life in Sixteenth-Century London*, Cambridge, Cambridge University Press, 1989, pp. 250–84; office holding in Valerie Pearl, 'Change and stability in seventeenth-century London', *London Journal*, 1979, vol. 5/1, p. 16.

22 Number of London schools in Pearl, 'Change and stability', p. 6; benefit of clergy in O'Day, *Education and Society*, p. 15, and 'benefit of the belly', Frances E. Dolan, 'Reading, writing, and other crimes', in Valerie Traub, M. Lindsay Kaplan and Dymphna Callaghan (eds), *Feminist Readings of Early Modern Culture*, Cambridge, Cambridge University Press, 1996, pp. 145–6; 'a woman hath no clergy, she is to die by the law, if guilty', the trial of Mary Carleton, 1663, in Elspeth Graham, Hilary Hinds, Elaine Hobby and Helen Wilcox (eds), *Her Own Life. Autobiographical Writings by Seventeenth-Century Englishwomen*, London and New York, Routledge, 1989, p. 133; Merchant Taylors' attendance in Richard Mulcaster, *Positions Concerning the Training Up of Children*, 1581, William Barker (ed.), Toronto, University of Toronto Press, 1994, p. lxvi; education charges in Houston, *Scottish Literacy*, pp. 120–1, O'Day, *Education and Society*, p. 32; Bury and Wolverhampton Schools in O'Day, pp. 36–7; Harrison, 'Of Universities', Furnivall, pp. 77–8, Edelen, p. 71.

23 London migration in Wrightson, *English Society*, pp. 28–9; city anxieties and libido in Graunt, *Observations*, p. 46.

24 Elizabeth Cary in Greer *et al.* (eds), *Kissing the Rod. An Anthology of Seventeenth-Century Women's Verse*, London, Virago, 1988, p. 54; Katherine Philips in *The Collected Works of*

Katherine Philips The Matchless Orinda, edited by Patrick Thomas, vol. 1, Stump Cross, Stump Cross Books, 1990, p. 2.

25 Yeomanry in local administration in Amussen, *An Ordered Society*, p. 51. Harrison, Furnivall, pp. 132–3, Edelen, p. 118.

26 Harvest failures in C. J. Harrison, 'Grain price analysis and harvest qualities 1465–1634', *The Agricultural History Review*, 1971, vol. XIX, p. 145; yeoman literacy in Cressy, *Literacy and the Social Order*, p. 127; spiritual autobiographies in Margaret Spufford, 'First steps in literacy: the reading and writing experience of the humblest seventeenth-century spiritual autobiographers', in Harvey J. Graff (ed.), *Literacy and Social Development in the West: A Reader*, Cambridge, Cambridge University Press, 1981, pp. 125–50; literacy and innovation in Houston, *Scottish Literacy*, p. 216.

27 Harrison, Furnivall, p. 134, Edelen, p. 118; for the exclusion of the lower ranks from the polity, Christopher Hill, 'The poor and the people in seventeenth-century England', in Frederick Krantz (ed.), *History from Below. Studies in Popular Protest and Popular Ideology*, Oxford, Basil Blackwell, 1988, pp. 29–52.

28 'Whosoever labour', Peacham, *The Complete Gentleman*, p. 23; artisan literacy in David Cressy, 'Literacy in context', p. 315; Houston, *Scottish Literacy*, p. 60, and Earle, 'The female labour market', p. 343.

29 Stageplayers and tumblers in Peacham, *Complete Gentleman*, p. 23; all materials on Alleyn from S. P. Cerasano, 'Edward Alleyn: 1566–1626', Susan Foister, 'Edward Alleyn's collection of paintings' and J. R. Piggott, 'Edward Alleyn's books', in Aileen Reid and Robert Maniura (eds), *Edward Alleyn. Elizabethan Actor, Jacobean Gentleman*, exhibition catalogue, London, Dulwich Picture Gallery, 1994: 'my poor original', Cerasano, p. 29; 'mouthing words', *The Second Part of the Return from Parnassus*, lines 1927–8, in *The Three Parnassus Plays (1598–1601)*, edited with an introduction and commentary by J. B. Leishman, London, Ivor Nicholson and Watson Ltd, 1949, p. 350; 'Shakesper sonetts', Piggott, p. 63; 'Master Ruler', Piggott, p. 65; see also *Mr Cartwright's Pictures. A Seventeenth Century Collection*, Dulwich Picture Gallery, 1987; beasts of the Bear Garden in Taylor, *Bull, Bear, and Horse, Cut, Curtail and Longtail*, 1638, pp. 54–62, in *Works of John Taylor the Water Poet Not Included in the Folio Volume of 1630*, Third Collection, London, The Spenser Society, 1867, vol. 19, reprinted New York, Burt Franklin, 1967.

30 Barbara Lewalski, 'Re-writing patriarchy and patronage: Margaret Clifford, Anne Clifford, and Aemilia Lanyer', in Cedric Brown (ed.), *Patronage, Politics, and Literary Traditions in England, 1558–1658*, Detroit, Wayne State University Press, 1991, pp. 59–78; 'England's first all-round professional woman writer', Janet Todd, *The Secret Life of Aphra Behn*, London, Andre Deutsch, 1996, p. 16, and a possible education for her, pp. 20–30; glovers' status in L. A. Clarkson, 'The leather crafts in Tudor and Stuart England', *The Agricultural History Review*, 1966, vol. xiv, pp. 25–30. For Mary Shakespeare's familiarity with a quill pen, Park Honan, *Shakespeare. A Life*, Oxford, Oxford University Press. John Shakespeare in the Stratford records and his application to the College of Heralds in F. E. Halliday, *A Shakespeare Companion 1564–1964*, Harmondsworth, Penguin, 1962, 'Arden Family', pp. 35–6, 'Arms, Grant of', pp. 37–8, 'Shakespeare, John', pp. 441–2; and see David Thomas, *Shakespeare in the Public Records*, London, HMSO, 1985, pp. 2–3.

31 Plebian graduands in O'Day, *Education and Society*, pp. 90–7.

32 Reconsideration of John Shakespeare's Spiritual Testament in Patrick Collinson, 'William Shakespeare's religious inheritance and environment', in *Elizabethan Essays*, London and Rio Grande, The Hambledon Press, 1994, pp. 218–52. Shakespeare at Hoghton Tower, Richard Wilson, 'Shakespeare and the Jesuits. New connections supporting the theory of the lost Catholic years in Lancashire', *Times Literary Supplement*, 19 December 1997, vol. 4942, pp. 11–13; the argument made extensively by E. A. J. Honigman, *Shakespeare: The 'Lost Years'*, Manchester, Manchester University Press, 1985.

33 Numbers in service in Laslett, *Family Life*, p. 34; 'poor young men and maids' in Henry Peacham, *The Art of Living in London*, 1642, in *The Complete Gentleman*, p. 243; New Exchange shop girls in O'Day, *Education and Society*, p. 182, and James Knowles, 'Cecil's shopping centre. The rediscovery of a Ben Jonson masque in praise of trade', *Times Literary Supplement*, 7 February 1997, pp. 14–15; Edward Barlow's diary in Illana Krausman Ben-Amos,

Adolescence and Youth in Early Modern England, New Haven and London, Yale University Press, 1994, p. 98; gentry apprentices in Wrightson, *English Society*, p. 28; apprentice numbers in Pearl, 'Change and stability', p. 14; Latin for apprentices in Mark Thornton Burnett, 'Apprentice literature and the "crisis" of the 1590s', *The Yearbook of English Studies*, 1991, vol. 21, p. 28; apprentice literacy in Ben-Amos, pp. 197–9; Paul Griffiths, *Youth and Authority. Formative Experiences in England, 1560–1640*, Oxford, Oxford University Press, 1996; debating artisan status in Ian Gadd, 'The mechanicks of difference: a study in Stationers' Company discourse in the seventeenth century', in Robin Myers and Michael Harris (eds), *The Stationers' Company and the Book Trade 1550–1990*, Winchester, St Paul's Bibliographies, and New Castle, Delaware, Oak Knoll Press, 1997, pp. 93–112.

34 Husbandmen earnings from P. J. Bowden, 'Agricultural prices, farm profits, and rents', in J. Thirsk (ed.), *The Agrarian History of England and Wales*, vol. IV, '1500–1640', Cambridge, Cambridge University Press, 1967, pp. 657–9, quoted in Wrightson, *English Society*, p. 33; population and dearth in Roger Schofield, 'The impact of scarcity and plenty on population change in England, 1541–1871', *The Journal of Interdisciplinary History*, 1983, vol. XIV: 2, pp. 265–91, and Scottish famine in Kishlansky, *A Monarchy Transformed*, p. 27; book prices, Watt, *Cheap Print*, p. 261.

35 Spufford, *Small Books and Pleasant Histories*, p. 2.

36 J. A. Sharpe, *Early Modern England. A Social History 1550–1760*, Part II: 'The social hierarchy and social change', London, Edward Arnold, 1987, p. 208; Ben-Amos, 'The labouring child', *Adolesence and Youth*, pp. 40–5; 'family economy', Amussen, *An Ordered Society*, p. 94.

37 Sir William Temple, 'Of Poetry', in *Miscellanea. The Second Part. In Four Essays*, 1705, fifth edition, pp. 360–1.

3 'TOWARDNESS'

1 *The Diary of Samuel Pepys*, vol. VIII, '1667', a new and complete transcription edited by Robert Latham and William Matthews, London, Bell and Hyman, 1974, pp. 338–9.

2 Wycliffite bibles in Anne Hudson, *The Premature Reformation. Wycliffite Texts and Lollard History*, Oxford, The Clarendon Press, 1988, pp. 198–206; vernacular devotional reading, Eamon Duffy, 'How the Plowman learned his Paternoster', *The Stripping of the Altars. Traditional Religion in England c. 1400–c. 1580*, New Haven and London, Yale University Press, 1992, pp. 53–88; Richard Rex, 'Vernacular religious culture', in *Henry VIII and the English Reformation*, London and Basingstoke, Macmillan, 1993, pp. 104–32; Andrew Taylor, 'Into his secret chamber: reading and privacy in late medieval England', in James Raven, Helen Small and Naomi Taylor (eds), *The Practice and Representation of Reading in England*, Cambridge, Cambridge University Press, 1996, pp. 41–61.

3 John Foxe, 'The Life and Story of Master William Tyndale', in, *Acts and Mouments of these latter and perilous days, touching matters of the Church, wherein are comprehended and described the great persecutions and horrible troubles, that have been wrought and practised by the Romish prelates, specially in this realm of England and Scotland*, 1563, p. 514, column b; David Daniell, 'The 1534 New Testament', in *William Tyndale: A Biography*, New Haven and London, Yale University Press, 1994, p. 317.

4 David Cressy, 'Literacy in context', pp. 305–19, and 'Levels of illiteracy in England 1530–1730', in Graff, *Literacy and Social Development*, pp. 105–24; David Vincent, *Literacy and Popular Culture. England 1750–1914*, Cambridge, Cambridge University Press, 1989, p. 1.

5 'The local geography', David Cressy, *Literacy and the Social Order*, p. 96; Ayr schooling, William Boyd, *Education in Ayreshire through Seven Centuries*, University of London Press, London, 1961, p. 16; Euphame Halcro in Houston, *Scottish Literacy and the Scottish Identity*, p. 297.

6 The range of literacies, Maureen Bell reviewing Tessa Watt, *Cheap Print and Popular Piety, 1500–1640*, Cambridge, Cambridge University Press, 1991, in *Publishing History*, 1993, vol. XXXIII, pp. 101–4, and Adam Fox, 'Popular verses and their readership in the early seventeenth century', in *The Practice and Representation of Reading*, pp. 125–37.

7 William Dell, *The Right Reformation of Learning, Schools and Universities According to the State of the Gospel, and the True Light that Shines Therein* (1646), in *Select Works of William Dell*,

London, 1773, pp. 579–81; Gerrard Winstanley, 'Education of mankind, in schools and trades', in *The Law of Freedom in a Platform: Or, True Magistracy Restored* (1652), in *The Law of Freedom and Other Writings*, edited with an introduction by Christopher Hill, Harmondsworth, Penguin, 1973, p. 362; attitudes to illiteracy, François Furet and Jacques Ozouf, *Reading and Writing. Literacy in France from Calvin to Jules Ferry* (1977), Cambridge, Cambridge University Press, and Paris, Editions de la Maison des Sciences de l'Homme, 1982, pp. 126–7; 'low literacy rates', Cressy, 'Literacy in context', p. 306.

8 *Gold Tried in the Fire; or, The Burnt Petitions Revived* (1647), attributed to William Walwyn, in *The Writings of William Walwyn*, edited by Jack R. McMichael and Barbara Taft, Foreword by Christopher Hill, Athens and London, The University of Georgia Press, 1989, p. 284.

9 Black-letter type discussed in Cressy, 'Literacy in context', p. 312; Ciceronian attitudes to illiteracy, William V. Harris, *Ancient Literacy*, Cambridge, MA and London, Harvard University Press, 1989, p. 6.

10 Egil Johansson, 'The history of literacy in Sweden', in Graff, *Literacy and Social Development*, pp. 152–3; 'following the minister', T. C. Smout, 'Born again at Cambuslang: new evidence on popular religion and literacy in eighteenth-century Scotland', *Past and Present*, 1982, vol. 97, p. 126; in 1742, 110 individuals were interviewed, an early exercise in oral popular cultural studies, 'all the women and men could read...over a third but perhaps not as many as three quarters of the men could write...there is no evidence that much above a tenth of the women could write' (p. 121).

11 The hornbook, Mitford M. Mathews, *Teaching to Read Historically Considered*, Chicago and London, University of Chicago Press, 1966, pp. 16–17, and see 'Christ-cross, criss-cross', *OED*; Dell, *The Right Reformation*, p. 579.

12 John Kerrigan, 'The editor as reader: constructing Renaissance texts', in *The Practice and Representation of Reading*, p. 115; John M. Wallace, ' "Examples are best precepts": readers and meanings in seventeenth-century poetry', *Critical Inquiry*, 1974, vol. 1, pp. 273–90; Mary Thomas Crane, 'Educational practice in early sixteenth-century England', in, *Framing Authority: Sayings, Self, and Society in Sixteenth-Century England*, Princeton, Princeton University Press, 1993, pp. 77–92; Eugene R. Kintgen, *Reading in Tudor England*, Pittsburgh, University of Pittsburgh Press, 1996, p. 210ff.; for the possible influence of these conventions on early modern acting, see Joseph R. Roach, 'Changeling Proteus: rhetoric and the passions in the seventeenth century', in *The Player's Passion. Studies in the Science of Acting*, Newark, University of Delaware Press, London and Toronto, Associated University Presses, 1985, pp. 23–57; and for possible audience response, 'In Shakespeare's own time the pleasures of discovering singularity in the plays would have been outweighed by those of recognizing exemplarity', Jonathan Bate, *Shakespeare and Ovid*, Oxford, Clarendon Press, 1993, p. 198.

13 Aphorism XC in *The New Organon; or, True Directions Concerning the Interpretation of Nature*, in *The Works of Francis Bacon*, collected and edited by James Spedding, Robert Leslie Ellis and Douglas Denton Heath, vol. IV, 'Translations of the Philosophical Works', London, Longman, 1870, p. 89.

14 *The Diary of Ralph Josselyn 1616–1683*, edited by Alan MacFarlane, London, published for the British Academy by Oxford University Press, 1976, p. 62; Cressy, *Literacy and the Social Order*, p. 149; 'Elizabeth Jane Weston: her life, acquaintance and writings', in J. W. Binns, *Intellectual Culture in Elizabethan and Jacobean England. The Latin Writings of the Age*, Leeds, Francis Cairns (Publications) Ltd, 1990, pp. 110–14; O'Day, *Education and Society*, p. 62.

15 *Walwyn's Just Defence...* (1649), in *The Writings of William Walwyn*, p. 397.

16 O'Day, *Education and Society*, p. 67.

17 O'Day, *Education and Society*, pp. 185–7; L. A. Pollock, ' "Teach her to live under obedience": the making of women in the upper ranks of early modern England', *Continuity and Change*, 1989, vol. 4, pp. 238–44; Norfolk widows in Patricia Crawford, *Women and Religion in England 1500–1720*, London, Routledge, 1993, p. 88.

18 'The Great Tew Circle', in Hugh Trevor-Roper, *Catholics, Anglicans and Puritans: Seventeenth Century Essays*, Chicago, University of Chicago Press, 1988, pp. 166–230; pious readers in Suzanne Trill, 'Religion and the construction of femininity', in Helen Wilcox (ed.), *Women and Literature in Britain 1500–1700*, Cambridge, Cambridge University Press, 1996, p. 33; the

Virgin and St Anne, in Rex, *Henry VIII and the English Reformation*, p. 110; radical embroiderers, Margaret Swain, *Figures on Fabric. Embroidery Design Sources and Their Application*, London, A. and C. Black, 1980, and personal communication; *Paradise Lost*, Book VIII, line 173, in *The Poems of John Milton*, edited by John Carey and Alastair Fowler, London, Longman, 1968, p. 824. Chapter 6 discusses the ways in which early modern assumptions as to what was appropriate for women to study could be circumvented in daily life.

19 'Education is the bringing up of one', from Richard Mulcaster, *Positions wherein those primitive circumstances be examined which are necessary for the training up of children, either for skill in their book or health in their body* 1581, p. 185; this edition lightly modernized and edited by William Barker, Toronto, Buffalo, London, University of Toronto Press, 1996, p. 186. All later quotations given by page number in the 1581 text and Barker's edition.

20 'The Virtuous Education of Youth…A Discourse upon Proverbs XXII, Verse 6' (1683), in *Twelve Sermons and Discourses on Several Subjects and Occasions*, 1717, vol. V, pp. 4–5, later page numbers in text; for South's new sermon rhetoric, David Norton, *A History of the Bible as Literature*, vol. 1, 'From Antiquity to 1700', Cambridge, Cambridge University Press, 1993, pp. 252–8.

21 The dissenting academies in O'Day, *Education and Society*, pp. 212–15, and Irene Parker, *Dissenting Academies in England. Their Rise and Progress and their Place Among the Educational Systems of the Country*, Cambridge, Cambridge University Press, 1914.

4 'MECHANICS IN THE SUBURBS OF LITERATURE'

1 'Mechanics…in the Suburbs of Literature' from *The Printers' Humble Remonstrance* (1643), in Edward Arber (ed.), *A Transcript of the Registers of the Company of Stationers of London 1554–1640 A.D.*, five vols, London, printed privately, 1875–94, vol. 1, p. 584, discussed by Ian Gadd, 'The mechanicks of difference: a study in Stationers' Company discourse in the seventeenth century', in Myers and Harris, *The Stationers' Company and the Book Trade*, pp. 93–112; Caxton's *Dicts or Sayings*, N. F. Blake, 'Dating the first books printed in English', in *William Caxton and English Literary Culture*, London and Rio Grande, The Hambledon Press, 1991, p. 75; Robert Greene, 'The Art of Cony-Catching', in *A Notable Discovery of Cozenage* (1591), in Gamini Salgado (ed.), *Cony-Catchers and Bawdy Baskets. An Anthology of Elizabethan Low Life*, Harmondsworth, Penguin, 1972, p. 162; for the early history of the site, Ann Saunders, 'The Stationers' Hall', in Myers and Harris, *The Stationers' Company and the Book Trade*, pp. 1–10.

2 Steinberg, *Five Hundred Years of Printing*, pp. 54–5; 'In continental terms', James Raven, 'Selling books across Europe, c. 1450–1800', *Publishing History*, 1993, vol. XXXIV, p. 14; the European book fairs, Lucien Febvre and Henri-Jean Martin, *The Coming of the Book. The Impact of Printing 1450–1800* (1958), translated by David Gerard, edited by Geoffrey Nowell-Smith and David Wootton, London, Verso, 1984, pp. 224–33; wandering chapmen, Watt, *Cheap Print*, p. 267, and woodblock recutting, p. 147.

3 Lisa Jardine, 'The Triumph of the Book', in *Worldly Goods. A New History of the Renaissance*, London and Basingstoke, Macmillan, 1996, pp. 143–52.

4 *Humble Remonstrance*, in Arber, *A Transcript*, vol. 1, p. 584.

5 This overview compiled from H. S. Bennett, *English Books and Readers 1558 to 1603. Being A Study in the History of the Book Trade in the Reign of Elizabeth I*, Cambridge, Cambridge University Press, 1965, Chapter VI, 'Printers and Booksellers'; John Feather, *A History of British Publishing*, London, Routledge, 1988, pp. 19–43, and Marjorie Plant, *The English Book Trade. An Economic History of the Making and Sale of Books*, London, George Allen and Unwin, 1965; Innerpefray borrowings, R. A. Houston, *Scottish Literacy and the Scottish Identity. Illiteracy and Society in Scotland and Northern England 1600–1800*, Cambridge, Cambridge University Press, 1985, p. 176; pictorial primers, O'Day, *Education and Society*, p. 54, and Lily's 'Grammar', p. 67.

6 John Feather, 'The Printed Book', in Martin Coyle, Peter Garside, Malcolm Kelsall and John Peck (eds), *Encyclopedia of Literature and Criticism*, London, Routledge, 1990, p. 830.

7 Cyprian Blagden, *The Stationers' Company. A History, 1403–1959*, London, George Allen and Unwin, 1960, Chapters I and III; Feather, *A History of British Publishing*, Part One; Clegg, *Press Censorship*, pp. 14–25 for the Company.

8 *Brief Discourse Concerning Printers and Printing*, London, 1663, p. 13.

9 Opportunism of the Crown and Stationers, Clegg, *Press Censorship*, pp. 22, 220; Martin Lowry, *Nicholas Jenson and the Rise of Venetian Publishing in Europe*, Oxford, Blackwell, 1991.

10 Sheila Lambert, 'State control of the press in theory and practice: the role of the Stationers' Company before 1640', in Robin Myers and Michael Harris (eds), *Censorship and the Control of Print in England and France 1600–1910*, London, St Paul's Bibliographies, 1992, p. 2; for the City Guilds, Steve Rappaport, *Worlds within Worlds*, pp. 184–93.

11 Numbers of women stationers in Bell *et al.*, *A Biographical Dictionary of English Women Writers*, 'Critical Appendices', p. 293; 'Women printers, publishers and booksellers' listed in Hilda L. Smith and Susan Cardinale (eds), *Women and the Literature of the Seventeenth Century*, New York, Westport, Connecticut, London, Greenwood Press, 1990, pp. 313–4; the 1636 election, Sheila Lambert, 'The printers and the government, 1604–1637', in Robin Myers and Michael Harris (eds), *Aspects of Printing from 1600*, Oxford, Oxford Polytechnic Press, 1987, p. 10; Joanna Nye, Blagden, *The Stationers' Company*, p. 162; women and apprenticeship, Ilana Krausman Ben-Amos, Chapter 6, 'Women's youth: the autonomous phase', in *Adolescence and Youth in Early Modern England*, New Haven and London, Yale University Press, 1994, pp. 133–55; 'London the great Stage and Shop', John Graunt, *Natural and Political Observations...Made upon the Bills of Mortality* (1662), in *The Earliest Classics*, 'Pioneers of Demography', introduced by Peter Laslett, n. p., Gregg International Publishers, 1973, p. 47.

12 Number of freemen, Valerie Pearl, 'Change and stability in seventeenth-century London', *The London Journal*, 1979, vol. 5/1, p. 13.

13 *Royal Commission Enquiring into Printing*, 1583, State Papers Domestic, Elizabeth I, vol. 161, art. 1, in W. W. Greg (ed.) *A Companion to Arber. With Text and Calendar of Supplementary Documents*, Oxford, Clarendon Press, 1967, p. 126.

14 Quoted in Plant, *The English Book Trade*, pp. 113–4.

15 Febvre and Martin, *The Coming of the Book*, p. 163; Clegg, *Press Censorship*, pp. 7–14 for the most recent work on licences and privileges; Ariosto and Daniel, Mark Rose, *Authors and Owners. The Invention of Copyright*, Cambridge, MA, London, Harvard University Press, 1993, p. 17.

16 Crown privileges in religious texts, Clegg, *Press Censorship*, p. 13; Bernard Capp, *Astrology and the Popular Press. English Almanacs 1500–1800*, London, Faber, 1979; Tessa Watt, *Cheap Print*, throughout; guild ownership, Rose, *Authors and Owners*, p. 14; a revealing history of privileges, patents and conflicts of interest in Peter Blayney, 'William Cecil and the Stationers', in Robin Myers and Michael Harris (eds), *The Stationers' Company and the Book Trade 1550–1990*, Winchester, St Paul's Bibliographies, and New Castle, Delaware, Oak Knoll Press, 1997, pp. 13–27.

17 Non-registration of titles and copyright, Blagden, *The Stationers' Company*, p. 44; Maureen Bell, 'Entrance in the Stationers' Register', *The Library*, 1994, 6th series, vol. 16, pp. 50–4; 'In 1596', Clegg, *Press Censorship*, p. 61, 'The benefits', p. 19.

18 Sir Philip Sidney, *The Countess of Pembroke's Arcadia*, edited with introduction and commentary by Jean Robertson, Oxford, Clarendon Press, 1973, p. [3]; proportion of dedicated works, Bennett, *English Books and Readers*, p. 51; for the culture of scribal publication, H. R. Woudhuysen, *Sir Philip Sidney and the Circulation of Manuscripts, 1558–1640*, Oxford, Clarendon Press, 1996.

19 Cecil's patronage, Jan Van Dorsten, 'Literary patronage in Elizabethan England: the early phase', in Guy Fitch Lytle and Stephen Orgel (eds), *Patronage in the Renaissance*, Princeton, Princeton University Press, 1981, pp. 194–9; Ortelius in Jardine, *Worldly Goods*, p. 178.

20 *Stationers' Petition* 1643, cited Plant, *The English Book Trade*, p. 113.

21 Plant, *The English Book Trade*, p. 74. Alleyn and Henslowe's income, Aileen Reid and Robert Maniura (eds), *Edward Alleyn*, pp. 12–18; see also Arthur F. Marotti, *John Donne, Coterie Poet*, Madison, University of Wisconsin Press, 1986, and *Manuscript, Print, and the English Renaissance Lyric*, Ithaca, New York, Cornell University Press, 1995.

22 Blagden, *The Stationers' Company*, pp. 92–109.

23 George Unwin, *The Gilds and Companies of London* (1908), with a new introduction by William F. Kahl, fourth edition, London, Frank Cass and Co., 1963; Lambert, 'The printers and the government', p. [1].

24 1637 Decree in Arber, *Transcript*, vol. 4, pp. 529–36, discussed in Lambert, 'State control of the press', pp. 22–3.

25 Lambert, 'State control of the press', p. 27, note 33. For Prynne's *Histrio-Mastix*, see Chapter 5.

26 *Scintilla, or A Light Broken into Dark Warehouses. With Observations upon the Monopolists of Seven several Patents, and Two Charters. Practised and Performed by a Mystery of some Printers, Sleeping Stationers, and Combining Book-sellers. Anatomised and laid open in a Breviat, in which is only a touch of their forestalling and ingrossing of Books in Patents, and Raising them to excessive prices. Left to the consideration of the High and Honourable House of Parliament now assembled*, 1641, p. 6.

27 *Scintilla*, p. 3.

28 Joad Raymond, *The Invention of the Newspaper. English Newsbooks 1641–1649*, Oxford, Clarendon Press, 1996; William K. Sessions, *A World of Mischiefe. The King's Printer in York in 1642 and in Shrewsbury 1642–1643*, York, The Ebor Press, 1981; and *The King's Printer at Newcastle-upon-Tyne in 1639, at Bristol in 1642 and at Exeter in 1645–1646*, York, The Ebor Press, 1982; Nigel Smith, 'Writing, publishing and reading in the war', *Literature and Revolution in England 1640–1660*, New Haven and London, Yale University Press, 1994, pp. 21–92.

29 Lois Spencer, 'The professional and literary connexions of George Thomason', *The Library*, 1958, 5th series, vol. 13, pp. 102–18; 'The politics of George Thomason', *The Library*, 1959, 5th series, vol. 14, pp. 11–27; on the scale of printed output in the 1640s, John Barnard and D. F. McKenzie (eds), *A History of the Book in Britain*, vol. IV, '1557–1695', Cambridge, Cambridge University Press, forthcoming.

30 P. W. Thomas, *Sir John Berkenhead 1617–1679. A Royalist Career in Politics and Polemics*, Oxford, Clarendon Press, 1969; Raymond, *The Invention of the Newspaper*.

31 Blagden, *The Stationers' Company*, p. 146; Plant, *The English Book Trade*, p. 113; for the role of *The Humble Remonstrance of the Company of Stationers*, April 1643, Ian Gadd, 'The mechanicks of difference', throughout.

32 *Areopagitica; A Speech of Mr John Milton For the Liberty of Unlicenced Printing, To the Parliament of England*, in *The Complete Prose Works of John Milton*, vol. II, '1643–1648', edited by Ernest Sirluck, New Haven, Yale University Press, and London, Oxford University Press, 'The fraud', p. 570, 'Those which', p. 569; Abbe Blum, 'The author's authority. *Areopagitica* and the labour of licensing', in Mary Nyquist and Margaret W. Ferguson (eds), *Re-membering Milton: Essays on the Texts and Traditions*, New York and London, Methuen, 1987, pp. 74–96.

33 Blum, 'The author's authority', pp. 86–92.

34 Blagden, *The Stationers' Company*, p. 153.

5 CENSORSHIP AND STATE FORMATION

1 'Good grows with her', John Margeson (ed.), *King Henry VIII*, Cambridge, Cambridge University Press, 1990, 5.4.32–8, p. 184; 'peace, plenty', 5.5.47; 'Lent him our terror', N. W. Bawcutt (ed.), *Measure for Measure*, Oxford and New York, Oxford University Press, 1994, 1.1.20, p. 88 and note; and see Lois Potter (ed.), *The Two Noble Kinsmen*, Walton-on-Thames, Thomas Nelson and Sons Ltd, 1997, pp. 35–40, probably written by Fletcher and Shakespeare immediately after *Henry VIII*, for some relevant political and dynastic contexts.

2 Paul L. Hughes and James F. Larkin (eds), *Tudor Royal Proclamations*, vol. II, 'The Later Tudors (1553–1587)', New Haven and London, Yale University Press, 1969, p. 115; see the letter from the Lord Mayor to Sir Francis Walsingham, 3 May 1583, in E. K. Chambers, *The Elizabethan Stage*, 4 vols, Oxford, Oxford University Press, 1923, vol. IV, p. 294, and to John Whitgift, Archbishop of Canterbury, 25 February 1592, vol. IV, pp. 307–8; Paul Yachnin, 'The powerless theatre', *English Literary Renaissance*, 1991, vol. 21, p. 66; J. Leeds Barroll *et al.*, *The Revels History of Drama in English*, vol. 3, '1576–1616', London, 1975, pp. 3–27.

3 For 'the most significant event', see 'Censorship and English literature', in *Writing and Revolution in Seventeenth-Century England*, Brighton, Harvester Wheatsheaf, 1985, p. 40; Tina Krontiris, *Oppositional Voices. Women as Writers and Translators of Literature in the English Renaissance*, London and New York, Routledge, pp. 17–23; Gerald Eades Bentley, 'Regulation and censorship', *The Profession of Dramatist in Shakespeare's Time, 1590–1642*, Princeton, Princeton University Press, 1971, pp. 145–96; Annabel Patterson, *Censorship and Interpretation. The Conditions of Writing and Reading in Early Modern England*, Madison, University of Wisconsin Press, 1984, and *Fables of Power. Aesopian Writing and Political History*, Durham and London, Duke University Press, 1991.

4 For 'the fabric of Elizabethan press censorship', see Clegg, *Press Censorship in Elizabethan England*, p. 5; 'quite precisely in the politics of personality', p. 222; and:

> A sense of what the government regarded as 'transgressive' is far less clear than previous studies have suggested....It is a mistake however to see political press censorship as illustrative of the kind of cultural hegemony posited by Foucault that assumes the interdependence of knowledge and power. This denies entirely the possibility of any kind of press unsanctioned by authority. This was simply not the case in late sixteenth-century England, where, as we have seen, countless unlicensed texts appeared – few of which were suppressed.
>
> (p. 222)

5 For 'no consistent political, moral or cultural criteria', see Janet Clare, *'Art made tongue-tied by authority': Elizabethan and Jacobean Dramatic Censorship*, Manchester and New York, Manchester University Press, 1990, p. 211; Cade's uprising, p. 41; 'Leave out the insurrection wholly', quoted in Clare, p. 32; 'With new additions', quoted in Clare pp. 47–8; Clare developed criticism of new-historicist and cultural-materialist readings in 'Historicism and the question of censorship in the renaissance', *English Literary Renaissance*, 1997, vol. 27/2, pp. 155–76:

> it is evident that we cannot begin to understand the Renaissance and its theater in historical terms by imposing inflexible notions of 'power', 'theatricality', 'play' and 'license'. In practice, such economies are fluid and complex, and always subject to historical contingency.
>
> (pp. 174–5)

Shakespeare as 'hand D' the reviser in *Sir Thomas More*, Jonathan Bate, *The Genius of Shakespeare*, London, Picador, 1997, pp. 98–9.

6 Libel cases, Philip J. Finkelpearl, ' "The comedians' liberty": censorship of the Jacobean stage reconsidered', *English Literary Renaissance*, 1986, vol. 16, pp. 123–4; 'thirty instances of censorship', Lambert, 'State control of the press', p. 3; also Kevin Sharpe, 'Culture and politics, court and country: assumptions and problems, questions and suggestions', in *Criticism and Compliment. The Politics of Literature in the England of Charles I*, Cambridge, Cambridge University Press, 1987, pp. 36–9; Yachnin, 'The powerless theatre', pp. 69–74; see also Stephen Mullaney, *The Place of the Stage: License, Play, and Power in Renaissance England*, Chicago, Chicago University Press, 1988, and Richard Burt, *Licensed by Authority. Ben Jonson and the Discourses of Censorship*, Ithaca, Cornell University Press, 1993; 'when we observe the breadth of political observation', A. B. Worden, 'Literature and political censorship in early modern England', in A. C. Duke and C. A. Tamse (eds), *Too Mighty To Be Free. Censorship and the Press in Britain and the Netherlands*, 'Britain and the Netherlands', vol. IX, Zutphen, De Walburg Pers, 1987, p. 48; for censorship of manuscript and other forums, Harold Love, *Scribal Publication in Seventeenth Century England*, Oxford, Oxford University Press, 1993 and D. F. McKenzie, 'Speech-Manuscript-Print', *Library Chronicle*, 1989, vol. 20, pp. 87–109.

7 For a story which 'belongs to anti-art, as much as to art', Margaret Aston, *The King's Bedpost. Reformation and Iconography in a Tudor Portrait Group*, Cambridge, Cambridge University

Press, 1993, p. 1; Eamon Duffy, *The Stripping of the Altars. Traditional Religion in England c. 1400–c. 1580*, New Haven and London, Yale University Press, 1992.

8 Harold Jenkins (ed.), *Hamlet*, London and New York, Methuen, 1982, 3.2.227–8, p. 301; 'some dozen or sixteen lines', 2.2.535, p. 269; 'guilty creatures', 2.2.585, 588, p. 272.

9 For early attempts at censorship, Blagden, *The Stationers' Company*, pp. 28–31; Feather, *A History of British Publishing*, p. 16 ff.; Peter Blayney, 'William Cecil and the Stationers', p. 11; Cecil's involvement, pp. 29–30.

10 'powers of this kind', Lambert, 'State control of the press', p. 10; Barker, 'if no man were allowed', *Report on Patents*, quoted in Marjorie Plant, *The English Book Trade. An Economic History of the Making and Sale of Books*, London, George Allen and Unwin, 1965, p. 83; searchers in Arber, *A Transcript*, p. 42; John Stow in Arber, *A Transcript*, vol. I, p. 393; 'remarkably little control', John Sutherland, 'Production and reception of the literary book', in *Encyclopedia of Literature and Criticism*, p. 814.

11 Holinshed called in, Clare, *'Art Made Tongue-tied'*, p. 17; 'few of the books printed in England', Clegg, *Press Censorship*, p. 221.

12 Stressed-out clerk, Lambert, 'State Control', p. 11; availability of Catholic texts, Roberts, *Publishing History*, 1990, vol. 27, p. 104, reviewing E. S. Leedham-Green, *Books in Cambridge Inventories. Book Lists from Vice-Chancellors' Court Probate Inventories in the Tudor and Stuart Periods*, two vols, Cambridge, Cambridge University Press, 1987; 'too saucy in censuring princes', John Racin Jr, 'The early editions of Ralegh's *History of the World*', *Studies in Bibliography*, 1964, vol. XVII, p. 200.

13 'We would call Topcliffe a sadist: a word they did not have', Charles Nicholl, *The Reckoning. The Murder of Christopher Marlowe*, Chicago, University of Chicago Press, 1992, p. 111; 'They come either in the night', in A. G. Pett (ed.), *The Letters and Despatches of Richard Verstegan c. 1550–1640*, Catholic Record Society, 1959, vol. 52, p. 7.

14 'prosecutions rarely proceeded', Clegg, *Press Censorship*, p. 221; William Chillingworth and Francis Cheynell in C. V. Wedgwood, *The King's War 1641–1647*, London, Collins, 1966, pp. 269–70; 'puritans composed within the church' and 'Most people assumed' in Patrick Collinson, *English Puritanism*, London, The Historical Association, 1983, p. 19, and see Christopher Durston and Jacqueline Eales, 'The puritan ethos, 1560–1700', in Durston and Eales (eds), *The Culture of English Puritanism, 1560–1700*, Basingstoke and London, Macmillan 1996, pp. 1–31.

15 1624 Proclamation in Stephen Foster, *Notes from the Caroline Underground. Alexander Leighton, the Puritan Triumvirate, and the Laudian Reaction to Nonconformity*, Hamden, CT, The Shoe String Press Inc., 1978, p. 21; Rudyerd, 'They have brought it to pass' in Durston and Eales, 'The puritan ethos', p. 5; Bancroft's papal ambitions, *Sion's Plea*, pp. 76–7; 'desperate against the hierarchy', Laud, *Works*, vol. VII, 'Letters', edited by James Bliss, Oxford, Henry Parker, 1860, p. 317.

16 'Ireland is but swordland', Tadhg Dall Ó hUiginn, quoted in T. J. Dunne, 'The Gaelic response to conquest and colonisation: the evidence of the poetry', *Studia Hibernica*, 1980, vol. 20, pp. 14–15; Montaigne, 'An Apology of Raymond Sebond', *The Essays of Michael Lord of Montaigne* translated by John Florio, 1603, London, J. M. Dent, 1897, Book Two, Chapter Twelve, vol. 3, p. 210; for analogies drawn between the Scottish, Irish and New World 'Indians', see Steven Mullaney, 'Strange things, gross terms, curious customs: the rehearsal of cultures in the late Renaissance', *Representations*, 1988, vol. 3, pp. 49–50.

17 Derek Hirst, Chapter 7, 'The crisis of the three kingdoms 1640–1642', *Authority and Conflict. England 1603–1658*, London, Melbourne, Auckland, Edward Arnold, 1986, p. 188; Conrad Russell, *The Fall of the British Monarchies 1637–1642*, Oxford, Clarendon Press, 1991; for a useful overview, Raphael Samuel, 'British dimensions: four nations history', *History Workshop Journal*, 1995, vol. 40, pp. iii–xxii.

18 Donald MacAuley, 'The Celtic languages: an overview', *The Celtic Languages*, Cambridge, Cambridge University Press, 1992, pp. 1–8; R. A. Butlin, 'Land and people, c. 1600', in T. W. Moody, F. X. Martin, F. J. Byrne (eds), *A New History of Ireland*, pp. 146–7.

19 Steven G. Ellis, 'Pacata Hibernia, 1579–1603', *Tudor Ireland. Crown, Community and the Conflict of Cultures, 1470–1603*, London and New York, Longman, 1985, pp. 278–313; Derick Thomson, 'Clan and politics', *An Introduction to Gaelic Poetry*, pp. 116–55; the Act of 1537,

Michael Cronin, 'Translation, conquest and controversy', in *Translating Ireland. Translation, Languages, Cultures*, Cork, Cork University Press, 1996, p. 48; Tudor policy on Gaelic, Brian Ó Cuív, 'The Irish language in the early modern period', in Moody *et al.* (eds), *The New History of Ireland*, pp. 510–12.

20 W. P. Griffith, *Learning, Law and Religion: Higher Education and Welsh Society, c. 1540–1640*, Cardiff, University of Wales Press, 1996, pp. 387–90; W. P. Griffith, 'Schooling and society', in John Gwynfor Jones (ed.), *Class, Community and Culture in Tudor Wales*, Cardiff, University of Wales Press, 1989; Ceri W. Lewis, 'The decline of professional poetry', in R. Geraint Gruffydd (ed.), *A Guide to Welsh Literature*, vol. III, 'c. 1530–1700', Cardiff, University of Wales Press, 1997, pp. 29–74; Sidney, Geoffrey Shepherd (ed.), *An Apology for Poetry*, London, Thomas Nelson, 1965, pp. 97–8; Philips, 'On the Welch Language', in *The Collected Works of Katherine Philips*, vol. 1, p. 377; R. B. McDowell and D. A. Webb, *Trinity College, Dublin, 1592–1952: An Academic History*, Cambridge, Cambridge University Press, 1982, pp. 9–10.

21 'Bardic poetry', T. J. Dunne, 'The Gaelic response', p. 12; Nicholas Canny, 'The formation of the Irish mind: religion, politics and Gaelic Irish literature 1580–1750', *Past and Present*, 1982, vol. 95, p. 93; Ó hUiginn and Ó hIfearnáin in Dunne, 'The Gaelic response', pp. 14–5, and Ó Cuív, 'The Irish language', pp. 524–6, 538.

22 Eileen Knott (ed.), *Irish Classical Poetry*, Dublin, 1966, p. 79; 'hounds of great knowledge' in Ó Cuív, 'The Irish language', p. 539; 'a factory of booksellers', *Acts of the Privy Council*, quoted in Blagden, 'The Irish Stock', *The Stationers' Company*, p. 108; for a discussion 'what are the deep structural changes occurring in the ability of [early modern] Gaelic discourse to figure and structure its world', see Ann Dooley, 'Literature and society in early seventeenth-century Ireland: the evaluation of change', in Cyril J. Byrne, Margaret Harry, Pádraig Ó Siadhail (eds), *Celtic Languages and Celtic Peoples*, Saint Mary's University, Halifax, Nova Scotia, 1992, pp. 513–34.

23 Céitinn in Brendan Bradshaw, Andrew Hadfield and Willy Maley (eds), *Representing Ireland: Literature and the Origins of Conflict, 1534–1660*, Cambridge, Cambridge University Press, 1993, pp. 166–90.

24 Poets denigrated from the 1530s in Ó Cuív, 'The Irish language', pp. 520–1; *A View of the Present State of Ireland*, pp. 75, 72–7, 117–8, the passage also quoted in Thomas F. O'Rahilly, 'Irish poets, historians, and judges in English documents, 1583–1615', *Proceedings of the Royal Irish Academy*, 1921–4, vol. XXXVI, p. 86, listing over fifty 'rimers' pardoned in the Fiants [warrants] of Elizabeth; see also Patricia Coughlan (ed.), *Spenser and Ireland: An Interdisciplinary Perspective*, Cork, Cork University Press, 1989, N. Canny, 'Edmund Spenser and the development of an Anglo-Irish identity', *Yearbook of English Studies*, 1983, vol. XIII, pp. 1–19, and Ciarán Brady, 'Spenser's Irish crisis: humanism and experience in the 1590s', *Past and Present*, 1986, vol. 111, pp. 17–49.

25 Material on Irish music, singers and their persecutions from W. H. Grattan Flood, *A History of Irish Music*, second edition, Dublin, Belfast, Cork, Waterford, Browne and Nolan, 1927, pp. 120–9, quoted in James R. Cowdery, *The Melodic Tradition of Ireland*, Kent, Ohio, and London, The Kent State University Press, 1990; persecution of the singers in Flood, *A History*, pp. 185–6. Thanks to Peter Riley for this reference; primary sources in *The Irish Fiants of the Tudor Sovereigns*, with a new introduction by Kenneth Nicholls and preface by Tomás G. Ó Canaan, vol. 2, '1558–1586', Dublin for Éamonn de Búrea for Edmund Burke Publisher, 1994, for example Fiant 3612, p. 501.

26 The 'birth of modern Irish', Cronin, *Translating Ireland*, p. 63; *Seathan* given entire in Thomson, *Gaelic Poetry*, pp. 76–81; Fedelm meets Medb, *The Tain*, translated by Thomas Kinsella from the Irish Táin Bó Cuailnge, Mountrath, The Dolmen Press in association with Oxford University Press, 1970, p. 61; on female patrons in seventeenth-century Ireland, Bernadette Cunningham, 'Women and Gaelic literature, 1500–1800', in Margaret MacCurtain and Mary O'Dowd (eds), *Women in Early Modern Ireland*, Edinburgh, Edinburgh University Press, 1991, pp. 147–59; on the displacement of the bardic schools 'from their pivotal role in [Scottish] Gaelic culture', Allan I. Macinnes, 'Seventeenth-century Scotland: the undervalued Gaelic perspective', in Byrne *et al.* (eds), *Celtic Languages and Celtic Peoples*, pp. 535–54.

27 Women poets in Thomson, *Gaelic Poetry*, p. 118; see also Catherine Kerrigan, *Scottish Women Poets*, pp. 63–84; 'the tunes themselves', Somhairle Mac Gill-eain [Sorley MacLean], 'Some

thoughts about Gaelic poetry', *Ris a' Bhruthaich* [*The Criticism and Prose Writings*], p. 120; Donald Mór's pibroch, Ian Spink, 'Music and society', in Spink (ed.), *Music in Britain. The Seventeenth Century*, Oxford, Basil Blackwell, 1992, p. 7.

28 Jane E. Dawson, 'Two kingdoms or three? Ireland in Anglo-Scottish relations in the middle of the sixteenth century', in Roger A. Mason (ed.), *Scotland and England, 1286–1815*, Edinburgh, John Donald Publishers Ltd, 1987, pp. 113–38, and throughout; Jenny Wormald, 'The creation of Britain: multiple kingdoms or core and colonies?', *Transactions of the Royal Historical Society*, 1992, 6th series, vol. 2, pp. 175–94; Acts of Union between England and Wales, Gruffydd (ed.), *A Guide to Welsh Literature*, pp. 1–6; David Crystal, 'Language planning', *The Cambridge Encyclopedia of Language*, Cambridge, Cambridge University Press, 1987, pp. 364–7; Statutes of Iona and status of Scottish Gaelic, MacAuley, *The Celtic Languages*, p. 144; the Statutes of Icolmkill (Iona) in *The Register of the Privy Council of Scotland*, edited and abridged by David Masson, Edinburgh, H. M. General Register House, 1889, vol. IX, 'A.D. 1610–1613', pp. 26–30.

6 'PENNY MERRIMENTS, PENNY GODLINESSES'

1 'Penny merriments, penny godlinesses', Samuel Pepys's terms for his chapbook collection made in the 1660s, Watt, *Cheap Print*, p. 272; 'More solid Things', John Selden 'Libels', in S. H. Reynolds (ed.), *The Table Talk*, Oxford, Clarendon Press, 1892, p. 105; Peg Verney, Linda Pollock, " 'Teach her to live under obedience": the making of women in the upper ranks of early modern England', *Continuity and Change*, 1989, vol. 4/2, p. 243.

2 [Anon.], *Civil and Uncivil Life*, quoted in Watt, *Cheap Print*, p. 258; the Red Bull and Fortune repertories in Peter Burke, 'Popular culture in seventeenth-century London', in Barry Reay (ed.), *Popular Culture in Seventeenth-Century England*, London and Sydney, Croom Helm, 1985, pp. 40–1; 'the late Jacobean and early Carolinian period', Watt, *Cheap Print*, p. 278; book prices, Francis R. Johnson, 'Notes on English retail book prices, 1550–1640', *The Library*, 1950, 5th series, vol. 5, pp. 83–112; the 'second wave' of educational expansion, David Cressy, *Literacy and the Social Order*, pp. 168–71; Nehemiah Wallington, Paul S. Seaver, *Wallington's World: A Puritan Artisan in Seventeenth Century London*, Stanford, University of California Press, 1985, and Christopher Durston and Jacqueline Eales, 'The puritan ethos, 1560–1700', in Durston and Eales (eds), *The Culture of English Puritanism, 1560–1700*, Basingstoke and London, 1996, p. 12.

3 [Anon.], *The Compassionate Samaritan Unbinding the Conscience, and pouring Oil into the wounds which have been made upon the Separation...*, 1644, pp. 30–1, and in McMichael and Taft, *The Writings of William Walwyn*, p. 110.

4 Nicholas Bownde, *The Doctrine of the Sabbath*, 1595, quoted in Watt, *Cheap Print*, p. 12; Roger Chartier, 'General Introduction: Print Culture', in Chartier, *The Culture of Print*, (1987), p. 4; 'scotch cloth' in Watt, *Cheap Print*, p. 6; Linda Woodbridge, 'Patchwork: piecing the early modern mind in England's first century of print culture', in *English Literary Renaissance*, 1993, vol. 23/1, pp. 5–45.

5 'To any Reader', dedication to *A Thief*, 1624, Taylor, *All the Works*, II.115; 'Ben Jonson's Conversations with William Drummond of Hawthornden', in C. H. Herford and Percy Simpson (eds), *Ben Jonson*, vol. I, 'The Man and His Work', Oxford, Clarendon Press, 1925, p. 142, lines 371–2.

6 *Timber*, Herford and Simpson, vol. VIII, p. 582.

7 Edward B. Partridge (ed.), *Bartholomew Fair*, London, Edward Arnold, 1964, 5.3.106–12, 'ancient' 5.3.7, 'I have only' 106–12.

8 *Taylor's Revenge*, 1615, *All the Works*, II.143.

9 'I Care', in *Taylor's Motto*, 1621, *All the Works*, II.55.

10 *The True Cause of the Watermen's Suit Concerning the Players*, 1614?, *All the Works*, II.172; Victor Neuburg in his 'Introductory note' to the Scholar Press facsimile of *All the Works* comments on Taylor's 'value', 'What he wrote was pungent, articulate, lively, and it deserves more of posterity than either condescension or neglect' [5]. The first extensive notice of Taylor is Robert Southey, *The Lives and Works of the Uneducated Poets*, 1831, edited by J. S. Childers,

'in every General Collection of the British Poets there are authors to be found, whose pretensions to a place there are much feebler than what might be advanced on behalf of Taylor', Humphrey Milford, 1925, pp. 37–8.

11 Morag Shiach discusses the critical and social construction of '"Peasant Poets" 1730–1848' in *Discourse on Popular Culture. Class, Gender and History in Cultural Analysis, 1730 to the Present*, Cambridge, Polity Press in association with Basil Blackwell, 1989, pp. 35–70.

12 Traffic congestion in Victor E. Neuburg, *Popular Literature. A History and Guide from the Beginning of Printing to the Year 1897*, Harmondsworth, Penguin, 1977, p. 65; 'The players are men that I generally love', *The True Cause...*, 1614?, *All the Works*, II.175.

13 Alleyn's library, J. R. Piggott, in Aileen Reid and Robert Maniura (eds), *Edward Alleyn.*, p. 63; 'A Gentleman to whom I am so much obliged', Dedication to *The Pennyless Pilgrimage*, 1618, *All the Works*, I.121; John Jackson as trustee in F. E. Halliday, *A Shakespeare Companion 1564–1964*, Harmondsworth, Penguin, 1964, pp. 65, 248–9.

14 'Sack is the best lining or living', in *Drink and Welcome*, 1637, pp. 14–5 in Taylor's *Works*, vol. 14, The Spenser Society, 1873; Falstaff citations, Ernest Sirluck, in 'Shakespeare and Jonson among the pamphleteers of the First Civil War: some unreported seventeenth-century allusions', *Modern Philology* 1955–6, vol. 53, p. 91; 'the reform of popular culture', in Burke, *Popular Culture*, pp. 207–43, modified by Hutton, *The Rise and Fall of Merry England*, pp. 111–52, 245.

15 Simon Shepherd (ed.), *The Women's Sharp Revenge. Five Women's Pamphlets from the Renaissance*, London, Fourth Estate, 1985, 'perhaps the best statement', p. 161; 'it hath been', p. 170.

16 'Honest John', in Bernard Capp, *The World of John Taylor the Water-Poet 1578–1653*, Oxford, Clarendon Press, 1994, p. 195; 'the Players began to play', *All the Works*, II.172.

17 'the Mirror of Time', *All the Works*, II.59; 'though the Volume and the Work be small', *All the Works*, III.133; Joseph Hall, in Capp, *Taylor*, p. 70; 'good clothes', Dedication, *All the Works*, fol. A3v; promotional puffery, Franklin B. Williams Jr, 'Commendatory verses: the rise of the art of puffing', *Studies in Bibliography*, 1966, 19, p. 3.

18 Alleyn's pound, J. R. Piggott, *Edward Alleyn*, p. 64; 'The name of *London*', *The Fearful Summer*, Oxford, 1625, *All the Works*, I.58–9.

19 'And that four Printers', *All the Works*, fol. A4v; the three most powerful office-holders in Capp, *Taylor*, p. 63; copies unsold in Capp, *Taylor*, p. 190, note 5; for William Herbert as patron and second husband of Lady Anne Clifford, see Chapter 7.

20 'I had a great importunate desire', *Tailor's Travels*, 1648, title page, vol. 21, The Spenser Society, 1877; anonymous contributions in Capp, *Taylor*, p. 157; the Glastonbury thorn, *John Taylor's Wandering*, 1649, p. 6, vol. 7, The Spenser Society, 1870.

21 *Mad Fashions, Odd Fashions*, 1642, vol. 7, The Spenser Society, 1870; on cheap print's use of graphic imagery, Watt, *Cheap Print*, 'The Broadside Picture', pp. 131–235.

22 *The World Turned Upside Down* By 'T. J.', given to 'Thomas Jordan' in Wing J1072A, Donald Wing, *Short-Title Catalogue of Books...1641–1700*, 1972–88, 2nd edition, New York, The Modern Language Association, in vol. 7; fols A2r–A3, The Spenser Society, 1870.

23 The literature of social inversion in Burke, *Popular Culture*, pp. 85–91; Christopher Hill, *The World Turned Upside Down. Radical Ideas during the English Revolution*, Harmondsworth, Penguin, 1972; Roger Chartier, 'The world turned upside-down', in *Cultural History: Between Practices and Representation* (1985), translated by Lydia G. Cochrane, Cambridge and Oxford, Polity Press in association with Blackwell Publishers, 1988, pp. 115–26; Jonathan Sawday, '"Mysteriously divided": Civil War, madness and the divided self', in Thomas Healy and Jonathan Sawday (eds), *Literature and the English Civil War*, Cambridge, Cambridge University Press, 1990, pp. 127–43.

24 Giorgio Melchiori (ed.), *The Second Part of King Henry IV*, Cambridge, Cambridge University Press, 1989, 2.1.38–9, 43–4, p. 85: 'the Hostess's peculiar interjections are strictly modelled on those reported of Lady More in Sir Thomas More's biography written before 1557 by Nicholas Harpsfield, a forbidden book circulating in manuscript in the houses of Roman Catholic recusants' (p. 7); 'hempen homespuns', Peter Holland (ed.), *A Midsummer Night's Dream*, Oxford,

Oxford University Press, 3.1.72, p. 181; 'hempen caudle', Michael Hattaway, *The Second Part of King Henry VI*, Cambridge, Cambridge University Press, 4.7.75, p. 188.

25 Henry Knight Miller, 'The paradoxical encomium with special reference to its vogue in England, 1600–1800', *Modern Philology*, 1956, vol. 53/3, pp. 145–78, Taylor discussed as 'the most prolific writer of paradoxical encomia in the seventeenth century'; also Capp, *Taylor*, pp. 145–78.

26 Dedication in *All the Works*, III.60; subsequent references are given in the text.

27 'Ovid...Ne'er knew', *All the Works*, III.66; *Nashe's Lenten Stuff* and paradoxical encomium in R. B. Mckerrow (ed.), *The Works of Thomas Nashe* (1905), vol. IV, Oxford, Oxford University Press, 1958, pp. 389–95, 436–9; François Rabelais, 'de l'herbe nommée Pantagruelion', Chapitre xlix–lii, *Le Tiers Livre des Faicts et Dicts Heroïques du Bon Pantagruel...* (1552), in *Oeuvres complètes, édition établie, présentée et annotée par Mireille Huchon, avec la collaboration de François Moreau*, France, Gallimard, 1994, pp. 500–13; Anne Lake Prescott, *Imagining Rabelais in Renaissance England*, New Haven and London, Yale University Press, 1998, describes the 'chapbook histories' of Gargantua and the ways in which they reached England, p. 13 ff. (though a shared source may be Pliny's *Natural History* or sixteenth-century compendia), and notes John Taylor's parallels: 'It is hard to know what to make of the "Water Poet"', pp. 25–6.

28 *Crop-Ear Curried* and quotations from Shakespeare, Sirluck, 'Shakespeare and Jonson among the pamphleteers', pp. 95–6.

29 *Fair and Foul Weather*, 1615, pp. 7 and 11, vol. 21, The Spenser Society, 1877.

30 Stephen Orgel (ed.), *The Tempest*, 1.1.30, 32, 47, pp. 98–9, Oxford, Oxford University Press, 1967.

31 A. F. Falconer, *Shakespeare and the Sea*, 1964, in Orgel, Appendix A, pp. 207–8, on the seamanship of the first scene.

32 Shepherd, *The Women's Sharp Revenge*, p. 182.

33 Capp, *Taylor*, pp. 66–7.

34 *All the Works*, II.233.

35 For 'mere entertainers and hangers-on', see Capp, *Taylor*, p. 48; a much more skilful poet, Hyder E. Rollins, 'Lieutenant in the United States Army', 'Martin Parker, Ballad-Monger', *Modern Philology*, January 1919, vol. 16/9, pp. 113–38; Jonson detesting balladmakers, in Capp, 'Popular Literature', p. 205.

36 *The Life and Death of the Most Blessed amongst All Women*, *All the Works*, I.19–24, and see Watt, *Cheap Print*, p. 292, and 'Penny books and marketplace theology', pp. 296–320.

7 'DRESSED UP WITH THE FLOWERS OF A
LIBRARY'

1 'Dressed up with the flowers of a Library', Edward Rainbowe, *A Sermon Preached at the Interment of Anne, Countess of Pembroke, Dorset and Montgomery*, 1676, p. 40, quoted in Barbara Kiefer Lewalski, 'Claiming patrimony and constructing a self: Anne Clifford and her *Diary*', in *Writing Women in Jacobean England*, Cambridge, MA, London, England, Harvard University Press, 1993, p. 140; '300 authors producing over 800 first editions', Patricia Crawford, 'Women's published writings, 1600–1700', in Mary Prior (ed.), *Women in English Society, 1500–1800*, London, Methuen, 1985, pp. 211–82; Smith and Cardinale, *Women and the Literature of the Seventeenth Century*, annotate 637 titles by women.

2 The account of Dorothy Hazzard from Edward Terrill's memoir in *The Records of a Church of Christ, Meeting in Broadmead, Bristol. 1640–1687*, edited by Edward Bean Underhill with an Historical Introduction, London, Hanserd Knollys Society, 1848, p. 10, subsequent quotations by page number; on breaking the Christmas holiday, 'such views seem to have been extraordinarily rare', Ronald Hutton, *The Rise and Fall of Merry England. The Ritual Year 1400–1700*, Oxford, Oxford University Press, 1996, p. 179; rioting for the restoration of Christmas festivals in Canterbury, December 1647, signalled the beginning of the second Civil War of 1648, see Derek Hirst, *Authority and Conflict. England 1603–1658*, London, Melbourne, Auckland, Edward Arnold, 1986, p. 282; on 'churching', Keith Thomas, *Religion and the Decline of Magic*.

Studies in Popular Beliefs in Sixteenth- and Seventeenth-Century England, Harmondsworth, Penguin, 1973, pp. 42–3, 68–9.

3 Patricia Crawford, *Women and Religion in England 1500–1720*, London, Routledge, 1993, p. 51, and for the dispute between Susanna Parr, Mary Allein and their priest Lewis Stucley in Exeter, 1657, pp. 152–9; Parr's *Susanna's Apology Against the Elders* (1659) extracted in Elspeth Graham *et al.*, pp. 101–15.

4 For the national situation in these months, Hirst, *Authority and Conflict*, pp. 202–3; Katherine Chidley in Ian Gentles, 'London Levellers in the English revolution: the Chidleys and their circle', *Journal of Ecclesiastical History*, 1978, vol. 29, pp. 281–309; and Nigel Smith, 'Introduction' and 'The sense of self: from Saints to Quakers', in *Perfection Proclaimed. Language and Literature in English Radical Religion 1640–1660*, Oxford, Clarendon Press, 1989, pp. 1–103.

5 *The English Hexapla Exhibiting the Six Important English Translations of the New Testament Scriptures: Wiclif (1380), Tyndale (1534), Cranmer (1539), Genevan (1557), Anglo-Rhemish (1582), Authorised (1611). The Original Greek Text after Scholz*, London, Samuel Bagster and Sons, 1841, The Revelation of John the Divine, n. p.

6 On separatism, Patrick Collinson, 'The English Conventicle', in W. J. Sheils and Diana Wood (eds), *Voluntary Religion*, Studies in Church History 23, Oxford, 1986; for other women's 'conversion crises', Patricia Crawford, *Women and Religion*, p. 142.

7 Crawford, *Women and Religion*, p. 43.

8 See 'Religion and ethics', in Richard Grassby, *The Business Community of Seventeenth-Century England*, Cambridge, Cambridge University Press, 1995, pp. 271–301.

9 Claire Cross, ' "He-goats before the flocks": a note on the part played by women in the founding of some Civil War churches', in G. J. Cuming and Derek Baker (eds), *Popular Belief and Practice*, Studies in Church History 8, Cambridge, Cambridge University Press, 1972, p. 198; Patricia Crawford, 'Women and radical religion in the English Revolution 1640–60', in *Women and Religion*, pp. 119–82; Elaine Hobby, 'Prophets and prophecies', in *Virtue of Necessity. English Women's Writing 1646–1688*, London, Virago, 1988, pp. 26–53.

10 For the siege, C. V. Wedgwood, *The King's War 1641–1647. The Great Rebellion*, London, Collins, 1966, pp. 217–21; C. H. Firth, 'The siege and capture of Bristol by the royalist forces in 1643', *Journal of the Society for Army Historical Research*, 1925, vol. 4, p. 203; Joan Batten and the Frome Gate women in Bell *et al.*, *Biographical Dictionary*, p. 20.

11 William Prynne and Clement Walker, *A True and Full Relation of the Prosecution, Arraignment and Trial of Col. Nathaniell Fiennes*, 1644, pp. 32–3.

12 John Latimer, *The Annals of Bristol in the Seventeenth Century*, Bristol, William George's Sons, 1900, p. 186.

13 N. H. Keeble (ed.), *The Cultural Identity of Seventeenth-Century Woman. A Reader*, London and New York, Routledge, 1994, p. 264, and Bell *et al.*, *Biographical Dictionary*, p. 249.

14 Kate Aughterson (ed.), *Renaissance Woman. Constructions of Femininity in England*, London and New York, Routledge, 1995, p. 230; proportion of female authors by period in Bell *et al.*, *Biographical Dictionary*, p. 247; Dipesh Chakrabarty, 'Minority histories, subaltern pasts', *Humanities Research* 1, Winter 1997; thanks to Rick Rylance for this reference; see also the discussion in Smith and Cardinale, *Women in the Literature of the Seventeenth Century*, pp. xii–xv.

15 For 'the answers focus', Margaret J. M. Ezell, 'The myth of Judith Shakespeare: creating the canon of women's literature', *New Literary History*, Spring 1990, vol. 21/3, p. 582; 'The literary profession', Ezell, 'The myth', p. 586; the extent and possibilities offered by unedited collections of women's letters, in Bell *et al.*, *Biographical Dictionary*, pp. 270–8; and see also The Perdita Project (http://www.human.ntu.ac.uk/perdita/PERDITA.HTM), Brown Women Writers (http://www.stg.brown.edu/projects/wwp/wwp_home.html) and Harold Love, *Scribal Publication in Seventeenth-Century England*, Oxford, Oxford University Press, 1993.

16 Crawford, 'Women's published writings', p. 211; Hobby, *Virtue of Necessity*, pp. 19, 207; Bell *et al.*, *Biographical Dictionary*, p. 248; Hugh de Quehen (ed.), *Lucy Hutchinson's Translation of Lucretius: De rerum natura*, London, Duckworth, 1996; David Norbrook, 'Lucy Hutchinson's "Elegies" and the situation of the republican woman writer', *English Literary Renaissance*, 1997, vol. 27, pp. 468–521, with an edited text of twenty-three poems.

17 R. A. Houston, *Scottish Literacy and Scottish Identity*, Cambridge, Cambridge University Press, 1983, p. 58.

18 Chakrabarty, 'Minority histories', p. 27.

19 Virginia Woolf, 'The strange Elizabethans', in *The Common Reader*, 2nd series, London, Hogarth, 1935, p. 9.

20 Susan Amussen, 'The gendering of popular culture in early modern England', in Harris, *Popular Culture in England*, p. 50.

21 Hirst, *Authority and Conflict*, p. 278.

22 *To the Supreme Authority…*, 5 May 1649, quoted in Crawford, 'Women's published writings', p. 224, and Hobby, *Virtue of Necessity*, pp. 16–17; Bell *et al.*, *Biographical Dictionary*, pp. 263–70 for the petitioners.

23 *The Law's Resolutions of Women's Rights*, by T. E., 1632, pp. 125, 139, quoted by Lewalski, 'Claiming patrimony and constructing a self', p. 370, n. 14; Susan Dwyer Amussen, *An Ordered Society: Gender and Class in Early Modern England*, Oxford, Basil Blackwell, 1988, p. 72; Hobby, *Virtue of Necessity*, pp. 13–15.

24 L. A. Pollock, 'Teach her to live under obedience: the making of women in the upper ranks of early modern England', *Continuity and Change*, 1989, vol. 4, p. 231.

25 Linda Gordon, 'What is women's history?', in Juliet Gardner (ed.), *What Is History Today?*, London, Macmillan, 1988, p. 86.

26 'Sermon XXV preached at St Paul's upon Easter-Day, 1630', *Sermons*, 1640, p. 242.

27 *The Women's Sharp Revenge…performed by Mary Tattle-well and Joan Hit-him-home, spinsters*, 1640 [John Taylor], in Shepherd (ed.), *The Women's Sharp Revenge*, p. 176, but read as a woman's work by Crawford, 'Women's published writings', p. 281, n. 166; on conventions associated with the birthing chamber as an exclusively female space, see David Cressy, 'Gender trouble and cross-dressing in early modern England', *Journal of British Studies*, 1996, vol. 35/4, pp. 438–65.

28 On 'scope for independence and initiative', Illana Krausman Ben-Amos, *Adolescence and Youth*, p. 135; Bristol widows, Ben-Amos, p. 145; Mary Prior, 'Women and the urban economy: Oxford 1500–1800', in Prior (ed.), *Women in English Society 1500–1800*, London, Methuen, 1985, pp. 93–117.

29 On 'how careful must you be', Samuel Daniel, 'To the Lady Anne Clifford', *The Poetical Works of Mr Samuel Daniel*, 1718, vol. 2, p. 360, and lines 63–4, in Arthur Colby Sprague (ed.), *Poems and a Defence of Rhyme*, Chicago and London, University of Chicago Press, 1965, p. 120; 'able to discourse in all Commendable Arts', George Sedgwick, *Memoirs*, quoted in Lewalski, 'Claiming patrimony and constructing a self', p. 139; for the commissioning of the Great Picture, George C. Williamson, *Lady Anne Clifford, Countess of Dorset, Pembroke and Montgomery, 1590–1676. Her Life, Letters and Work*, (1922), second edition, Wakefield, S. R. Publishers Ltd, 1967, Chapter xix, 'The Great Picture', pp. 334–56; Richard T. Spence, *Lady Anne Clifford Countess of Pembroke, Dorset and Montgomery (1590–1676)*, Thrupp, Sutton Publishing Ltd, 1997, Chapter 9, 'History and legitimacy proclaimed: the manuscript records', pp. 160–4, and 'History and legitimacy proclaimed: the visual displays', pp. 181–99.

30 *A Summary of Records and also a memorial of that religious and blessed lady, Margaret Russell, Countess of Cumberland*, in J. P. Gilson (ed.), *Lives of Lady Anne Clifford and of Her Parents*, London, Roxburghe Club, 1916, p. 36, cited in Lewalski, 'Claiming patrimony and constructing a self', p. 127.

31 'To The Lady Anne Clifford', *Poetical Works*, vol. 2, p. 359, lines 3–6, in Sprague, *Poems and a Defence of Rhyme*, p. 119.

32 *A Summary of Records*, in Lewalski, 'Claiming patrimony and constructing a self', p. 137.

33 Spence, *Lady Anne Clifford*, Chapter 4, 'Anne, Countess of Dorset, 1609–24', pp. 59–79; aphrodisiac potatoes in Lewalski, 'Claiming patrimony and constructing a self', p. 128.

34 Spence, *Lady Anne Clifford*, p. 95, and Chapter 6, 'Countess of Pembroke, Dorset and Montgomery, 1630–50', pp. 96–113; on possible royalist 'character assassination' of Pembroke, see Margaret P. Hannay, Noel J. Kinnamon, and Michael G. Brennan (eds), *The Collected Works of Mary Sidney Herbert Countess of Pembroke*, vol. I, 'Poems. Translations, and Correspondence', Oxford, Clarendon Press, 1998, p. 10.

35 'I gave myself wholly', D. J. H. Clifford, *The Diaries of Lady Anne Clifford*, Thrupp, Sutton Publishing Ltd, 1992, 'The Years Between, 1620–1649', p. 94; Pembroke's 'uniquely vainglorious picture', Christopher Brown, 'Van Dyck's Pembroke family portrait: an inquiry into its Italian sources', in Arthur K. Wheelock Jr, Susan J. Barnes, Julius S. Held (eds), *Anthony Van Dyck*, National Gallery of Art, Washington, 1990, p. 39; 'The Family of Henry VIII', Spence, *Lady Anne Clifford*, p. 184, discussed in Margaret Aston, *The King's Bedpost. Reformation and Iconography in a Tudor Group Portrait*, Cambridge, Cambridge University Press, 1993, pp. 128–31; Flicke's portrait of Cranmer and its meaning in Diarmid MacCulloch, *Thomas Cranmer. A Life*, New Haven and London, Yale University Press, 1996, pp. 338–42. Thanks to Catherine Davies for this reference.

36 *Memorial of Margaret*, pp. 19–23, in Lewalski, 'Claiming patrimony and constructing a self', p. 133.

37 Williamson, 'The Inscriptions in full upon the Great Picture…from a 17th century manuscript', p. 494.

38 Spence, p. 197.

39 *A Summary of the Records of George, Lord and Baron of Clifford*, in Gilson, pp. 7–8, cited in Lewalski, 'Claiming patrimony and constructing a self', p. 132.

40 'Alchemist Extractions', see Cumbria Records Office Acc. A988/5; 'her husband's armour', Graham Parry, 'The Great Picture of Lady Anne Clifford', in David Howarth (ed.), *Art and Patronage in the Caroline Courts. Essays in Honour of Sir Oliver Millar*, Cambridge, Cambridge University Press, 1993, p. 208.

41 'To The Lady Margaret, Countess of Cumberland', *Poetical Works*, p. 355, lines 113–5, in Sprague, *Poems and a Defence of Rhyme*, p. 114.

42 Clifford, 'The Knole Diary', p. 27; Jenkins as boy musician to the Cliffords, Lynn Hulse, 'Musical apprenticeship in noble households', in Andrew Ashbee and Peter Holman (eds), *John Jenkins and His Time. Studies in English Consort Music*, Oxford, Clarendon Press, 1996, p. 75; and for the 'twelve-course double-headed lute' in the Picture, Matthew Spring, 'Jenkins' lute music: an approach to reconstructing the lost multitudes of lute lessons', Ashbee and Holman, p. 314–15.

43 *The Genius of Shakespeare*, London, Picador, 1997, p. 56; Daniel, 'to Henry Wriothesly Earl of Southampton', *Poetical Works*, vol. 2, p. 362–3, Sprague, pp. 122–3.

44 Edward Rainbowe, *A Sermon Preached*, p. 40, quoted in Lewalski, 'Claiming patrimony and constructing a self', pp. 139–40.

45 For 'she had no language', *Memorial*, pp. 19–23, quoted Lewalski, 'Claiming patrimony and constructing a self', p. 134; her memoir, Williamson, *George, Third Earl of Cumberland (1558–1605): His Life and His Voyages*, Cambridge, Cambridge University Press, 1920, pp. 285–8, quoted in Lewalski, 'Claiming patrimony and constructing a self', p. 136; for her patronage, Franklin B. Williams Jr, *Index of Dedications and Commendatory Verses in English Books before 1641*, London, Bibliographical Society, 1962.

46 'The Description of Cookham' in *The Penguin Book of Renaissance Verse*, selected and with an introduction by David Norbrook, edited by H. R. Woudhuysen, Harmondsworth, Penguin, 1992, p. 417; and see Tina Krontiris, Chapter 4, 'Women of the Jacobean Court defending their sex', in *Oppositional Voices. Women as Writers and Translators of Literature in the English Renaissance*, London and New York, Routledge, 1992, p. 109, and Lewalski, 'Re-writing patriarchy and patronage', pp. 59–78, and 'Claiming patrimony and constructing a self', pp. 224–5, 234–41.

47 Spence, pp. 19–22, Lewalski, 'Claiming patrimony and constructing a self', p. 128.

48 BL, Additional MS 15,232, quoted Lewalski, 'Claiming patrimony and constructing a self', p. 140.

49 On 'the Book of Job', Spence, p. 8; 'our English Seneca', in Jill Kraye, 'Moral philosophy', discussing Hall, Charron and Christian Neostoicism, in Charles B. Schmitt (general editor), *The Cambridge History of Renaissance Philosophy*, Cambridge, Cambridge University Press, 1988, pp. 367–74.

50 Glecko, Clifford, *The Diaries of Lady Anne Clifford*, p. 29; 19 April, p. 32; 'an Owl in the Desert', p. 33.

51 Spence, p. 194; Young Clifford's speech, 5.2.56–60 in *The Second Part of King Henry VI*, Hattaway, p. 211; Lady Anne's defence of John de Clifford in Clifford, *The Diaries of Lady Anne Clifford*, p. 8.

52 Fourteen titled women were dedicatees of specific plays from 1583 to 1633; see David Bergeron, 'Women as patrons of English Renaissance drama', in Guy Fitch Lytle and Stephen Orgel (eds), *Patronage in the Renaissance*, Princeton, Princeton University Press, 1981, pp. 274–90; Lucy Russell Countess of Bedford, Anne Clifford's aunt, was the leading patroness (Bergeron, p. 283–5).

53 Parry, 'The Great Picture of Lady Anne Clifford', p. 215, quoting William Haller, 'The honest liberty of free speech, 1644', in *Liberty and Reformation in the Puritan Revolution*, New York and London, Columbia University Press, 1955, pp. 169–72. Walwyn's text in *Walwyn's Just Defence*, in McMichael and Taft, *The Writings of William Walwyn*, p. 397.

54 *The Power of Love*, in McMichael and Taft, *The Writings of William Walwyn*, p. 80.

8 'THE POWER OF SELF AT SUCH OVER-FLOWING TIMES'

1 On 'such over-flowing times', Gerrard Winstanley, Preface, *Several Pieces Gathered in One Volume* (1650), in Hill, *Winstanley: The Law of Freedom and Other Writings*, pp. 155–6; the 'Land of Cockaigne' as a utopia of cost-free gratification in A. L. Morton, *The English Utopia*, London, Lawrence and Wishart, 1969; 'good people...no money', Hattaway, *The Second Part of King Henry VI*, 4.2.60, p. 174; 'O monstrous', 4.2.72–90, pp. 175–6.

2 On 'all records...most worthy to live', Hattaway, *The Second Part of King Henry VI*, 4.7.10–37, pp. 185–6, and see Hattaway's discussion, 'The play: a political documentary', pp. 6–10, 'Cade', pp. 21–34, and compare Janet Clare, *'Art Made Tongue-tied by Authority'. Elizabethan and Jacobean Censorship*, Manchester and New York, Manchester University Press, 1990, pp. 41–2, Richard Wilson, *Will Power. Essays on Shakespearean Authority*, New York, London, Toronto, Sydney, Tokyo, Singapore, Harvester Wheatsheaf, 1993, pp. 26–9, Thomas Cartelli, 'Jack Cade in the garden: class consciousness and class conflict in *2Henry VI*', in Richard Burt and John Michael Archer (eds), *Enclosure Acts. Sexuality, Property, and Culture in Early Modern England*, Ithaca, Cornell University Press, 1994, pp. 48–67, and Geraldo U. de Sousa, 'The Peasants' Revolt and the writing of history', in David M. Bergeron (ed.), *Reading and Writing in Shakespeare*, Newark, University of Delaware Press, London, Associated University Presses, 1996.

3 'The said Paul reads', in Lawrence Stone, 'The educational revolution in England, 1560–1640', *Past and Present*, 1964, vol. 28, p. 43; 'he shall die', Hattaway, *The Second Part of King Henry VI*, 4.7.90–1, p. 188.

4 Print and revolutionary turmoil, Nigel Smith, 'Writing, publishing and reading in the war', in *Literature and Revolution in England 1640–1660*, New Haven and London, Yale University Press, 1994, pp. 21–53; Winstanley, 'beaten out of both estate and trade, in Hill, Introduction, *Winstanley*, p. 12; 'the pleasant fruit trees of freedom', *A Watch-word to the City of London, and the Army*, (1649), p. 147; 'those diggers that remain', *A bill of account of the most remarkable sufferings that the diggers have met with from the great red dragon's power since April 1, 1649...* (1650), p. 147; 'Sometimes my heart', Preface, *Several Pieces Gathered in One Volume* (1650), pp. 155–6.

5 For 'all that I have writ', Preface, *Several Pieces Gathered in One Volume* (1650), in Hill, *Winstanley*, p. 157; see Nigel Smith, 'The theory and practice of radical religious language', in *Perfection Proclaimed. Language and Literature in English Radical Religion 1640–1660*, Oxford, Clarendon Press, 1989, for Winstanley breaking down 'the barriers between God, man, and nature, setting knowledge alongside power', p. 266, and throughout.

6 For 'the mob' (1691), *Oxford English Dictionary* second edition, Oxford, Clarendon Press, 1989; 'religious works predominated', Vernon F. Snow, 'An inventory of the Lord General's library, 1646', *The Library*, 1966, 5th series, vol. 21, p. 117.

7 Robert B. Shoemaker, 'Reforming the city: the Reformation of Manners campaign in London, 1690–1738', Lee Davison, Tim Hitchcock, Tim Keirn and Robert B. Shoemaker (eds), *Stilling*

the Grumbling Hive. The Response to Social and Economic Problems in England, 1689–1750, Stroud and New York, Alan Sutton and St Martin's Press, 1992, pp. 99–120; on the 'polarization of wealth and power within English society, and especially rural society, between about 1550 and 1650', see Ronald Hutton, *The Rise and Fall of Merry England. The Ritual Year 1400–1700*, Oxford and New York, Oxford University Press, 1996, p. 241 ff., who in crucial respects modifies the arguments of David Underdown, Chapter 3, 'Cultural conflict', *Revel, Riot, and Rebellion. Popular Politics and Culture in England 1603–1660*, Oxford, Clarendon Press, 1985, pp. 44–72, Keith Wrightson, Chapter 7, 'Learning and godliness', in *English Society 1580–1680*, London, Unwin Hyman, 1982, pp. 183–221, and A. J. Fletcher and J. Stevenson, 'A polarised society?', in A. Fletcher and J. Stevenson (eds), *Order and Disorder in Early Modern England*, Cambridge, Cambridge University Press, 1985, pp. 1–15; Keith Wrightson and David Levine, Chapters 5–7 in *Poverty and Piety in an English Village. Terling, 1525–1700*, second edition, Oxford, Clarendon Press, 1995.

INDEX

Note: the Constant Register of Public Facts has not been indexed.

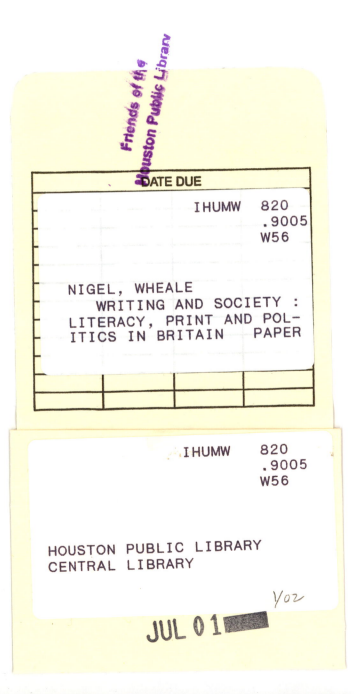